Encyclopedia of International Relations of India with SAARC Countries

Encyclopedia of International Relations of India with SAARC Countries

P.C. Mathur

AMIGA PRESS. INC
Delhi -110051

AMIGA PRESS. INC
H.O :- 28-A, Indra Park, Chander Nagar
Delhi :- 110051 (India)
Tel :- 011-22504028, +91-98736-57000
Email :- amigapress@gmail.com
amigaeditorial@gmail.com
amigapub@gmail.com
Website :- www.amigapress@co.in

This edition is published by Amiga Press.Inc

ISBN : 978-93-84533-21-2

First Published 2018

PRINTED : THOMSON PRESS INDIA

Preface

The book aims to provide an insight into India and its relations with other SAARC countries in the field of trade and economic cooperation. The author has carried out as in depth research into the subject and presents a comprehensive analysis of international trade theories, India's export import policies, India's foreign trade and its trade with other SAARC countries. The author also focuses on regional economic cooperation among SAARC countries and its impact on their economies.

The South Asian Association for Regional Cooperation, popularly known as SAARC was established on 8th December, 1985. It comprises of the States of Bangladesh, Bhutan, India, Maldives, Nepal, Pakistan and Sri Lanka. Afghanistan was added to this regional group on 13th November, 2005. SAARC provides a platform for its people to work together in a spirit of friendship, trust and understanding. The progress that the regional entity has made , or the problems it has encountered can be properly appreciated only through an adequate understanding of the respective constitutional system.

India's neighbourhood which the member-countries of the South Asian Association for Regional Cooperation (SAARC) namely Afghanistan, Bangladesh, Bhutan, Nepal, Maldives, Pakistan and Sri Lanka comprise, is a fairly complex geographical entity. This is to say the least. In fact India can be said to be living in a dangerous neighbourhood. The constituent countries-individually as well as collectively-represent a world of historical links, shared legacies, commonalities as well as diversities which are so elaborately reflected in their ethnic, linguistic, religious and political fabric. China and Myanmar, the other two neighbours, are no less complex.

The South Asian region is also full of contradictions, disparities and paradoxes. In the post-colonial period, the South Asia has been a theatre of bloody inter-state as well as civil wars; it has witnessed liberation movements, nuclear rivalry, military dictatorships and continues to suffer from insurgencies, religious fundamentalism and terrorism, besides serious problems associated with drugs and human trafficking. The region also has the dubious distinction of having over 540mn people who earn less than $ 1.25 a day and account for 44% of developing world's poor. The region has produced several powerful female leaders and yet in the overall much remains to be done for the empowerment of women. On the barometer of religious tolerance, the constituent countries range anywhere between flexible secular minded and rigidly fundamentalist.

The SAARC was designed to improve both the economic and social progress of its member states. But, unfortunately ever since its formation there have been hindrances to the regional cooperation. Differences in political system among the member countries make regional cooperation difficult. Asean countries must decide whether to retreat into protectionism or reaffirm their commitment to a more open approach. It does not have the kind of deep institutional ties and infrastructure links that bind together the European Union's members. If integration strategy is fully implemented and capturing a larger share of global manufacturing, the Asean countries could gain $280-625 billion in annual gross domestic product (GDP) by 2030.

This book elaborately describe the development of South Asia and particularly India. Details of SAARC summits and regional conventions are also included. History and evolution of SAARC finds description in detailed manner. India's relations with SAARC nations are analysed. The work aims at presenting the Indian policy perspective in South Asia in a larger context of the phenomenon of regional integration across the world.

—*Editor*

Contents

1

Introduction

SOUTH ASIAN ASSOCIATION FOR REGIONAL COOPERATION

The South Asian Association for Regional Cooperation (SAARC) is an economic and political organization of eight countries in Southern Asia. It was established on December 8, 1985 by Bangladesh, Bhutan, Maldives, Nepal, Pakistan, India and Sri Lanka. In April 2007, at the Association's 14th summit, Afghanistan became its eighth member.

HISTORY

In the late 1970s, Bangladeshi President Ziaur Rahman proposed the creation of a trade bloc consisting of South Asian countries. The idea of regional cooperation in South Asia was again mooted in May 1980. The foreign secretaries of the seven countries met for the first time in Colombo in April 1981.

The Committee of the Whole, which met in Colombo in August 1981, identified five broad areas for regional cooperation. New areas of cooperation were added in the following years.

The objectives of the Association as defined in the Charter are:

- to promote the welfare of the people of South Asia and to improve their quality of life;
- to accelerate economic growth, social progress and cultural development in the region and to provide all individuals the opportunity to live in dignity and to realize their full potential;
- to promote and strengthen collective self-reliance among the countries of South Asia;
- to contribute to mutual trust, understanding and appreciation of one another's problems;

- to promote active collaboration and mutual assistance in the economic, social, cultural, technical and scientific fields;
- to strengthen cooperation with other developing countries;
- to strengthen cooperation among themselves in international forums on matters of common interest; and
- to cooperate with international and regional organisations with similar aims and purposes.

The Declaration on South Asian Regional Cooperation was adopted by the Foreign Ministers in 1983 in New Delhi. During the meeting, the Ministers also launched the Integrated Programme of Action (IPA) in nine agreed areas, namely, Agriculture; Rural Development; Telecommunications; Meteorology; Health and Population Activities; Transport; Postal Services; Science and Technology; and Sports, Arts and Culture. The South Asian Association for Regional Cooperation (SAARC) was established when its Charter was formally adopted on 8 December 1985 by the Heads of State or Government of Bangladesh, Bhutan, India, Maldives, Nepal, Pakistan and Sri Lanka.

Afghanistan was added to the regional grouping at the behest of India on 13 November 2005, and became a member on 3 April 2007. With the addition of Afghanistan, the total number of member states were raised to eight (8). In April 2006, the United States of America and South Korea made formal requests to be granted observer status. The European Union has also indicated interest in being given observer status, and made a formal request for the same to the SAARC Council of Ministers meeting in July 2006. On 2 August 2006 the foreign ministers of the SAARC countries agreed in principle to grant observer status to the US, South Korea and the European Union. On 4 March 2007, Iran requested observer status. Followed shortly by the entrance of Mauritius.

Secretariat

The SAARC Secretariat was established in Kathmandu on 16 January 1987 and was inaugurated by Late King Birendra Bir Bikram Shah of Nepal. It is headed by a Secretary General appointed by the Council of Ministers from Member Countries in alphabetical order for a three-year term. He is assisted by the Professional and the General Services Staff, and also an appropriate number of functional units called Divisions assigned to Directors on deputation from Member States. The Secretariat coordinates and monitors implementation of activities, prepares for and services meetings, and serves as a channel of communication between the Association and its Member States as well as other regional organizations.

The Memorandum of Understanding on the establishment of the Secretariat which was signed by Foreign Ministers of member countries on 17 November 1986 at Bangalore, India contains various clauses concerning the role, structure and administration of the SAARC Secretariat as well as the powers of the Secretary-General. In several recent meetings the heads of state or government of member states of SAARC have taken some important decisions and bold initiatives to strengthen the organisation and to widen and deepen regional co-operation. The SAARC Secretariat and Member States observe 8 December as the SAARC Charter Day.

Criticism

Not enough is being done to for rapid economic integration of the region. Apart from the fact that the recently approved South Asian University and the creation of new rail lines linking the region, people to people contacts and connectivity of region needs to be strengthened.

Political Issues

SAARC has intentionally laid more stress on "core issues" mentioned above rather than more decisive political issues like the Kashmir dispute and the Sri Lankan civil war. However, political dialogue is often conducted on the margins of SAARC meetings. SAARC has also refrained itself from interfering in the internal matters of its member states. During the 12th and 13th SAARC summits, extreme emphasis was laid upon greater cooperation between the SAARC members to fight terrorism.

Free Trade Agreement

Over the years, the SAARC members have expressed their unwillingness on signing a free trade agreement. Though India has several trade pacts with Maldives, Nepal, Bhutan and Sri Lanka, similar trade agreements with Pakistan and Bangladesh have been stalled due to political and economic concerns on both sides.

India has been constructing a barrier across its borders with Bangladesh and Pakistan. In 1993, SAARC countries signed an agreement to gradually lower tariffs within the region, in Dhaka. Eleven years later, at the 12th SAARC Summit at Islamabad, SAARC countries devised the South Asia Free Trade Agreement which created a framework for the establishment of a free trade area covering 1.4 billion people. This agreement went into force on January 1, 2006. Under this agreement, SAARC members will bring their duties down to 20 per cent by 2007.

DHAKA 2005 SUMMIT

The summit accorded observer status to People's Republic of China, Japan, South Korea and United States of America. The nations also agreed to organize development funds under a single financial institution with a permanent secretariat, that would cover all SAARC programs and also ranging from social, to infrastructure, to economic ones.

Membership

Current members (alphabetically):

- Afghanistan
- Bangladesh
- Bhutan
- India
- Maldives
- Nepal
- Pakistan
- Sri Lanka.

Observers:

- Australia
- China
- European Union
- Iran
- Japan
- Mauritius
- Myanmar (Burma)
- South Korea
- United States.

Future membership:

- The People's Republic of China has shown its interest in joining SAARC. While Pakistan and Bangladesh support China's candidature, India is against the prospect of Chinese membership. China's entry in to SAARC will likely balance India's overbearing presence there. However, during the 2005 Dhaka summit, India agreed on granting observer status to the PRC along with Japan. During the 14th summit, Nepal along with Pakistan and Bangladesh, announced their support for the membership of China. China seeks greater involvement in SAARC, however, finds it too early to apply for full membership.

- Indonesia intends to become an observer as well, and is supported by Sri Lanka.
- Iran, a state with borders to two SAARC members, has traditionally enjoyed strong cultural, economic and political relationships with Afghanistan and Pakistan and has expressed its desire to become a member of the South Asian organization. On 22 February 2005, the Foreign Minister of Iran, Kamal Kharrazi, indicated Iran's interest in joining SAARC by saying that his country could provide the region with "East-West connectivity". On 3 March 2007, Iran asked to join the SAARC as an observer. SAARC Secretary-General Lyonpo Chenkyab Dorji responded by saying that Iran's request for observer status would be taken up during a meeting of ministers of foreign affairs of SAARC member countries in the 3 April summit in New Delhi.
- Russia intends to become an observer as well, and is supported by India.
- Myanmar has expressed an interest in joining as a full member. If done so, Myanmar will become the ninth member in the group. India is currently backing Myanmar. Myanmar's military regime officially applied for full SAARC membership in May 2008. However, the application is still being considered and the government is currently restricted to observer status.
- South Africa has participated in meetings.

SAARC Preferential Trading Arrangement

The Agreement on SAARC Preferential Trading Arrangement (SAPTA) was signed on 11 April 1993 and entered into force on 7 December 1995, with the desire of the Member States of SAARC (India, Pakistan, Nepal, Sri Lanka, Bangladesh, Bhutan and the Maldives) to promote and sustain mutual trade and economic cooperation within the SAARC region through the exchange of concessions. The establishment of an Inter-Governmental Group (IGG) to formulate an agreement to establish a SAPTA by 1997 was approved in the *Sixth Summit of SAARC* held in Colombo in December 1991.

The basic principles underlying SAPTA are:

1. overall reciprocity and mutuality of advantages so as to benefit equitably all Contracting States, taking into account their respective level of economic and industrial development, the pattern of their external trade, and trade and tariff policies and systems;
2. negotiation of *tariff reform* step by step, improved and extended in successive stages through periodic reviews;

3. recognition of the special needs of the Least Developed Contracting States and agreement on *concrete preferential measures* in their favour;
4. inclusion of all products, manufactures and commodities in their raw, semi-processed and processed forms.

So far, four rounds of trade negotiations have been concluded under SAPTA covering over 5000 commodities.

SAARC AND INDIA

Indian Prime Minister Narendra Modi undertook a two-day official visit to Nepal on August 2–3. Surprisingly, no Indian prime minister had visited Nepal—with whom India shares more than 1,700 kilometers of borders—for 17 years. Modi articulated his vision for Indo-Nepal relationship with four C's: cooperation, connectivity, culture, and constitution. As a part of his vision, he also spoke about developing a satellite to assist India's neighbors. Naturally, Modi is looking at satellite technology as a tool for cooperation and connectivity.

Narendra Modi became India's prime minister on May 27. On June 30, after witnessing the launch of PSLV-C23, carrying the French earth observation satellite SPOT-7, he addressed India's rocket scientists. While congratulating the Indian Space Research Organisation (ISRO) for the successful PSLV launch, he also outlined his vision for India's space program. He argued in favor of changing the perception that India's space program has an elitist agenda. He emphasized that space technologies are being used for socioeconomic development and, over the years, have proved their utility for common people.

During his speech, Prime Minister Modi also argued for the need to share India's space expertise with its neighbors. He proposed to develop a "SAARC satellite" for the region and also to expand the footprint of India's satellite navigation program to South Asia. This indicates that generally New Delhi is keen to use India's expertise in space as an instrument of foreign policy. It's worth examining and deliberating about the possible design of such a vision in the context of SAARC. The South Asian Association for Regional Cooperation (SAARC) was established in 1985. This organization has a key focus on economic and developmental issues. SAARC has eight members: Afghanistan, Bangladesh, Bhutan, India, Maldives, Nepal, Pakistan, and Sri Lanka. Additionally, there are some nations with observer status, including the United States, Australia, Japan, and China. Myanmar (Burma) also has the status of an observer, but is keen to become a full member. This country shares more than 1,600 kilometers of borders with India. Owing to geographical and political realities for this discussion, Myanmar is thus considered as a part of SAARC.

Over the years, SAARC has evolved various areas of cooperation, and science and technology is one such area of interest. They have developed a cooperation mechanism that includes areas like environment, energy, education, and media. In the areas of science and technology cooperation, SAARC established a Meteorological Research Centre (SMRC) in 1995. It undertakes collective research in meteorology in the SAARC region. It has a modern and advanced observing system with a reliable and timely communications network. Also, there is a network for regional cooperation on subjects like hydrology, oceanography, seismology, and atmospheric science. Obviously, such networks rely on satellite-derived data.

Amongst the SAARC member states, India is the only spacefaring nation with a number of satellites operating in various orbits. Pakistan is another state with reasonable interest in space field. However, in spite of its early start and its knowledge of "rocket science" (it has a well-developed missile program), Pakistan has not made much progress in space arena. Their space agency, known as Space and Upper Atmosphere Research Commission (SUPARCO), was established during 1961 as a committee and was granted the status of a Commission in 1981. Badr-1 (Badr-A) was Pakistan's first indigenously developed satellite and was launched from China on July 16, 1990. This satellite is no longer operational. Pakistan's second satellite, BADR-B, an Earth observation spacecraft, was launched on December 10, 2001. Subsequently, Paksat 1, its first geostationary satellite, was acquired in 2002. China launched Paksat-1R, a communication satellite for Pakistan, on August 12, 2011. In November 2013, a CubeSat called iCUBE-1 was launched in a polar orbit to take low-resolution images of the planet.

There are two other SAARC states with satellites in their inventory. One is Sri Lanka. Its first satellite is actually a commercial satellite and was launched by China in 2012. Otherwise, Sri Lanka is likely to launch its first geostationary communications satellite by 2015, in collaboration with a Chinese company. The other nation is Afghanistan, which started using its first satellite in May of this year. This satellite, called Afghansat 1, was acquired to boost the telecommunications sector. This is an orbiting Eutelsat satellite that was launched in December 2008 and with is designed to last until 2020. Afghan's Ministry of Communications and Information Technology is renting this satellite for US$4 million per year.

Apart from these two nations, Bangladesh has shown some interest in research related to space. The Bangladesh Space Research and Remote Sensing Organization (SPARRSO), established in 1980, is a state agency concerned with astronomical research and the application of space technology. They propose to launch their first satellite, called Bangabandhu-1, around 2015. There are some unconfirmed reports that Maldives could be assisted by China to evolve their space agenda in near future.

This is the existing "SAARC space footprint" that is providing assistance to a limited population. By contrast, India's proposed SAARC satellite would be serving the interests of entire SAARC population, almost 1.5 billion people. The SAARC region included many nations plagued by poverty and conflict. In this region, in a relative sense, India is an island of prosperity surrounded by states fighting to win over security and economic challenges. At the same time, within India there are also visible disparities between rich and poor. It's also worth noting that two nuclear weapon states are the part of this grouping and there are some inherent security contradictions amongst some of the states in the region.

The geography of the SAARC region is unique, with coastlines, forests, deserts, and mountains. It has one of the youngest mountain ranges in the world, the Himalayas. They influence the major rain providing system for the region, the monsoon. The major rivers in South Asia are the Ganges, the Indus, and the Brahmaputra. Major deserts include the Thar Desert, which covers large areas of both Pakistan and India, with an approximate area of 175,000 square kilometers. Mainly tropical weather systems influence the Indian peninsula and other island states. Extra-tropical weather systems influence the survival of people staying close to Himalayan region. The region is prone for earthquakes, and a few tsunamis have taken place in the recent past.

These geophysical and geopolitical realities of the region should be taken into account before suggesting any model for the SAARC satellite. India needs to evolve a joint mechanism involving representatives from all member states to decide on the expectations from the proposed SAARC satellite. Before designing such a satellite, it would be important to identify and zero in on the specific and urgent needs of the nations in the region. Broadly, the various socioeconomic challenges of SAARC nations could be at least partially addressed by communications satellites, weather satellites, and remote sensing satellites.

Considering the issues like necessities of member states, cost, time, and expertise required for development and launch of a satellite, the best option for India could be to develop an Earth observation satellite as the first SAARC satellite. Basically, such a satellite could be of much use for land and water resources management for the entire region. India would also be expected to assist member states to develop ground infrastructure and create expertise. Some analysts believe that, at times, SAARC gets held hostage to the divergence of the India-Pakistan relationship. In fact, satellite technology could come very handy to silence such critics. As confidence building measures, such technology could be used to undertake joint surveillance of the border regions and resolve issues related to infiltration, water sharing, and more.

India's Regional Satellite Navigational Network is likely to become operational by the end of 2015. As suggested by Prime Minister Modi, India could offer these facilities to the SAARC states as well. To assist civilian aircraft for navigation and non-precision approaches over India airspace, ISRO has developed a GPS-Aided Geo Augmented Navigation (GAGAN) system. India could also allow access to this system to aircraft operating within SAARC airspace.

Presently, what is important for India is not to limit itself with the idea of a SAARC satellite but instead to effectively use its existing capabilities in space to assist the various SAARC members. Most of these nations, being novices in the field of satellite technology, may not be in a position to ask India for specific assistance. India needs to become proactive and share with these nations imagery and other relevant data. In 2005, the Asia-Pacific Space Cooperation Organization (APSCO) was established, which is the only multilateral space mechanism presently available for the region. Among the SAARC members, only Bangladesh and Pakistan are members of APSCO and, from the SAARC point of view, such a body is not of much use. India could take a lead to establish a SAARC space cooperation mechanism, which could also bring more transparency into the system. Such agency could play a major role towards coordinating various data sharing and training related activities.

In SAARC, India is the dominant player; in the space arena, it is the only player. It is important for India to guard against developing any form of so-called "big brother attitude." While establishing a relationship with other nations, India should not play only the role of assister. India needs to develop a system where these nations could be made partners in various activities. To reduce rivalry (if any) and promote solidarity among members, India could engage these nations in important space projects to create a sense of belonging. Presently, India is working on a program to develop Astrosat, a dedicated astronomy satellite that is likely to be launched in 2015. India could involve SAARC members in this project and could call this satellite "SAARC Astrosat." Also, with the Sri Lankan government, India could undertake a feasibility study for developing a joint spaceport in that country.

SAARC region is bound together not only by geography but also (in some sense) by culture, ethnicity, traditions, religion, and languages. At the same time, this region has various strategic fault lines with strong differences on issues among some member nations. Any proactive collaboration in the outer space arena is unlikely to resolve all issues of differences. However, in an era of tremendous growth in information technologies, the Internet, mobile telephony, and social media, satellite technology could form the basis to establish a common SAARC identity.

THE NEW IDENTITY FOR THE SAARC

With one-fifth of the world's population, the countries of South Asia face formidable challenges resulting from poverty, underdevelopment, and conflict within and among themselves. Their low levels of production, unemployment, and population pressures are not helped by historic exploitation and other adverse legacies. In an historical, cultural, physical and linguistic sense, South Asia is an integrated region, but any commonality across nations has been made impossible by deep-rooted divisions and animosities across the whole region. The latter is hugely polarized, and it has to grapple with gross violations of human rights. Consequently, governments in the region lack the effective initiative and political commitment needed to meet their obligations to respect, protect, and fulfil human rights and fundamental freedoms. Internal conflicts, civil strife, poverty and so-called state anti-terror legislation and measures have resulted in violations of the civil liberties of the people.

The South Asian Association for Regional Cooperation (SAARC) was established in 1985 with the objective of promoting regional cooperation between seven South Asian countries: Bangladesh, Bhutan, India, Nepal, the Maldives, Pakistan and Sri Lanka. Despite the extremely slow pace at which SAARC moves and its very limited achievements, the association did receive an increase in its membership when Afghanistan became the 8th member in 2007. However, the Association has from its very beginning been up against hard politics, mutual fear, and a strong sense of rivalry between its two principle members: India and Pakistan. One reason for SAARC's unimpressive progress is a lack of agreement among the member states on what should be the guiding force towards regionalism. SAARC has consequently been unable in any way to achieve its basic objective of promoting regional cooperation and solidarity. It is a disgrace that after nearly 30 years it has nothing to show and nothing to celebrate.

Even now SAARC is still trying to steady itself. It may not have made any great mark, but at least it has not been disbanded and it continues to function, albeit in a haphazard manner. Sadly, the presence of this regional organization has done nothing to remove historical irritants between members or to lower the levels of suspicion and distrust among neighbors.

Disputes between member states have led to outright wars, low-intensity conflicts, cross-border terrorism, a debilitating arms race and some very hostile propaganda. SAARC has failed to prevent any of these and they in turn have held up SAARC's progress. Belonging to a regional forum for nearly 30 years has led to no shared values or norms and, despite some points of commonality in the past, the member states have been unable to map out a common future.

South Asia today is a black spot for the gross violation of human rights and civil liberties. The people of Bhutan have as yet seen no glimpse of democracy, and they are deprived of all kinds of freedoms under the rule of an assertive kingship.

Pakistan enjoys a pseudo democracy. Nepal has been faced with a serious political crisis from more than a decade: it has no proper government, no constitution, a dead civil society, and a puppet media. India, a so-called growing economy and the largest democracy on earth, faces political crises and internal instability from Kashmir to Assam. Kashmir is regarded as 'a legal black hole' in terms of human rights violations perpetrated by the armed forces. Most importantly, throughout the SAARC region, the poor are getting poorer and the rich richer: the gap between the two is widening further while the dynastic political elite and business people can enjoy whole states' welfare facilities and opportunities. Why is this happening? Why there is so much that is unjust in this region? Is it not time for a radical rethink? Who is responsible? Is it not high time for the people of SAARC as a whole to seek common answers to common problems?

Despite a serious human rights crisis throughout much of the region, SAARC has not even given thought to adopting a specific, detailed and uniform human rights convention or charter despite the existence of these in all other major regions of the world. Is it not high time then for SAARC states to think seriously about it?

What is required is a widespread formal commitment to human rights across the whole region. This should take the form of bills of rights, the establishment of national human rights institutions, declarations by IGOs, and the establishment of regional human rights regimes. The latter would be relatively independent but coherent human rights sub-regimes operated within the larger framework of international human rights practice. Examples of major regional mechanisms are the European human rights monitoring mechanism, the Inter-American system, and the African system. All these regional mechanisms have created, under their human rights charter, bodies such as a commission and a court of human rights. These have broad mandates to monitor human rights compliance by states parties, to receive reports from states, to receive complaints from individuals and states, to investigate and to order interim measures to prevent any escalation of human rights violations. They also provide appropriate reparations for victims by the violators, and they publish their findings and make recommendations to pressurize the state parties concerned.

Many questions need to be asked today: has SAARC achieved anything in nearly three decades of existence? Why, compared with other regions, are they so backward in terms of everything? In almost every other region there is some kind of regional human rights mechanism: since a fifth of the world's population resides in the SAARC region, why have the SAARC nations never thought having one? Can a region so politically, socially, and economically volatile afford to go on ignoring this issue? Most importantly, can South Asia gear itself for real regional cooperation? Can national and regime interests become sufficiently harmonized in order to promote cooperative trust and mutual confidence among the power elites of the region? The very diversity of South Asia demands the gradual implementation of conceptual steps that build towards a distinct regional identity. One such conceptualization could well be the establishment of a SAARC regional human rights mechanism.

Towards Setting up a South Asian Human Rights Mechanism

Many questions need to be asked: Why is a separate charter for the promotion of human rights so important for the SAARC region? What would it add to existing practices? SAARC countries have signed already several conventions on narcotics, trafficking in women and children for prostitution, promotion of child welfare, and there have been several agreements on food security and various social issues.

However, there has been no regional agreement that specifically focuses on human rights and fundamental freedoms. A regional instrument would be regarded as an appropriate complement to the universal human rights instruments of the United Nations. Such regional human rights mechanisms are already established in the Americas, Europe, Africa and most recently the Arab States: the last major geographic area, therefore, without its own mechanism is the SAARC region. The Council of the League of Arab States adopted its own Arab Charter on Human Rights in 2004, and it has been in force since 2008. The Charter grants a number of human rights and fundamental freedoms to the people, and it provides for the election of a seven-person Committee of Experts on Human Rights to consider states' reports and to monitor states' compliance with the Charter.

Most SAARC countries have common problems concerning torture, trafficking, internal displacement due to conflict, refugees, rights over resources, urban shelter and demolition, domestic violation against women, the practice of the death penalty, and extra-judicial detention and forced disappearances. A few countries of SAARC have national human rights institutions. All SAARC countries have, or in the case of Nepal should soon have, a written constitution under which human rights are recognized as fundamental. Despite these provisions and initiatives, however, there is a deteriorating human rights situation in the region brought about by the anti-terrorism measures adopted in some South Asian countries, by internal political crises and civil strife and by the hostility of governments towards human rights despite their claims to be democratic. The SAARC region has suffered for centuries from the absence of a rule of law and constitutionalism and from a culture of impunity that affects almost all the countries. Is there not then an urgent need to formulate a regional human rights mechanism?

The majority of SAARC member states have still to ratify the optional protocols to the International Convention on Civil and Political Rights (ICCPR) and the Convention on the Elimination of All Forms of Discrimination against Women (CEDAW). Moreover, Bhutan has still to ratify the ICCPR, the International Convention on Economic, Social and Cultural Rights (ICESCR), and the Convention against Torture.

Even where treaties have been ratified, though, implementation has been restricted by the reservations of some countries that follow a narrow interpretation of treaties relating to civil and political rights, and by a limited political commitment to implement economic, social, and cultural rights. An effective regional human rights mechanism would ensure the protection and promotion of human rights in the region especially common issues including the rights of migrant workers, human trafficking, minority rights, the right to development, and, most importantly, it would challenge the existing culture of impunity and lawlessness in the region. Such a mechanism could also provide a less costly, more accessible and effective redress alternative to existing international processes and procedures.

Not all SAARC nations are democratic and those that claim to be on the way to being so easily slide into authoritarianism, as in the case of Bangladesh, Pakistan, and Nepal. The prospect, therefore, of ideological homogeneity across the region would seem to be anything other than bright. With over sixty per cent of its population still forced to survive below the poverty line, how could this region even claim to be democratic? Moreover, how could it claim to have a fully-fledged democracy until human rights are protected and enshrined in the international covenants? The SAARC region faces serious challenges in consolidating democracy and strengthening and promoting human rights and the fundamental freedoms of its people. SAARC should now seriously consider establishing a regional human rights mechanism similar to those of the Inter-American or European Systems. The mechanism would certainly help states to promote and protect rights and freedoms effectively within their jurisdiction. It would ensure that international human rights laws were respected and promoted effectively throughout the SAARC nations. Moreover, such a mechanism could help people in the region to develop a common understanding of universal human rights issues, norms, values and perspectives.

By way of example, the Organization of American States governs human rights protection in the Americas. Both states and individuals can file cases and complaints. Under the American Convention on Human Rights, two bodies protect, promote and monitor human rights: a) The Inter-American Commission whose the primary function is to make a complaint to the Inter-American system whenever an American state is proved to have violated individual human rights; and b) The Inter-American Human Rights Court, which has jurisdiction over contentious cases mostly forwarded by the Commission. In the Inter-American system, both the Commission and the Court have made a major contribution to recognizing human rights, developing human rights jurisprudence and protecting human rights in the Americas. Elsewhere, the Council of Europe drafted a European Convention on Human Rights after Second World War in response to a call issued by Europeans from all walks of life. The Convention was designed to incorporate a traditional civil liberties approach to securing effective political democracy. The Convention created the European Court of Human Rights in Strasbourg, and any person, who feels that a state party has violated his or her rights under the Convention, can take a case to the Court. Judgments confirming violations are binding on all.

To be credible and able to meet both the promotion and protection requirements effectively and practically, a future regional human rights mechanism for SAARC, based on a human rights charter, should have a minimum set of characteristics. These would include an ability to receive and decide upon individual and interstate complaints of human rights violations by the state party. It should have the potential to develop additional mechanisms such as special procedures and subsidiary bodies on thematic issues, working groups, etc. There would be a SAARC Human Rights Commission, with broad powers to investigate, make site visits, receive reports and complaints by states and individuals, and a SAARC Human Rights Court empowered to make binding decisions on human rights issues and grant reparations for victims of human rights violations by states. The human rights mechanism, as with other regional practices, would be able to cooperate with international human rights mechanisms. This would permit reinforcement of the existing human rights framework and the overcoming of procedural and institutional weaknesses in domestic jurisdictions as well as in the international system. It would also help to overcome any lack of expertise or experience in human rights jurisprudence and to ensure effective implementation and enforcement of human rights norms and standards.

National human rights mechanisms are more important and effective in addressing local issues: the regional mechanism would play a complementary role, especially with regard to cross-border matters. The regional mechanism would also be a useful platform for South Asian countries to utilize opportunities under the United Nations's Universal Periodic Review system, which monitors the human rights performance of all UN members. A future SAARC charter on human rights, similar that of the Inter-American system, would be a great breakthrough for the SAARC region.

A Human Rights Culture in the Region

Enough is enough—SAARC must no longer be a hostage of rival powers in the region. The South Asian states have been too reluctant to take forward the regional project in a manner that it deserves. The provisions of the SAARC Charter have been ignored. Regional cooperation remains at a very rudimentary stage, and there is little evidence of any desire to act regionally by building trust and avoiding force. Prominent Nepalese Professor Lok Raj Baral has argued: 'So whatever commonalities and shared values exist in the region, they hardly matter for making SAARC more meaningful for the peoples of the region. Unless the South Asian regimes are reconstructed (and this is perhaps a challenging task for South Asian power elites who come from a variety of backgrounds) for transforming the nature of the region, SAARC cannot make headway.' In the absence of the right political atmosphere no economic, political or social integration is feasible. Establishing a proper regional human rights mechanism could provide an alternative way of establishing a favorable political environment and of reconstructing the region politically, socially and economically.

Of course, there would be enormous challenges in establishing a regional human rights mechanism in South Asia because of the legal and geo-political hurdles. The politics of the South Asia continue to be affected heavily by the continuing tensions in Indo-Pakistan relations. There are contentious issues, too, in South Asia—such as water, migrant workers, trafficking, minority and indigenous communities, refugees, and border disputes—which need to be settled through bilateral and multi-lateral mechanisms. If the SAARC countries fail to address these factors, its very future is bleak. Most importantly, political commitment, sincerity, and establishing a culture of human rights and the rule of law across borders are essential. Now is the time to create a SAARC Charter on Human Rights in treaty form, a consensus document. This must be the primary focus of all SAARC nations. It is essential. It needs to be the departure point for all SAARC agendas; it needs to be the alpha and omega for SAARC's future plans, programs and cooperation. The basic norms and values of human rights guaranteed by the international human rights covenants and national constitutions has to be the guiding force for any economic, social, developmental, and political cooperation among the South Asian countries.

Human rights must also be the guiding force for South Asian politics and for its democratic processes. These values must be above partisan politics and above the narrow interests of one or two nations. It has to be the means to common goals and agendas. Establishing the proposed human rights institution to monitor, promote, and consolidate human rights will bring the SAARC nations together to achieve common aims and ambitions towards peace and prosperity. The new future human rights body must be the common forum and a milestone to bring the South Asian society together as a single body of humanity regardless of religious, political, cultural or ideological differences. The essence of human rights has the power to mend all differences!

SAARC: INDIA NEEDS TO LEAD THE WAY

The upcoming summit of South Asian Association for Regional Cooperation (Saarc) will be held against the backdrop of important global and regional developments. On one hand, it is increasingly clear that the advanced Western economies are unlikely to see off the economic downturn in the short-run. This will have a knock on economic effects on South Asian countries in the form of weakening the demand for their products.

On the other hand, the context in the subcontinent is changing in a manner that augurs well for closer regional economic linkages. Taken together, these trends could provide an opportunity to infuse a muchneeded sense of purpose to Saarc. India should take the lead in re-programming Saarc for the next decade and ahead.

South Asia is one of the least economically integrated regions of the world. Intra-regional trade is just about five per cent of total official trade.

The contrast with other sub-regions of Asia — let alone other parts of the world — is sobering. For instance, intra-regional trade in East Asia accounts for over 50 per cent of total trade. The current situation in South Asia seems all the more stark when we set it against its past record as well as its future potential. Before 1947, this region boasted of more or less open borders, allowing for easy movement of goods and services.

Furthermore, the subcontinent also enjoyed close economic ties with other parts of Asia. The regional arc stretching from Kolkata to Singapore was a vibrant network of trade, finance and entrepreneurs that formed the economic heartland of the British empire in Asia. South Asia does not have to rest on its history. It continues to have tremendous potential to grow through trade. The region has the highest population density in the world. It has a large number of cities close to the borders. And there is considerable cultural, ethnic and linguistic overlap of populations across the borders.

What, then, has prevented closer regional and sub-regional economic integration? At one level, the answer can be found in the economic policies and outlook of the countries of South Asia since independence. The experience of colonialism led the newly independent countries — with the notable exception of Sri Lanka — to regard the idea of an open trading system with some suspicion and to pursue more autarkic economic policies and plans.

India and Pakistan also struggled to come to terms not only with the political consequences of Partition but also with its economic implications. The two countries were at odds on economic issues ranging from division of assets to exchange rates — differences that put paid to the idea of free trade between them. The problem was compounded by India's propensity to treat its borders as fences to keep others out rather than using them as gateways for the movement of goods, people and ideas. The under-development of India's own border areas, which were wont to be seen as buffer zones, undermined India's ability to promote regional trade.

These economic issues have been overlaid by political differences. Reconciling the two is not all that simple. Economic affairs tend to have a win-win logic. It is easy to see how cooperative exchange could work to the material benefit of all parties. But in politics moral considerations such as identity and honour can outweigh material interests. This is a problem that India faces with almost every one of its neighbours. What's more, if political differences have a national security angle to them, it becomes all the more difficult for the logic of economic integration to assume primacy. Economic affairs are about absolute advantages accruing from interchange, but security affairs are about relative advantages gained by one side or another.

Here too, India's immense lead in size and power as well as outstanding political disputes have worked to reduce the attraction of closer economic ties in the subcontinent.

The issues will not go away any time soon. But there are some indications that South Asian countries are willing to try according greater importance to economic linkages as opposed to political and security considerations. For one thing, India's economic growth in the last two decades has positioned it to credibly play the role of a regional dynamo. India's neighbours are slowly realising the tremendous opportunity that India presents for their growth prospects. India's free trade agreements with Sri Lanka and Bhutan, and the trade and transit agreement with Nepal have highlighted the potential benefits of regional economic integration.

It is not surprising that Bangladesh wants to greatly enhance trade and connectivity with India, or that Pakistan has at last agreed to confer "Most Favoured Nation" status on India. In the context of the continuing economic downturn in the West, India could become rather more important to its neighbours.

For another, India too has understood the fact that allowing its neighbours to partake of its growth is essential both to draw the sting from political differences and to enable India to play a role on the global stage. Once the largest recipient of foreign aid, India now extends aid and developmental assistance to most of its neighbours. These bilateral programmes are important, but India needs to help institutionalise pan-regional economic cooperation and eventually integration. The South Asian Free Trade Agreement (Safta) needs to be worth more than the piece of paper on which it was written. It's time India took concrete measures to hasten the implementation and expand the provisions of Safta.

CLIMATE CHANGE: INDIA TO SIGN TREATY WITH SAARC NATIONS

Marking a shift from its earlier position of staying within the United Nations Framework Convention on Climate Changes, India now appears ready to collaborate with various countries on climate change. On top of the list are the US, China and Japan. In a bid to present itself as a leader on climate change issues in the SAARC region, India is set to sign a treaty on environment with SAARC countries, the draft text of which is ready, *The Indian Express* has learnt. India has also discussed the possibility of a bilateral cooperation with Japan on thermal technology which cuts down on greenhouse gases.

Minister of Environment and Forests Jairam Ramesh met Japanese Environment Minister Sakihito Ozawa on Monday on the issue. SAARC Environment Ministers are at present in New Delhi. On Tuesday, the SAARC delegates are expected to release a joint environmental statement.

Ministry officials said the cooperation will chiefly be in the regions of forestry, biodiversity and wildlife and coastal management. Ramesh, speaking to *The Indian Express*, indicated that India needed to look beyond the Kyoto Protocol. "India has multiple messages to give on climate change, and India cannot be Doctor No," he said. "We are engaging with China, Japan and the US on climate change." This includes, he said, "being open to the discussion of a bilateral with Japan on climate change technologies." The focus is on reducing greenhouse gases through better coal-based thermal power technologies. "We are discussing with Japan coal-based power generation with less greenhouse gases. Japan is helping us with that."

In yet another shift, India seems set to be a donor in the issue of tackling climate change. It will give one-time grants for forestry and coastal management, Ramesh said. "We are looking at assuming a prominent role for climate change and environment in South Asia. The draft for a new environment agreement is also ready from India's side. The crux will be technology and financial transfer. Climate change is becoming a very important issue for SAARC, the theme of the April 2010 SAARC meet at Thimpu will be climate change. We are making one time grants of one million dollars to the SAARC forestry Centre, Thimpu, and one million dollars to SAARC Coastal Management Zone, Maldives.," he said. On a bilateral agreement with the US, Ramesh said: "We are open to it. The PM will discuss this with US President Barack Obama next month. The discussions are likely to be on energy security."

SOUTH ASIAN FREE TRADE AREA

The Agreement on the South Asian Free Trade Area is an agreement reached at the 12th SAARC summit at Islamabad, capital of Pakistan on 6 January 2004. It creates a framework for the creation of a free trade area covering 1.4 billion people in India, Pakistan, Nepal, Sri Lanka, Bangladesh, Bhutan and the Maldives. The seven foreign ministers of the region signed a framework agreement on SAFTA with zero customs duty on the trade of practically all products in the region by end 2016. The new agreement i.e. SAFTA, came into being on 1 January 2006 and will be operational following the ratification of the agreement by the seven governments.

SAFTA requires the developing countries in South Asia, that is, India, Pakistan and Sri Lanka, to bring their duties down to 20 percent in the first phase of the two year period ending in 2007. In the final five year phase ending 2012, the 20 percent duty will be reduced to zero in a series of annual cuts. The least developed nations in South Asia consisting of Nepal, Bhutan, Bangladesh and Maldives have an additional three years to reduce tariffs to zero. India and Pakistan have signed but not ratified the treaty.

Bimstec

Bay of Bengal Initiative for Multi Sectoral Technical and Economic Cooperation (BIMSTEC) is an international organisation involving a group of countries in South Asia and South East Asia. The member countries of this group are: Bangladesh, India, Myanmar, Sri Lanka, Thailand, Bhutan and Nepal.

Background

On 6 June 1997, a new sub-regional grouping was formed in Bangkok and given the name BIST-EC (Bangladesh, India, Sri Lanka, and Thailand Economic Cooperation). Myanmar attended the inaugural June Meeting as an observer and joined the organization as a full member at a Special Ministerial Meeting held in Bangkok on 22 December 1997, upon which the name of the grouping was changed to BIMST-EC. Nepal was granted observer status by the second Ministerial Meeting in Dhaka in December 1998. Subsequently, full membership has been granted to Nepal and Bhutan in 2004. In the first Summit on 31 July 2004, leaders of the group agreed that the name of the grouping should be known as BIMSTEC or the Bay of Bengal Initiative for Multi-Sectoral Technical and Economic Cooperation.

Aims and Purposes

According to the Bangkok Declaration on the Establishment of BIST-EC, the aims and purposes of BIST-EC/BIMST-EC are to create an enabling environment for rapid economic development, accelerate social progress in the sub-region, promote active collaboration and mutual assistance on matters of common interest, provide assistance to each other in the form of training and research facilities, cooperate more effectively in joint efforts that are supportive of, and complementary to national development plans of member states, maintain close and beneficial cooperation with existing international and regional organizations, and cooperate in projects that can be dealt with most productively on a sub-regional basis and which make best use of available synergies.

Bimstec was initiated with the goal to combine the 'Look West' policy of Thailand and Asean with the 'Look East' policy of India and South Asia. So it could be explained that Bimstec is a link between Asean and Saarc. Seven members of Bimstec covers 13 Priority Sectors led by member countries in a voluntary manner namely, Trade & Investment, Technology, Energy, Transport & Communication, Tourism, Fisheries, Agriculture, Cultural Cooperation, Environment and Disaster Management, Public Health, People-to-People Contact, Poverty Alleviation and Counter-Terrorism and Transnational Crimes.

What make Bimstec different from other organization would be that Bimstec represent one of the most diverse regions of the world, be it, way of life, religion, language, culture, etc. Bimstec clearly separates issues of development into 13 Priority Sectors besides focusing only on economic cooperation which make Bimstec covers all aspects regarding the word 'developing'. Bimstec provides a unique link between South Asia and Southeast Asia bringing together 1.3 billion people - 21 percent of the world population, a combined GDP of US$750 billion, and a considerable amount of complementarities. A study shows the potential of US$ 43 to 59 billion trade creation under Bimstec FTA. Regarding economic aspect, Bimstec has Trade Negotiating Committee (Bimtec TNC). The 16th TNC meeting was held during 17-21 March 2008 in India. The 17th TNC meeting was held during 15-17 October 2008 in Colombo, Sri Lanka. TNC Meeting is now working on the List of Goods regarding the Framework Agreement that has been signed in 2004. So far, Bimstec has been working on the FTA and looking forward to finalise our agreement soon.

Membership Criteria

Eligibility: Countries seeking membership should satisfy the conditions of territorial contiguity to, or direct opening into, or primary dependence on the Bay of Bengal for trade and transportation purposes. Procedure: All applications should be submitted in writing to the Chairman of BIMSTEC. The decision on admitting new members will be taken on the basis of consensus by all the BIMSTEC members. Institutional Structure and Arrangements The BIST-EC Declaration provides for the following institutional mechanisms:

- Annual Ministerial Meetings, which shall be hosted by the Member States on the basis of alphabetical rotation.
- Senior Officials Committee, which shall meet on a regular basis as and when required.
- A Working Group, under the chairmanship of Thailand and having as its members the accredited Ambassadors to Thailand, or their

representatives, of the other Member States, to carry on the work in between Annual Ministerial Meetings.

- Specialized task forces and other mechanisms as may be deemed necessary by the senior Officials to be coordinated by Member States as appropriate.

BIMSTEC Priority Sectors

BIMSTEC has thirteen priority sectors cover all areas of cooperation. Six priority sectors of cooperation were identified at the 2nd Ministerial Meeting in Dhaka on 19 November 1998. They include the followings:

1. Trade and Investment, led by Bangladesh
2. Transport and Communication, led by India
3. Energy, led by Myanmar
4. Tourism, led by India
5. Technology, led by Sri Lanka
6. Fisheries, led by Thailand After the 8th Ministerial Meeting in Dhaka on 18-19 December 2005, a number of new areas of cooperation emerged. The number of priority sectors of cooperation increased from 6 to 13. The 7 new sectors were discussed in the 1st BIMSTEC Summit and there has been various activities to enhance those co-operations ever since. The sectors are as follows,
7. Agriculture, led by Myanmar
8. Public Health, led by Thailand
9. Poverty Alleviation, led by Nepal
10. Counter-Terrorism and Transnational Crime, led by India
11. Environment and Natural Disaster Management, led by India
12. Culture, led by Bhutan
13. People to People contact, led by Thailand.

Chairmanship

BIMSTEC uses the alphabetical order for the Chairmanship. The Chairmanship of BIMSTEC has been taken in rotation commencing with Bangladesh (1997 - 1999), India (2000) Myanmar (2001-2002), Sri Lanka (2002 - 2003), Thailand (2003 – 2005), Bangladesh (2005-2006). Bhutan asked for the skip. So it's turned to India (2006-2009).

In November 2009, Myanmar hosted the 12th Ministerial Meeting and assumed BIMSTEC Chairmanship.

Cooperation with ADB

ADB has become BIMSTEC's development partner since 2005, to undertake a study which is designed to help promote and improve transport infrastructure and logistic among the BIMSTEC countries. So far, ADB has already finished the project so called BIMSTEC Transport Infrastructure and Logistic Study (BTILS). The final report of the said study from ADB has already been conveyed to all members and being awaited for the feedback. Other fields of cooperation will be designed later on.

BIMSTEC Centre

At the Sixth BIMSTEC Ministerial Meeting on 8 February 2004 in Phuket, Ministers endorsed the setting up of a Technical Support Facility (TSF). As reflected in the Ministerial Joint Statement, this Technical Support Facility would "serve the BIMSTEC Working Group (BWG) and to coordinate BIMSTEC activities, including those of the BIMSTEC Chamber of Commerce, for a trial period of two years". The decision by the Ministers was based upon the recommendation proposed by BIMSTEC Senior Officials who met in Bangkok during 17-19 September 2003. On this particular item, the SOM had with them a draft report prepared by Mr. David Oldfield, an ESCAP consultant, on "Towards Setting up a BIMSTEC Technical Support Facility and Permanent Secretariat: Considerations and Options". The report recommended that a TSF should be set up in Bangkok and would initially serve just the BWG during the trial period of 2 years. Since the Establishment of the Permanent Secretariat is awaited to consider in the 2nd Summit, which will be held on 12-13 November 2008 in India, Thailand had already extended the contract of the BIMSTEC Centre for another year from June 2007 - May 2008. So far, the Ministry of Foreign Affairs of Thailand had recently extended the contract for another year from 1 June 2008 – 31 May 2009.

NEWS ANALYSIS OF SAARC SOUTH ASIAN ASSOCIATION FOR REGIONAL COOPERATION

The South Asian Association for Regional Cooperation (SAARC) was established when its Charter was formally adopted on 8 December 1985 by the Heads of State or Government of Bangladesh, Bhutan, India, Maldives, Nepal, Pakistan and SriLanka. The Association provides a platform for the peoples of South Asia to work together in a spirit of friendship, trust and understanding. It aims to promote the welfare of the peoples of South Asia and to improve their quality of life through accelerated economic growth, social progress and cultural development in the region.

Cooperation in the SAARC is based on respect for the principles of sovereign equality, territorial integrity, political independence, noninterference in internal affairs of the Member States and mutual benefit. Regional cooperation is seen as a complement to the bilateral and multilateral relations of SAARC Member States. Decisions are taken on the basis of unanimity. Bilateral and contentious issues are excluded from the deliberations of SAARC. The SAARC Secretariat is based in Kathmandu. It coordinates and monitors implementation of activities, prepares for and services meetings, and serves as a channel of communication between the Association and its Member States as well as other regional organizations. The Secretariat is headed by the Secretary General, who is appointed by the Council of Ministers from Member Countries in alphabetical order for a three-year term. Mr. Q.A.M.A. Rahim from Bangladesh is the current Secretary General. The previous Secretaries General were from Bangladesh, India, Maldives, Nepal, Pakistan and Sri Lanka. The next Secretary General is to be from Bhutan.

The availability of real time maritime intelligence from South and South East Asian countries has been a key factor in the Sri Lankan navy's recent stunning successes against the intrepid and innovative naval wing of the LTTE. (Intelligence Key To Navy's Success: Source, *Hindustan Times*, Correspondent or Reporter, Oct 31, 2007) Pakistan said Monday that it would go ahead with the multi-billion Iran-Pakistan-India (IPI) gas pipeline project.

Pakistan will join hands with India to combat extremism and work with other SAARC countries to develop a mechanism for exchanging information to curb terrorism and drug trafficking, interior minister Aftab Ahmed Khan Sherpao has said. There was solid basis for New Delhi's response to the blasts in Karachi. The two countries are in the process of evolving a mechanism for police cooperation against terrorism and it is in India's interest to make Benazir conform to the....

The SAARC members on Thursday decided to strengthen cooperation in combating terror and crime, with a meeting of home ministers, chaired by Union Home Minister Shivraj Patil, agreeing to a bi-annual meeting of police chiefs.

Saarc countries on Thursday decided to have regular exchange of information to combat terrorism and to work towards establishing a convention for mutual legal assistance in criminal matters. Viewing terrorism as a "serious threat" to South Asia's peace and development, SAARC countries today decided to have regular exchange of information to combat the menace and push efforts for establishing a convention for mutual legal assistance... (SAARC Vows To Combat Terror, *Hindu*, Correspondent or Reporter, Oct 26, 2007)

Home Ministers of SAARC countries on Thursday said terrorism remained a serious threat to peace and development in the region and called upon the member-states to strengthen institutional mechanisms to fight it effectively. (Terrorism A Serious Threat: SAARC, *Hindu*, Correspondent or Reporter, Oct 26, 2007)

Acknowledging that terrorism remains a serious threat to sustainable peace and development of South Asia, SAARC countries underlined the need to give an added push to evolving a treaty on mutual legal assistance with the home or interior ministers... (SAARC Nations For Evolving Treaty On Mutual Legal Aid, *Tribune*, A N Sudarsan Rao, Oct 26, 2007)

After the Karachi bloodbath on October 19 the global condemnation of the terrorists' act and commiseration for Pakistan and Ms Benazir Bhutto was on the expected lines. (Cooperate To End Terrorism, *Tribune*, Gen V.P. Malik (retd), Oct 26, 2007)

Home Secretaries of SAARC countries on Wednesday resolved to move forward in the matter of mutual assistance to check terrorism and trans-border crimes and expressed the need for better cooperation among police organisations of member-countries. (SAARC Ministers On Mutual Assistance To Check Terrorism, *Pioneer*, Correspondent or Reporter, Oct 25, 2007)

Agreeing to share information to check trans-border crimes, police chiefs from SAARC nations on Tuesday suggested a database that could help security agencies combat terrorism, narcotics smuggling and cyber crime. (SAARC Meet: New Database To Combat Terrorism, *Indian Express*, Correspondent or Reporter, Oct 24, 2007). Member countries of the South Asian Association for Regional Cooperation on Tuesday proposed the creation of a database among them for a coordinated action against terrorism, drug trafficking, cyber crimes and financial frauds. (S. Asian Terror Database Proposed, *Dawn*, Jawed Naqvi, Oct 24, 2007) High-voltage talks are on this week to counter terrorism in the subcontinent, and it may just be coincidental that the move comes in the wake of explosions in Ajmer, Ludhiana and Karachi. (Edits, *Statesman*, Editorial, Statesman, Oct 24, 2007)

India and Pakistan today agreed to work together for identifying measures to beef up the anti-terror mechanism in the light of information shared earlier by the two on terrorist incidents and terror-related activities. (India, Pakistan Agree To Work On Anti-Terror Mechanism, *Statesman*, Correspondent or Reporter, Oct 23, 2007)

The second annual meeting of the SAARC home ministers will begin here tomorrow to hammer out a treaty on mutual legal assistance in criminal matters, forming a regional police forum and evolving a comprehensive mechanism for tackling terror...... (SAARC Home Ministers' Meeting Today, *Tribune*, Correspondent or Reporter, Oct 23, 2007)

India will host the second meeting of SAARC Interior/Home Ministers from Tuesday preceded by second meeting of SAARC Home Secretaries and the sixth SAARC Cooperation on Police Matters. (India To Host SAARC Ministerial Meet, *Pioneer*, Correspondent or Reporter, Oct 23, 2007)

The Pakistani link to the recent terror strikes in Hyderabad, Ajmer and Ludhiana came to the fore on Monday as India sought Pakistan's help in tracking down suspects who are believed to have cross-border links. (At Anti-Terror Meet, India Seeks Pak'S Help In Tracking Bombers, *Indian Express*, Correspondent or Reporter, Oct 23, 2007)

India and Pakistan will hold the second meeting of the Joint Anti-Terrorism Mechanism (JATM) here on Monday, during which Islamabad is expected to raise the issue of Samjhauta Express blast inquiry report. (Second Round Of Indo-Pak Jatm Talks On Monday, *The Economic Times*, Correspondent or Reporter, Oct 22, 2007)

With the British government more or less towing the American line on Iran albeit indirectly and the American pressure on India to clear its stand on the "errant" Iranian President, it looks like from SAARC (South Asian Association for Regional.... (India, Afghan And The Nam, Deccan Herald, Deepali Gaur Singh, Oct 10, 2007)

MODI'S SPACE DIPLOMACY: LEVERAGING SCIENCE IN REGIONAL INTEGRATION

On Aug 3, 2014, while addressing the parliament of Nepal, Indian Prime Minister Narendra Modi, the first foreign leader to address Nepal's Constituent Assembly-cum-parliament, stressed the need to launch a satellite for South Asia. Earlier, on June 30, at the launch ceremony of the Polar Satellite Launch Vehicle (PSLV – C23) in Sriharikota in Andhra Pradesh, Modi asked the country's scientists to develop a satellite for the South Asian region.

The prime minister saw an opportunity in leveraging India's leadership position in space applications and satellite launch capabilities to inject further momentum to his fledgling "neighbours first" foreign policy. Modi's proposal indicates his intent to add substance to ties with neighbours and further his agenda for regional integration.

The idea of a South Asian Association for Regional Cooperation (SAARC) satellite is not new. On April 26, 1998, the idea of a SAARC satellite was discussed by information ministers of the member states. Then SAARC secretary–general, Naeem Hasan, had pointed out: "We will examine the financial and technical feasibility of establishing a SAARC satellite." However, the idea was shelved, largely due to tensions between India and Pakistan. A year later, the Kargil conflict broke out between the two countries, and the idea of a SAARC satellite was relegated to the background. Modi feels it is an idea whose time has come.

India has always recognised that space has dimensions beyond national considerations and can only be addressed through international partnerships. Internationally, India is viewed by space faring nations as an emerging space power, with the Indian Space Research Organization (ISRO) capable of achieving its goals in a cost effective and time-efficient manner compared to its Western peers. Antrix Corporation limited, the commercial arm of ISRO, has successfully launched around 40 foreign satellites into the earth's orbit. The Indian-French joint satellite mission, MEGHA-TROPIQUES, was launched in 2011 for the study of the tropical atmosphere and climate related aspects such as monsoons, cyclones, etc.

Space technology is cost intensive, hence questions are raised about the relevance of space programmes for developing countries like India. However, despite the cost involved, space programmes have the potential to leapfrog infrastructure bottlenecks and provide basic services to the marginalised. The history of South Asia serves to remind us that natural disasters, mainly cyclones, earthquakes and droughts have destroyed life of the region. It is the need of the hour to generate and compile realtime scientific data to avoid natural disasters. India's remote sensing (IRS) satellites are time- tasted and have a proven track record.

IRS data has been of immense use not only in India but also for the region. The proposed SAARC satellite may prove helpful in addressing these imminent issues and reduce the risk and impact of natural disasters. Besides, space technology makes it feasible to develop a Tsunami Early Warning and protection system and is therefore relevant for those South Asian states having a coastline. Incidentally, India has already developed the Tsunami Early Warning system which warns about impending tsunamis in the Indian Ocean. It would add teeth to regional institutions like the SAARC Disaster Management Centre established in New Delhi.

Another use of a SAARC satellite is to resolve water woes in the region. Water is a burning issue and disputes related to sharing of water are common in South Asia. Water management is one of the ways to provide amicable solution to such disputes. By applying space technology we can undertake resource mapping as a first step towards carrying out water management of the Himalayas, which is the water source for a large part of South Asia.

In addition, Bangladesh, Maldives and India are facing a Herculean challenge in climate change. Rising sea levels have threatened the livelihood of millions of coastline residents of these countries. The proposed SAARC satellite could study the exact nature of the threat and may offer solutions.

The Indian National Satellites (INSAT) series is established for communication, television broadcasting and meteorological services that may prove instrumental in improving the fragile communication infrastructure of rural parts of South Asia. Further, INSAT could be put to use for aid in search and rescue operations during times of natural calamities. At the time of disasters space technology comes in handy to locate human beings and installations of economic importance.

India can push for establishment of a SAARC Space Applications Centre and train countries in the use of space technology. Also, India can assist its neighbours in the establishment of their own space programmes. Besides, India can replicate the Pan African e-Network project in South Asia to enable access to, and share expertise in the areas of tele-medicine, tele-education, resource mapping among others.

The South Asian region is struggling with plenty of problems and this reminds us of the need to work beyond national territories. A SAARC satellite is not a panacea for all of these evils but provides opportunity for South Asian states to work closely for common cause and eradicate many urgent predicaments. Modi should make a strong pitch for developing this idea in the forthcoming SAARC summit in November.

The idea of a SAARC satellite may be a ray of hope for one-fourth of humanity. By inviting all leaders of SAARC, in addition to Mauritius, for his May 26 swearing-in ceremony, Modi already pulled off a diplomatic coup and has now launched 'space diplomacy' through reviving the old idea of a SAARC satellite.

Modi is known for his out-of-the-box thinking, and development of a SAARC satellite will add a new feather to his cap.

A FORGOTTEN NEIGHBOUR THAT HOLDS THE KEY TO A REGION BEYOND SAARC

While the presence of leaders from the South Asian Association of Regional Cooperation was considered one of the most memorable aspects of Prime Minister Narendra Modi's swearing-in ceremony last May, this attachment to a regional organisation that has achieved little by way of economic integration, connectivity, or people to people contacts is, to say the least, strange.

In the brief period since India became a "dialogue partner" of ASEAN, we have achieved a far more rapid transformation of economic ties and connectivity — especially by air and now hopefully by road — than we have with our SAARC neighbours over the past three decades. One of the reasons for this has been the fact that the economies of our eastern neighbours in ASEAN are far more dynamic than those of the neighbouring SAARC countries, where only Sri Lanka and Bhutan can be said to have comparable rates of growth. Moreover, Pakistan is interested neither in connectivity nor economic integration with India, which is the only SAARC country sharing land/maritime boundaries with all other members. Islamabad's primary role in SAARC is to seek to isolate and embarrass India.

While Myanmar was regarded in colonial times as linked to India, the years following independence saw that country isolating itself progressively from the rest of the world. The advent of economic liberalisation in India and Narasimha Rao's "Look East Policy," coincided with efforts by the military junta in Myanmar to seek membership of ASEAN and open their doors for trade, investment and other ties, with the world. Mercifully, Rao and his successors chose not to follow western double standards and ostracise the military junta. What has followed has been a fruitful partnership with Myanmar that has safeguarded the security of our northeast, where four Indian States — Arunachal Pradesh, Manipur, Nagaland and Mizoram share borders with it.

Ignoring Myanmar

While our engagement with Myanmar has been of immense benefit to both countries, public knowledge of, and political interest in, this relationship have been abysmal. The net result is that while an unfriendly Pakistan and a distant Maldives were invited to Modi's inauguration, no representative from friendly Myanmar, with whom we share a 1640 kilometre land border and a well demarcated maritime boundary was invited. This, despite the fact, that Myanmar soldiers have, in the past, shed their blood fighting Indian insurgents. Moreover, Myanmar is today going through a quiet, but significant transformation in both its internal and foreign policies, which few in India have noted.

While the military junta, which took over in 1988, discarded General Ne Win's socialistic inclinations and isolationism, the country is now finally headed for a high growth path, after a decade of relatively slower growth.

The primary reason for this change is the end of US-led efforts to isolate Myanmar, ostensibly because of the absence of democratic freedoms. This change in American and western policies came about in 2010, when a new constitution came into force. While the US has called for a further reduction of the role of the military, which nominates 25% of the members of parliament and effectively blocks constitutional change, it appears unlikely that such change will be effected before general elections scheduled for later this year. Myanmar has been afflicted since its birth by ethnic insurgencies. Even today there are 16 armed ethnic groups committed to waging war against Yangon, under the umbrella of a "United Nationalities Federation Council". While the ethnic minorities may not vote for Aung San Suu Kyi, they do share her views on diluting the constitutional powers of the military.

China factor

Ever since the military Junta took over in 1988, New Delhi has viewed growing Chinese influence in Myanmar with increasing concern. New Delhi wisely discarded an ill-advised policy of joining Western efforts to criticise and isolate the military Junta and opted for a process of constructive engagement. While India had no intention of matching Chinese assistance in areas like infrastructure and arms supplies, substantial assistance was rendered in skill development of Myanmar personnel in areas ranging from remote sensing and military training to hotel management and Information Technology. The possibility of China establishing a military presence in the Bay of Bengal was pre-empted by India agreeing to develop the Bay of Bengal Port of Sittwe and building a road and river corridor linking Sittwe to its north-eastern States through Mizoram. India has also successfully participated in off-shore exploration for oil and gas.

The fears that existed in India just over a decade ago about Myanmar providing naval and radar bases on its mainland and the offshore Coco Islands to China have been assuaged. Myanmar looked the other way on aerial and satellite surveillance of activities on the Coco Islands by India. While there is still concern in New Delhi at some of the separatist groups from Nagaland, Assam, Manipur and Bodoland operating from Myanmar territory, there is broad satisfaction on both sides about continuing cooperation on this issue.

There are limits to the actions that Myanmar can presently take, as Indian insurgents have found haven in Kachin State, where large areas are controlled, not by the government, but by the Kachin Independence Army, which is known to enjoy links with people in China's bordering Yunnan province. In the meantime, as Myanmar's international isolation had ended and western and Japanese assistance has grown, there are strains in its relations with China. The Myanmar government has, in recent years, rejected Chinese projects for copper mining, a hydro-electric dam and a proposed rail link between Kunming and Kyaukphyu, in western Myanmar. Many Chinese-aided projects are primarily for exploitation of raw materials in recipient countries. They are administered by Chinese state-run enterprises like CNPC or PetroChina, with supplies of equipment and machinery coming from Chinese enterprises like Huawei. Their partners receive few benefits and, in fact, face problems of displacement of people and environmental degradation. Myanmar also suspects China, with good reason, of allowing its territory in Yunnan to be used by ethnic Han insurgents in Myanmar's Shan state. Matters escalated when the Myanmar Air Force bombed suspected bases of "Kokang" insurgents in Yunnan, resulting in the deaths of 4 Chinese farmers.

Wider regions

In these circumstances, India would do well to focus increasing attention on issues like energy corridors and connectivity in BIMSTEC, which links ASEAN members Thailand and Myanmar, across the Bay of Bengal, with Bangladesh, Sri Lanka, India and landlocked Nepal and Bhutan. This will allow India to demonstrate that Pakistani negativism cannot hinder its efforts at regional cooperation. Once Chabahar port in Iran is available for trade with Afghanistan and Central Asia, Pakistan will find itself bypassed. This would involve diminishing the salience and importance of SAARC as a forum for regional cooperation. That may not be a bad development, considering the limitations of SAARC as a useful forum for regional cooperation.

INDIA AND SAARC: INTERLINKED DREAMS

It may be a pure coincidence, but it's a serendipity laden with enormous symbolic significance. Exactly six months after taking charge of the world's largest democracy and pulling off a diplomatic masterstroke by inviting leaders of all South Asian countries for his swearing-in ceremony in New Delhi, Prime Minister Narendra Modi will be in Kathmandu for the 18th SAARC summit, signalling the pre-eminence of the 'neighbourhood first' template in his evolving foreign policy.

The focus on South Asia was visible from Day 1 of the Modi government and was reinforced by the prime minister's travels to Bhutan and Nepal and External Affairs Minister Sushma Swaraj's trips to Dhaka, Thimphu, Male and Kathmandu. It's also fitting that Mr Modi returns to a neighbouring country to galvanise India's South Asia diplomacy and spur the dream of an economically and culturally integrated region after engaging dozens of world leaders and attending a slew of big-ticket multilateral summits, for the destinies of the countries in the region are intimately intertwined.

Interlinked Dreams

Intertwined Destinies, Interlinked Dreams – expressions like these may appear ornate clichés for sceptics, but in reality it would be an understatement to underscore the enormous stakes each country has in fructifying immense potential of the region. India, the largest economy and the most populous country in the region, is an idealist as well as a realist in its ongoing efforts to revitalise the SAARC as the preeminent forum of regional cooperation and integration. For the India Story can't be delinked from the state of South Asia, its choices and its conflicts and its surging hopes and aspirations.

Why South Asia Matters

Eight nations, vibrant and emerging democracies, growing economies, and home to 1.7 billion people and major religions of the world, South Asia has all the makings of a regional dynamo itching for its place under the global sun. Twenty-nine years after its founding and in the run-up to the 30th anniversary in 2015, it's time for SAARC to bridge the gap between grand-sounding declarations and concrete action that can make South Asia a potent and effective player in the region and the world at large.

However, SAARC has been unfairly derided by sceptics as all talk and no action grouping; this critique is misplaced as SAARC may have miles to go achieve the required traction, but in its nearly three-decade journey, it has taken some important steps to cement the architecture of regional cooperation like the setting up of a South Asian University, SAARC Development Fund, a SAARC Food Bank to supplement national efforts in times of crises, and SAARC Disaster Management Centre to bail out each other in case of calamities and natural disasters.

These are all laudable steps, and only underlines the need to accelerate the pace of implementation of a whole range of ideas that are waiting to take off. And this ongoing collective effort to empower the SAARC and make the South Asia narrative of opportunity resonant will be the overarching scope of the November 26-27 Kathmandu summit –- the agenda which India wishes to proactively partner and bring it to fruition.

Regional Economic Integration

Imparting a renewed energy and momentum to regional economic integration will top the agenda at the Kathmandu summit, which is appositely themed: "Deeper Integration for Peace, Progress and Prosperity." The agreement on South Asian Free Trade Area (SAFTA) has led to a scaling up of intra-regional exports to about US$ 22 billion in 2013 from US$ 10 billion in 2006, but experts say this is just the tip of the iceberg.

The best is yet to come, and India is expected to proactively join efforts with other countries for actualising the vision of a South Asia Economic Union. The economic union envisages greater trade liberalisation, the development of cross-border trade infrastructure and the removal of non-tariff barriers, which is hindering the free movement of goods and services in the region. With the Modi government looking to make India a manufacturing powerhouse, Prime Minister Modi is expected to push for creating new cross-border production networks and joint manufacturing projects. India should also be pushing for proactive implementation of the SAARC agreement on services as the long-range goal of creating a seamless economic space in the region can only be achieved by free movement of not just goods, but through the liberalisation of services and the free movement of professionals.

Intensifying energy cooperation will be another key priority. In this context, the SAARC summit is expected to seal a pact on energy-sharing, a defining agreement that could pave the way for opening new pathways of economic cooperation among countries of the region.

Only Connect

Connectivity is the reigning theme of the Kathmandu summit. And India's focus, too, will be on weaving the region together in a web of rail, road and air links. One can expect SAARC countries to sign a pact for the regulation of passenger and cargo vehicular traffic and finalise modalities for stepping up trans-regional rail networks. The wish list of connectivity projects is a long one, and there are many ideas on the table, which includes, among others, a container service that connects Bangladesh and Nepal to India through the India-Pakistan Peshawar route.

Cultural Synergies

Connectivity can't be just physical; in the end, it's forging connections of mind and heart that matters. India is, therefore, expected to unveil new initiatives and highlight the need for promoting and deepening people-to-people, educational and cultural linkages.

Harnessing cultural and spiritual energies of the region will complement the larger project of regional integration.

South Asia is the cradle of four important religions of the world - Hinduism, Buddhism, Sikhism and Jainism - and its multicultural mosaic includes nearly half a billion Muslims who live across countries in the region.

Some of Sikhism's holiest shrines are in Pakistan. Except for Lumbini in Nepal, the birthplace of Lord Buddha, Buddhism's most important shrines are located in India, and Buddhism links India, Sri Lanka, Nepal and Bhutan.

Besides religion, one can see a literary alchemy binding the region. Nobel-winning sage-poet Rabindranath Tagore is equally popular in India and Bangladesh. Couplets penned by Urdu poets like Mirza Ghalib and Iqbal are recited with equal fervour in both India and Pakistan, and across the region.

Moving into Higher Orbit

With such a confluence of literary, cultural and religious affinities, and reinforced by a common impulse for regional economic integration and development, it's clearly time for South Asia. In an imaginative initiative, Prime Minister Modi has called for jointly developing a SAARC satellite that could become a powerful symbol of regional solidarity and a realistic vehicle of providing the much-needed data for averting natural disasters and meteorological data to optimise agriculture potential of individual economies and the region.

Initiatives like these show that the SAARC grouping, if it wants to, is ready to move into a different orbit, literally as well as metaphorically. It's time to raise the sights, dream big and prove that even the sky is not the limit for regional integration. Leaders should seize this SAARC moment of a potential South Asian renaissance, and unleash collective prosperity for the 1.7 billion people of the region.

2

India-Bangladesh Relation

For far too long has India been oblivious to the playing of the 'Indian-Card' (for or against) in Bangladesh's domestic politics. For far too long has India tolerated the use of Bangladesh as a springboard for Pakistan's strategic de-estabilisation of India's North-Eastern states. India could borrow a leaf from Myanmar's dealing with the Rohinggya problem emanating from Saudi based organizations in Bangladesh. Al Qaeda's tentacles exist in Bangladesh.

Bangladesh too is a fit case where Indian foreign policy objectives could gain a convergence with United States national interests. The China-Bangladesh Defence Cooperation Agreement adds an additional dimension to the other threats as analysed in an earlier Paper of this author.

India needs to draw red-lines in terms of India's national interests which Bangladesh must not overstep with impunity. In tandem, India through its big business houses should integrate Bangladesh into more commercial linkages. Increased Indian economic investments in Bangladesh could generates thousands of job and remove the root cause of Bangladesh's instability and move towards Islamic fundamentalism.

Historical Background

During the Partition of India after independence in 1947, the Bengal region was divided into two: East Bengal (present-day Bangladesh) and West Bengal. East Bengal was made a part of the Islamic Republic of Pakistan due to the fact that both regions had an overwhelmingly large Muslim population, more than 86%. In 1955, the government of Pakistan changed its name from East Bengal to East Pakistan.

There were some confrontations between the two regions though. Firstly, in 1948, Muhammad Ali Jinnah declared that only Urdu would the sole official language of the entire nation, though more than 95% of the East Bengali population spoke Bengali. And when protests broke out in Bangladesh on

February 21, 1952, Pakistani police fired on the protesters, killing hundreds. Secondly, East Bengal/East Pakistan was allotted only a small amount of revenue for its development out of the Pakistani national budget. Therefore, a separatist movement started to grow in the isolated province. When the main separatist party the Awami League, headed by Sheikh Mujibur Rahman, won 167 of 169 seats up for grabs in the 1970 elections and got the right to form the government, the Pakistan president under Yahya Khan refused to recognize the election results and arrested Sheikh Mujibur Rahman.

This led to widespread protests in East Pakistan and in 1971, the Liberation War, followed by the declaration (by Sheikh Mujibur Rahman on 7 March 1971) of the independent state of Bangladesh.

India under Indira Gandhi fully supported the cause of the Bangladeshis and its troops and equipment were used to fight the Pakistani forces. The Indian Army also gave full support to the main Bangladeshi guerrilla force, the Mukti Bahini. Finally, on 26 March 1971, Bangladesh emerged as an independent state. Since then, there have been several issues of agreement as well as of dispute.

Areas of Agreement

1. India played a central role in the independence of Bangladesh. About 250,000 Indian soldiers fought for, and 20,000 losing their lives for the cause of an independent Bangladesh. India sheltered over 10 million refugees who were fleeing the atrocities of the occupying West Pakistan Army. India and its ally Bhutan were the first countries to recognize Bangladesh as an independent nation. Bangladeshis have some awareness of their obligation and gratitude towards India.
2. Sheikh Mujibur Rahman's first foreign visit as Prime Minister and the Founding Father of the newly born nation was to India and it was then decided Indo-Bangladesh relations would be guided by principles of democracy, socialism, nonalignment and opposition to colonialism and racism. Indira Gandhi too visited Bangladesh in 1972 and assured that India would never interfere in the internal affairs of the country.
3. In 1972, both the countries signed a 'Treaty of Friendship and Peace'. An Indo-Bangladesh Trade Pact was also signed.
4. The mainstream party Awami League is generally considered to be friendly towards India.

Areas of Contention

1. A major area of contention has been the construction and operation of the Farakka Barrage by India to increase water supply in the river

Hoogly. Bangladesh insists that it does not receive a fair share of the Ganga waters during the drier seasons, and gets flooded during the monsoons when India releases excess waters.

2. There have also been disputes regarding the transfer of Teen Bigha Corridor to Bangladesh. Part of Bangladesh is surrounded by the Indian state of West Bengal. On 26 June 1992, India leased three bigha land to Bangladesh to connect this enclave with mainland Bangladesh. There is dispute regarding the indefinite nature of the lease.
3. Terrorist activities carried out by outfits based in both countries, like Banga Sena and Harkat-ul-Jihad-al-Islami. Recently India and Bangladesh had agreed to jointly fight terrorism.
4. The Sharing of Ganges Waters was also a matter of dispute.

A VIEW FROM THE INDIA-BANGLADESH BORDER

On 18 December 2013, the Indian National Congress party government introduced a bill in parliament to facilitate the realisation of the 1974 Land Boundary Agreement with Bangladesh. This bill was the latest in a long series of attempts to enable the exchange of 161 enclaves — tiny pieces of Indian territory completely bounded by Bangladesh and vice-versa — by absorbing them into their bounding states.

Residents of these enclaves face an absurd territorial dilemma, where to effectively exercise their rights as citizens they must illegally cross two borders. Yet, enclave exchange has proved a persistent and proverbial fly in the ointment of India-Bangladesh relations. Even the bill's introduction was heatedly contested, with members of a range of opposition parties raising vociferous protests calling the bill a 'Bangladesh giveaway'.

What are we to make of such protests? And what do they tell us about the India-Bangladesh border more generally? The Land Boundary Agreement's controversy hinges on both local and national disputes over the meaning of the border and its broader relationship to nationalist politics. Indeed, such struggles offer clues to the politics of postcolonial territory that haunt discussions of Bangladesh and its futures in both countries.

India's border with Bangladesh (formerly East Pakistan) has been a locus of contention since 1947. Hastily and haphazardly demarcated, the line dividing Bengal occasioned massive migration and violent dislocation of both Hindus fleeing the newly formed East Pakistan for India and Muslims moving in the opposite direction. Since Partition, the border has in practice gradually been worked out, formalised, and ossified into a highly securitised political boundary.

The border, itself, is a communal marker — the nominal division of a Muslim majority population from a Hindu majority one. And, indeed, that religious divide continues to dominate much debate over border politics.

Communal division is salient in discussions of migration and the steady illegal flow of people and goods across the border (in both directions). While an ongoing political debate continues between the two states over the scale of migration, the reality*and* imagination of (Muslim) Bangladeshis entering India on a permanent or temporary basis has long been a central lever in nationalist politics within India.

Another key issue is the spectre of violence at the border, particularly the debates over the regular exercising of lethal justice by India's Border Security Forces (BSF) on peasants and 'smugglers' crossing it.

Between 2007 and 2010, Human Rights Watch found that there were at least 315 Bangladeshi nationals reported killed by the BSF. As geographer Reece Jones persuasively argues, the BSF exercises a de facto right to carry out lethal justice, a reality that has made reporting on border shootings by the Bangladeshi media so regular as to have become banal.

An even more visibly present marker of this communal divide is the 3300-km floodlit border fence erected by India and surrounding much of Bangladesh. The fence has become a site of often graphic displays of violence. A troubling case-in-point is the 2011 shooting of Falini Khatun, a 15-year-old girl shot while crossing from India into Bangladesh and left tangled in the barbed wire at the fence's top to die. In Bangladesh, photos of Falini's hanging body became a potent marker of lethal border security. Its iniquities were further highlighted by the acquittal of the BSF officers charged with her death by an Indian court in 2013.

While the border thus dramatises the Partition's unfinished business — the incomplete communal division of Bengal — it would be a mistake to imagine that its politics are only influenced by communal debates and religious nationalism.

The fence also lays bare complex questions related to climate change — particularly the expectation that ecological transformation in the deltaic state will directly produce countless so-called climate refugees in the coming years. Indeed, a number of recent commentators have claimed that the India-Bangladesh border offers a preview of the ways that climate transformation is likely to effect political boundaries in the rest of the world.

Such arguments oversimplify the complex politics of migration and ecology at the border, but highlight the sensitive nature of border securitization in Bengal. It is also important to note that the border, and the bilateral relationship, is far from static. Indeed, particularly since the restoration of democracy in Bangladesh in 1991 with the ousting of General Mohammed Ershad from power, tensions along the border have dynamically fluctuated with elections in both states. The border, as residents report, is markedly less tense when the nominally secular Awami League is in power in Bangladesh and the Congress party is in power in India. Indeed, many critics of the Land Boundary Agreement bill saw its introduction as a Congress party attempt to provide support to Sheikh Hasina's Awami League government in Bangladesh's January elections.

In the summer of 2013, residents of a border enclave in Northern Bangladesh described to me the ways in which local border economies are intimately tied to such shifts. As they told it, a profitable boom in feed corn production in the enclave was, in fact, underwritten by cartels who had secured capital through cattle smuggling in the more relaxed border climate following the Awami League's 2008 return to power.

Such fluctuations mark life in the borderland, on both sides of the fence, with uncertainty. Moreover, they raise questions about what might happen to border life should Narendra Modi and the Hindu-right BJP ride the wave of Gujarat's economic miracle to power in India in 2014.

Given all this, it is not hard to see why so many policy initiatives to address border complications fail, or to see why the exchange of tiny amounts of territory should prove such a fraught and intractable proposition. The fate of the latest attempt to realise the Land Boundary Agreement remains unclear, though a short survey of border history leaves one skeptical about its prospects. The Agreement, and its 40-year history, are about much more than just the enclaves and their residents.

They take on symbolic dimensions, coming to represent both unfinished pasts and uncertain futures. The dramas of such legislative initiatives obscure the real costs of repeated political failure — the ongoing uncertainty and anxiety of life for residents who must navigate the dangerous complexities of the border on a daily basis.

INDO-BANGLADESH ENCLAVES

The Indo-Bangladesh enclaves, also known as the chitmahals, are the enclaves along the Bangladesh–India border, in Bangladesh and the Indian state of West Bengal. There are 106 Indian enclaves and 92 Bangladeshi enclaves. Inside the main part of Bangladesh, 102 of these are first-order

Indian enclaves, while inside the main part of India, 71 of these are Bangladeshi first-order enclaves. Further inside these enclaves are an additional 24 second order- or counter-enclaves (21 Bangladeshi, 3 Indian) and one Indian counter-counter-enclave, called *Dahala Khagrabari #51*. They have an estimated combined population between 50,000 and 100,000.

In September 2011, the Prime Ministers of the two countries (Manmohan Singh of India and Sheikh Hasina of Bangladesh) signed an accord on border demarcation and exchange of adversely held enclaves; however, the Indian parliament has yet to ratify it. Under this intended agreement, the enclave residents could continue to reside at their present location or move to the country of their choice.

HISTORY

According to an unverified popular legend, the enclaves were used as stakes in card or chess games centuries ago between two regional kings, the Raja of Koch Bihar and the Maharaja of Rangpur. As far as history records, the little territories were apparently the result of a confused outcome of a 1713 treaty between the Kingdom of Koch Bihar and the Mughal Empire. Possibly, the Kingdom and the Mughals ended a war without determining a single boundary for what territories had been gained or lost.

After the partition of India in 1947, Rangpur was joined to East Pakistan, and Koch Bihar was merged in 1949 with India. The desire to "de-enclave" most of the enclaves was manifested in a 1958 agreement for an exchange between India and Pakistan, but the matter then worked into a Supreme Court case in India. With that agreement unratified, the negotiations had to restart after East Pakistan became independent as Bangladesh in 1971. In 1974, both countries agreed either to exchange the enclaves or at least to provide easy access to the enclaves; Bangladesh quickly ratified, but in India the matter was rife with political sensitivity, and little materialised. Talks between the two countries on the issue resumed in 2001, but the lack of a concrete time frame relegated the issue to the back burner.

The residents of the enclaves live in abysmal conditions, with a lack of water, roads, electricity, schools and medicines. Crime also is rampant, as complaining would mean crossing the international boundary due to the lack of law enforcement resources. Residents of the enclaves may go to their respective countries only on the production of an identity card, after seeking permission from the border guards, causing much resentment. Recently the countries have moved towards an agreement to absorb the enclaves, but the resulting nationality of the current residents remains an impediment, as it could have implications for border disputes in other parts of the region. In September 2011, the governments of India and Bangladesh announced an intention to resolve the issue by means of swapping 162 enclaves, giving residents a choice of nationality. India will receive 51 enclaves (out of 74 Bangladeshi chhits inside India proper) of 7,110 acres, while Bangladesh will get 111 enclaves (out of the 119 Indian chhits inside Bangladesh proper) of 17,149 acres. Apparently Bangladesh would retain the 4617 acres of its Dahagram-Angarpota exclave. India planned to submit a constitutional amendment to Parliament to approve the agreement in August 2013. Bangladesh has already ratified the agreement. The bill was submitted to the India's Rajya Sabha on 18 December 2013.

NOTABLE ENCLAVES

Bangladesh

Dahagram–Angarpota: The largest Bangladeshi composite enclave (combining the first- and third-largest Bangladeshi chhits by area), administered as part of Patgram upazila in Lalmonirhat zila, lies within the Indian province of West Bengal. It is separated from the contiguous area of Bangladesh at its closest point by less than 200 meters. The enclave has an area of 25.95 km^2 (10 sq mi) with a resident population of 20,000 people. The enclave lacks all facilities. The lone health complex remains virtually useless for lack of power supply, as India refused to allow Bangladesh to run power lines to the enclave.

The Tin-Bigha Corridor, the 178 x 85 meter strip of Indian territory separating the Dahagram–Angarpota composite enclave from other Bangladeshi territory, was leased to Bangladesh for 999 years for access to the enclave. It is available for use by the residents of Dahagram–Angarpota during specified hours of the day.

India

Dasiar Chhara, the fourth largest Indian chhit by area, is the largest stand-alone Indian enclave (i.e., not a composite of adjoining chhits). It lies 3 km (2 mi) from the main part of India and has an area of 6.65 km^2 (3 sq mi).

According to the Census Report issued by Bharat Bangladesh Enclave Exchange Co-ordination Committee (31 July 2010), the total population of 9510 includes: male 4941, female 4569; Hindu 640, Muslim 8870; cultivator 2426, non-cultivator 840; literate 4148; disabled 6; with Indian EPIC 193, with BD EPIC 1173; under 5 years 378; 6 to 18 years 1072.

Dahala Khagrabari, the world's only third-order enclave (counter-counter-enclave, India in Bangladesh in India in Bangladesh).

ISSUES BETWEEN INDIA AND BANGLADESH

India and Bangladesh share a unique bond and a special relationship rooted in a common cultural heritage, shared principles and values and forged by common aspirations and sacrifices of its peoples. India is committed to carry forward the mission of strengthening the historic bonds and impart a vision for the future that is durable and sustainable and conducive for the collective prosperity of the region. Bangladesh's geopolitical importance for India is due to three factors. First, Bangladesh's location is a strategic wedge between mainland India and Northeastern seven states of the Indian Union. Each of these states is land-locked and has shorter route to the sea through Bangladesh. Currently, Kolkata port is used by these states for both domestic and imported cargo. Bangladesh is a natural pillar of "Look East Policy". A friendly Bangladesh that ensures no anti-India terror or insurgent activities can be carried out from its soil unlike in the past will substantially assist India in handling security problems in some of its restive north-east States. Importantly, a 'neutral' Bangladesh also ensures containment of an assertive China in this region, including along the strategic sea-lanes of the Bay of Bengal.

Further the navigable rivers in India's Northeast that could connect West Bengal or Orissa ports pass through Bangladesh. The only entry to and exit from the Northeastern region of India is through the Shiliguri Corridor that is close to the Chinese border and within striking distance of Bangladesh. The Shiliguri Corridor is the most sensitive 'choke point' for the Indian Union.

But unfortunately, there exist many contentious issues between the two countries.

Water Dispute

India and Bangladesh share 54 trans-boundary rivers, big and small. In 1996, the sharing of the Ganga waters was successfully agreed upon between the two nations. However, the major area of dispute has been India's construction and operation of the Farakka Barrage. The aim of construction of the Farakka Barrage was to increase the lean period flow of the Bhagirathi-Hooghly branch of Ganga to increase the water depth at the Kolkota port which was threatened by siltation. As irrigation withdrawals increased in Bangladesh, dispute arose between India and Bangladesh over the sharing of the lean season flow at Farakka. The inadequacy of water during the lean season to meet the assessed demands in the two countries is the root cause of the conflict.

The Bangladesh government feels that the reduction in flow caused damage to agriculture, industry and ecology in the basin in Bangladesh. Because of the inability of the concerned governments to come to any lasting agreement over the last few decades on sharing the river water, this problem has grown and now it is also viewed as a case of upstream-downstream dispute.

The other reason for water dispute is Teesta River – which has its source in Sikkim – flows through the northern part of West Bengal in India before entering Bangladesh, where after crosssing through about 45km of irrigable land, merges with the Brahmaputra River (or Jamuna when it enters Bangladesh). In 1983, an ad-hoc water sharing agreement was reached between India and Bangladesh, whereby both countries were allocated 39% and 36% of the water flow respectively. The new bilateral treaty expands upon this agreement by proposing an equal allocation of the Teesta River. However, the deal fell through when the then newly elected Chief Minister of West Bengal, Ms. Mamata Banerjee, refused to approve the treaty, fearing that the loss of higher volume of water to the lower riparian would cause problems in the northern region of state, especially during drier months.

Construction of the Tipaimukh Dam is another contentious issue between India and Bangladesh. Tipaimukh Dam is a hydel power project proposed on the river Barak in Manipur. Bangladesh's objection is that it would have adverse ecological effects in its eastern Sylhet district. In spite of India's reiteration that no dam would be constructed overlooking Bangladesh's objections, the controversy is far from over. The popular arguments in Bangladesh against the Tipaimukh project are:

- India should not decide what is good for people of Bangladesh without taking them into confidence;
- No study has been undertaken in Bangladesh to assess the impact of the ecosystems that exist and depend on the natural flow of the water in Surma-Kusiyara-Meghna and their tributaries.

India and Bangladesh have agreed on a joint study group to examine the points raised by Bangladesh.

Boundary Dispute

India's land border with Bangladesh as per the Ministry of Defence is 4351 km. running through five states, viz., West Bengal (2217kms), Assam (262 kms), Meghalaya (443kms), Tripura (856 kms) and Mizoram (318 kms), including nearly 781 kms of riverine border. The border traverses through 25 districts.

The border is used as a route for smuggling livestock, food items, medicines and drugs from India to Bangladesh. Moreover, illegal immigrants from Bangladesh cross the border to India in search of improving their lives. Because of a large number of illegal immigrants crossing from Bangladesh into India, a controversial shoot-on-sight policy has been enforced by the Indian border patrols. This policy was initiated with reports of violence between the illegal migrants and Indian soldiers. The border has also witnessed occasional skirmishes between the Indian Border Security Force and the Border Guards Bangladesh, most notably in 2001.

The killing of Bangladeshi nationals by Border Security Force (BSF) has become a major irritant between the two countries in the recent past. It has evoked strong public sentiments in Bangladesh. According to a report of Bangladesh Human Rights Watch organization Odhikar, BSF has, from January 1, 2001 to March 31, 2012, killed 907 Bangladeshis. Bangladesh wants no time lost in stopping these killings.

Further the Agreement on the demarcation of Land Boundary between Bangladesh and India and related matters had been signed in May 1974 between the two great statesmen, Bangabandhu Sheikh Mujibur Rahman, and Smt. Indira Gandhi. This comprehensive agreement was intended to resolve all lingering and vexing problems that history had bequeathed on the two nations. But it has not full filled by both Governments.

During the State visit of the Prime Minister to Bangladesh in September 2011, a "Protocol to the Agreement between the Government of India and the Government of Bangladesh Concerning the Demarcation of the Land Boundary Between India and Bangladesh and Related Matters (LBA)" was signed. It settles the long outstanding land boundary issues related to un-demarcated segment of 6.1 Kms; territories in adverse possession; and exchange of enclaves.

The Cabinet has, on 13 February 2013, approved the draft of a Constitution (Amendment) Bill for implementing the India-Bangladesh Land Boundary Agreement (LBA) 1974 and the Protocol to LBA signed in 2011. The Protocol envisages that 111 Indian Enclaves in Bangladesh and 51 Bangladesh Enclaves in India, as per the jointly verified cadastral enclave maps, shall be exchanged. As per Article 3 of the LBA 1974, when the Enclaves are transferred, people living in these areas shall be given the right of staying on where they are as nationals of the State to which the areas are transferred.

The delay in implementation of the land boundary agreement signed during the Indian Prime Minister's visit has increased the differences. The

Bangladesh Parliament has ratified the agreement, but it awaits ratification by the Indian Parliament. Bangladesh is urging India to take necessary steps at the earliest to make it functional. The reason for the parliamentary delay is the reservation expressed by some sections, mainly people living on the border, who complain that they had not been consulted before signing the treaty. They also argue that implementation of the treaty would have adverse impact on their lives.

INDIA-BANGLADESH RELATIONS: TOWARDS INCREASED PARTNERSHIP

The last decade has seen a new development in India's foreign policy. Both the Congress-led United Progressive Alliance (UPA) and the BJP-led National Democratic Alliance (NDA) governments have sought to improve political relations and deepen economic partnerships with neighbouring countries.

India's quest for self reliance, initiated soon after Independence, steadily reduced the salience of economic engagement with its neighbours. This approach cost India economically and diplomatically; trade barriers within South Asia have limited growth potential. Certain key unresolved issues between the two countries resulted in the under-exploitation of the potential for mutual growth. While India played a critical role in 1971 in the birth of Bangladesh, this did not however result in close bilateral ties. India was even present in Bangladesh's threat perception, with public opinion in Bangladesh accusing India of embracing a heavy-handed approach.

But the opening up of India's economy and the renewed political emphasis on building a peaceful periphery represented a unique opportunity for India to realise its ambition of resecuring strategic ties in its immediate neighbourhood. Additionally, geo-strategic equations with China, whose rise has cast a lengthening shadow over the subcontinent, presented an added urgency in New Delhi to transform its regional policy.

Bangladesh formed an important component in this strategy. India and Bangladesh, two sub-continental neighbours, have always shared strong cultural, linguistic and geographical ties. Historically the destiny of the Bangladeshi people has never been far removed from that of the other communities that make up the Indian sub-continent. Bangladesh has fought alongside India twice in the cause of the right of peoples to self determination, and the two countries have shared a porous border for over 40 years. Today, as the recent improvement in relations suggests, there is a growing realisation that increased cooperation will bring substantial socio-economic benefits that can no longer be overlooked. Bangladesh Prime Minister Sheikh Hasina's landmark visit to India in 2010 was followed by Prime Minister Manmohan Singh calling on Dhaka in September 2011. These visits unveiled a sweeping agenda for the transformation of bilateral relations by committing the two leaders to resolve all major outstanding issues left behind since the partition.

The ambition in 2010 was to reaffirm their shared history and build a new basis for a cooperative relationship, with both sides making a substantive effort to overcome issues. A comprehensive framework of cooperation for development aimed at promoting trans-border cooperation in the management of shared water resources, hydro-power potential and eco-systems and in the areas of connectivity and trade and economic cooperation was signed between the two countries.

However, some of the progress that was made in the run-up to the second visit was undermined when the Teesta Waters Agreement did not fructify at the last minute. Given the emotion attached to the water issue in Bangladesh, there was some disappointment during Indian Prime Minister Dr. Manmohan Singh's visit to Dhaka. Neverthless, it is to be noted that the Joint Communiqué of 2010 and the Joint Statement of 2011 were major steps in charting the future course of relations between India and Bangladesh. It is now up to both the countries to restore confidence and rebuild upon what has already been achieved and advance the bilateral relationship.

DOMESTIC SITUATION IN BANGLADESH

The evolving political situation in Dhaka has always played a key role in determining Bangladesh's foreign policy and its relations with India. The 2008 general elections saw the Awami League come to power in Bangladesh, with the Sheikh Hasina-led government decimating Khaleda Zia's Bangladesh Nationalist Party (BNP) in the polls.

Over the years, India has enjoyed strong relations with Bangladesh under an Awami League government. This was further demonstrated by Bangladesh cracking down on insurgent groups operating within its borders and tempering anti-Indian Islamist sentiments within the country. The success or failure of Sheikh Hasina's policies will not only affect the future prosperity of Bangladesh, but will also impact the prospects of Indo-Bangladesh relations.

The spectacular manner in which the Awami League came to power in 2008 has allowed the government to undertake certain bold decisions that it was not capable of making during its previous term. In a bid to remove the caretaker system of government during elections, the government passed the

15th amendment to the constitution in 2011. The BNP, which is extremely critical of the amendment, is afraid that the Awami League will take advantage of the highly politicized nature of Bangladesh's institutions like the judiciary, police force and election commission and has threatened to boycott the elections.

The last time elections were boycotted by the opposition party, the army was forced to step in amidst allegations that the caretaker government was partisan. Crucially, going forward, India must be aware of developments occurring in real time in Bangladesh, lest it be caught off guard by unfavourable political changes.

One concern experts cite is that India may be relying too heavily on Sheikh Hasina and the Awami League to maintain stable relations with Bangladesh. While the Awami League shall remain in power till 2013, and might even return to power in an unprecedented fashion, it is imperative that India cultivate relations with the opposition party. It is no secret that India shares a certain affinity with Sheikh Hasina's liberal and pro-democratic government, but a propensity to vote incumbents out of power necessitates that India engages all shades of Bangladeshi public opinion.

Conscious of the present mindset of the people of Bangladesh, the BNP has also significantly toned down its anti-India stand of late. Certain BNP leaders have voiced the need to improve and strengthen India-Bangladesh relations, indicating that they can no longer exploit anti-India sentiments for narrow and immediate political gains. With the political situation precariously balanced in Bangladesh, taking this window of opportunity, the Indian government must look to the future and engage all sides of Bangladesh's political spectrum.

BORDER MANAGEMENT AND LAND BOUNDARY AGREEMENT

The India-Bangladesh border that stretches for over 4094 km and is extremely porous facilitates the illicit flow of goods across the border and illegal migration from Bangladesh into India. In fact, illegal trade and smuggling has led to violent incidents in the past with Bangladesh accusing India's Border Security Force (BSF) of shooting innocents. India, which has always maintained that the supposed innocents were in fact gangs of cattle smugglers, has now issued strict guidelines for the use of non-lethal weapons against illegal trespassers. With the majority of the trespassers evading security forces, it is evident that not enough resources are being allocated to the border. India's greater focus on the Indo-China and Indo-Pak borders has relegated the India's border with Bangladesh to relative obscurity over the last few decades, with the neglected border only receiving the central government's attention in the last decade only, due to rapidly escalating security concerns.

While both countries now recognise the significance of checking cross border crime they also acknowledge that the border guarding forces must exercise restraint. In July 2011 both nations signed the Coordinated Border Management Plan to effectively control cross border illegal activities. Both governments directed the concerned agencies to meet regularly to discuss coordination efforts, share information and identify vulnerable areas.

Related to the border issue is the problem of illegal migration from Bangladesh into India. Historically, migration has been a recurring cause of concern in India-Bangladesh relations; and Bangladesh's role in facilitating the movement of its population beyond its borders has always been a question mark. Today, with population pressures beginning to tell in several Indian states and influx from Bangladesh rising at an alarming rate, the issue has taken on great significance. Over and above the economic and demographic risk that migration poses to India through drain of resources and employment strains, migration has also led to a rise in crime and other subversive activities that pose a considerable challenge for India's security apparatus.

With the termination of the Illegal Migrants Determination by Tribunal Act (IMDT), the government took an important step in detecting and deporting illegal immigrants. However, in order for the Indian government to make considerable headway with the migration issue it needs the support of the sending country, in this case Bangladesh. Many European countries that are faced with the same migration problem are increasingly resorting to re-admission agreements in order to tackle the problem. Whether India should enter into a similar readmission agreement with Bangladesh remains unclear; yet it is evident that it needs to engage with Bangladesh on this issue. The Land Boundary Agreement signed on the 6th of September 2011 was meant to mark a watershed in India-Bangladesh relations and resolve a decade old boundary dispute between the two countries. This long overdue exchange of territory concentrated over 200 enclaves would give India a clear and demarcated border with Bangladesh and would bring these enclaves, which are like islands of Indian and Bangladeshi territory surrounded by each other's land, out of isolation and abject poverty.

The Indira-Mujib Land Boundary Agreement of 1974 (upon which the current agreement was built) was meant to do just that, but was not ratified by the Indian parliament. However, the agreement which has yet to be ratified by the parliament, was stalled when UPA ally Trinamool Congress and sections of the opposing NDA voiced reservations against the historic deal, arguing that the deal gives away too much territory to Bangladesh. The non-resolution of the enclaves remains a major problem for the current Bangladeshi government which has repeatedly been criticised by opposition parties for extending too much support to India.

INDIA'S FOREIGN POLICY IN COMPARISON WITH BANGLADESH'S FOREIGN POLICY

India's policies towards Bangladesh can be studied within the broad parameters of its policy towards its friendly neighbours. The basic objective of such policies can be acknowledged as:

(a) India's aspiration to see a forthcoming, secular and democratic regime in Bangladesh.

(b) To ensure that, Bangladesh does not pose any security challenge to India.

(c) To seek trade and transit for its North East (NE) region and have an integrated move towards socio - economic developments.

(d) To implement a bilateral approach to resolve all issues between the two countries.

These above mentioned four steps have substantially influenced India's policy towards Bangladesh. Unlike Pakistan, India always had the aspirations to become a regional super power through its own military and economic capacity. In this chase for supremacy, India has always considered Pakistan and China to be the major hindrances or impediment. India's clear fixation with these two countries has apparently reduced the significance of Bangladesh to her.

The foreign policy of Bangladesh, like that of any other democratic and secular state is a projection of the country's socio-economic and political commitments and restrictions in the international amphitheatre. Due to obvious reasons, India has always occupied the centre stage of Bangladesh's foreign policy. However many feel that India has displayed a lackadaisical attitude towards her. Unfortunately, Bangladesh has been perceived more as a safe haven for insurgents and illegal immigration.

Political and Sociological Faultlines

The polity of Bangladesh is marked by confrontation. There are two major and dominant political parties and their problem is that, these parties have not demonstrated any common move on how to deal with India on issues like water, transit, trade and NE insurgents. Each move is considered through a populist gauge and the perceived political mileage. One of them is over friendly to India, while the other one bears the extreme 'Anti-India' posture. Perhaps, India-Bangladesh relations have suffered cyclic phases of ups and downs, largely reflecting the shifting governments both in Dhaka and New Delhi. The public perception in Bangladesh is that, India, as a bigger country, should be giving more concessions to Bangladesh; since, it argues that it supported the war on humanitarian and political grounds.

Water Issues

One of the major irritant in the relationship has been the perennial debate over the 54 common rivers, running between Bangladesh and India. If one single issue that has degraded India in Bangladesh to the optimum, is Farakka. Because of Farakka, Bangladesh has suffered and even India has not benefited out of it. Since the time Farakka issue had started becoming evident, anti-Indianism in Bangladeshi people became far more popular and to some extent, turned into an aspect of main stream politics and the relationship has turned into an extreme astringent one.

India undertook more projects on the common rivers; namely, river linking project, Tipaimukh Dam and Gazaldoba Barrage, etc. Bangladesh feels that both Gazaldoba and Tipaimukh, have been constructed or planned to deprive Bangladesh of an equitable share of water, which has been proved otherwise by India, scientifically. Bangladesh contests that anything, which amounts to denial of this right (of water) would be perceived by the Bangladeshis, as stabbing on their sovereignty and as an example of India's "hegemony," "high-handedness," "big brotherly attitude" and "a desire to dominate ". The sharing of the river waters, therefore, is a highly emotive issue for the policy makers, people and media in both the nations.

Security Related Issues

India's concern for security is axiomatic and recognizable. India's sympathies with democratic forces and its aversion to extra-regional presence are all geared to optimise its security interest, which is ensconced in its principal belief of a stable neighbourhood while engaging in a mutually beneficial relationship.

However, India on its own, can do very little to augment its security environment, and it requires the active cooperation and assistance of its neighbours. An increasing number of Bangladeshis have of late been getting involved in terror activities inside Indian territories. The issue of terrorist camps of Indian Insurgent Groups, inside Bangladesh had been one of the controversial issues between the two nations. To curb insurgency and ensure political stability, India has repeatedly sought Dhaka's assistance without which, it would be almost impossible for India to irradiate these radical groups.

The transformation of security scenario began, as the incumbent government led by Sheikh Hasina assumed power in Dhaka. Bangladesh had taken decisive steps to limit the activities of militant organisations. Terrorist activities are being actively carried out by outfits based in both countries, like Banga Sena and Harkat-ul-Jihad-al-Islami. Bangladesh has apprehended and handed over some terrorists to Indian authorities. India is satisfied with Bangladesh's efforts as the United Liberation Front of Assam (ULFA) insurgency in Assam, has already begun to dissolve.

Bilateral Trade and Imbalances

Post independence India has grown many folds from a status of a struggling underdeveloped country to an economically recognised super power that has posted an impressive 8% average annual growth for over a decade. The economy of Bangladesh is also rising, however at a much slower rate of 6% to 8%. Although it will be correct to assume that Bangladesh is totally dependent on India due to its geostrategic location and other known reasons, it can also be assumed that India too has been benefiting economically due to its exports to Bangladesh. Therefore it is a complete matter of mutual dependence in the field of trade and economy. Issues like the Non-Tariff Barriers and Para-Tariff Barriers are seen by Bangladesh, as India's reluctance to open up its market and has lead to trade imbalances in favour of India.

Transit Facility to Indian States of NE

The geographical position of Bangladesh allows it to be a passage country, connecting the larger part of South Asia with the South-East Asia. Bangladesh has consistently denied India transit facility to the landlocked NE Regions of India. Although India has a narrow land link to this North Eastern region, which is famously known as "India's Chicken Neck" for better connectivity, India has always wanted transit facility from Bangladesh.

India's aspiration to develop insurgency-infested NE region, is inextricably linked to the issue of transit through Bangladesh. Bangladesh had agreed to accord transit facility to India through waterways, railways and roadways by signing Indo- Bangladesh Trade Agreement on 28 March 1972. However the Bangladeshi politicians have always been against providing transit to India on the pretext that they did not want Bangladesh to be unnecessarily dragged into a future Indo-China conflict. Therefore, despite economic benefits, providing connectivity to India, it remains a dubious issue; as it could have troublesome effect on Bangladesh's bilateral relationship with India or China in isolation.

Border Issues

India and Bangladesh share a land boundary of 4096.7 km, the fifth longest border in the world. This border is marked by porosity, complexities, spread over a varied terrain to include riverine, hilly and mountainous terrain; which has made guarding of this vast stretch of land, very tricky. The temperament of political relation between the two countries definitely has an influence on the borderland and vice versa.

The terrain and demographic composition of the bordering areas and lax governance make it convenient for populace of either side to slip into the other side. The wide-spread illegal migration from Bangladesh has reached such an astounding level, that it had begun to alter the demographic profile and threaten the socio-political fabric of the bordering. Recently a number of mass congregations and riots were witnessed in Assam to protest the deep seepage of the Bangladeshi migrants into the state. Thus, Indian prime concerns ie. illegal migration, cross border movement of Insurgent Groups and security of the state are entwined with the border. Killing of illegal migrants and trespassers (Bangladeshis or Indians) by BSF, rampant smuggling of arms and drugs, recurrent problem of cattle trade etc, are other border related problems which have negatively undermined the bilateral relation.

2001 BANGLADESHI-INDIAN BORDER SKIRMISH

The 2001 Bangladeshi-India border skirmish took place in the third week of April 2001 between companies of theBangladesh Rifles and the Indian Border Security Force on the poorly marked international border between the two countries.

Cause

The Partition of Bengal in 1947 left a poorly demarcated international border between India and Bangladesh (then-East Pakistan). Ownership of several villages on both sides of the de facto border were disputed and claimed by both countries. The dispute over the demarcation of the Indo-Bangladeshi border worsened due to the existence of over 190 enclaves.

One of the disputed areas was a small sliver of land near the village of Pyrdiwah which the Indian Border Security Force (BSF) had occupied since the 1971 liberation of Bangladesh. The village was one of the Indian exclaves near the border of Bangladesh with the Indian state of Meghalaya. Bangladesh claimed that the village was within its territory.

Conflict

The April 16–19 fighting was the worst since the creation of Bangladesh in 1971. It took place around the village of Padua (known as Pyrdiwah in India), which adjoins the Indian state of Meghalaya and the Timbil area of the Bangladesh border in the Sylhet district. In that area, 6.5 kilometres of the border have remained in dispute for the past 30 years.

The trigger for the clash appears to have been an attempt by Indian forces to construct a footpath from an army outpost in Padua across a disputed territory some 300 metres wide to Indian Meghalaya. When the Indian Border Security Force refused to withdraw, the Bangladeshi border force attacked and retook Pyrdiwah village. As per the Bangladesh Rifles chief, the village had been illegally occupied by India since Bangladesh's war of independence in 1971. A few days later, Indian border guards retaliated and tried to enter Boroibari, more than 100 km to the west of Padua/Pyrdiwah. Boroibari is another disputed area between India and Bangladesh. In a violent confrontation 16 Indian border guards died and 2 were injured. The attack also left 3 Bangladeshi border guards dead and 5 injured. About 10.000 civilians fled the area after some 24 were wounded in the shooting.

Result

Top Indian border security sources claimed that the BDR personnel had withdrawn from the occupied territories in the Meghalaya sector, while in the Assam sector, the Indian BSF had vacated positions seized from Bangladesh. Fresh clashes erupted along the India–Bangladesh border just hours after both sides voiced regret for the recent killings, but by midnight of 20 April firing had again stopped.

An article reported that 6,000 Indian civilians had fled the region, and Indian government officials were attempting to convince villagers to return to their homes. Bangladesh later agreed to return 16 dead Indian soldiers the next day. Upon examining the bodies of the dead personnel, India alleged that the BSF men were tortured before being shot dead. On the other hand three Bangladeshi soldiers were also killed: two during combat and another who died of woundssustained during operations.

Aftermath

The Prime Ministers of Bangladesh and India, Sheikh Hasina and Atal Bihari Vajpayee, spoke over telephone and agreed to order a high-level investigation into the incident. Indian Foreign Ministry spokesman Raminder Jassal reported that both India and Bangladesh would improve diplomatic channels and promised to exercise restraint in the future. India and Bangladesh started talks in March 2002 to resolve their border disputes. By July 2001, the two sides established joint working groups to establish the un-demarcated sections of the border.

Officially, Bangladesh denied it had initiated hostilities. This was the first armed conflict between India and Bangladesh, two nations that had maintained friendly relations since Bangladeshi independence in 1971. The end of the brief conflict saw an upsurge of nationalism in Bangladesh. In parliamentary elections, the four-party right-wing alliance led by the Bangladesh Nationalist Party and Jamaat-e-Islami Bangladesh won a majority of 196 seats out of 300. Both sides desisted from any further hostilities and began border talks to discuss disputes along their 4,000-kilometre (2,500 mi) border. Relations were cooled down shortly afterwards. India later began constructing a fence along the entire length of the international border with Bangladesh. India is still in the process of constructing the Indo-Bangladeshi barrier. Bangladesh protested that construction of the fence within 150 yards of the border was a gross violation of the Indo-Bangladeshi Treaty of Friendship, Cooperation and Peace. The Bangladesh government also protested frequent BSF incursions into Bangladesh, and shootings which resulted in the deaths of Bangladeshi citizens inside Bangladeshi territory. In a news conference in August 2008, it was stated that 97 people had been killed (69 Bangladeshis, 28 Indians, rest unidentified) trying to cross the border illegally during the prior six months.

3

India-Bhutan Relation

While Bhutan shares borders with both China and India, its relationships with the two are not of equal length and depth. It is a lot closer to India, and the two share intimate bonds in the areas of foreign affairs, economy, trade, education and technology, and national defence and security.

Bhutan used to build its foreign relations completely around India. The two signed the Treaty of Perpetual Peace and Friendship Between the Government of India and the Government of Bhutan in Darjeeling, India on August 8, 1949. The treaty does not mention Bhutan's status as a sovereign state. Article 2 says that, "The Government of India undertakes to exercise no interference in the internal administration of Bhutan. On its part the Government of Bhutan agrees to be guided by the advice of the Government of India in regard to its external relations."

This means that Bhutan needs to seek "advice" from India in foreign relations in exchange for India's recognition. Bhutan is heavily dependent on India for financial assistance and foreign relations. India agrees to provide 500,000 INR to Bhutan every year, which is much higher than the 200,000 INR a year from Britain, and also offers to return the 32 square mile of land at Dewangiri to Bhutan as a friendly gesture.

India and Bhutan established formal diplomatic ties on August 8, 1978, but support from India came long before that, as India has been showering Bhutan with financial and technical assistance since 1960s, helping Bhutan set up highways as well as water and power stations. Bhutan has always supported India on the international scene, taking the side with India in the United Nations, SAARC, and other international conventions. Examples include Bhutan's support for India to become a permanent member of the United Nations Security Council. The Bhutanese Minister of Foreign Affairs Lyonpo Khandu Wangchuk, on the 59th United Nations Conference in September 2004, explicitly expressed Bhutan's support for India and Japan to become permanent members of the United Nations Security Council. India is Bhutan's leading provider of economic assistance. The majority of investment in Bhutan's successive five-year economic development projects (hereinafter "five-year projects") comes from India. Under the suggestion of India Prime Minister Jawaharlal Nehru, Bhutan launched the first five-year project in 1961. The first and the second five-year projects were completely funded by India. The third to eighth saw India providing 90% to 27.6% of the funds. India recently agreed to subsidize Bhutan's ninth five-year project.

India is Bhutan's biggest trade partner in terms of import and export. Take year 2001 as an example, Bhutan's export to India in that year amounts to 4.7 billion Bhutanese ngultrums (including electricity), accounting for 94% of Bhutan's total export. Bhutan's import from India in that year amounts to 7 billion Bhutanese ngultrums, accounting for 77% of Bhutan's total export.

Each year, India provides scholarship to 50 Bhutanese students studying medicine, law, engineering, computer science, science, humanities, and business at universities in India. Bhutan has two higher education institutions, namely the Royal University of Bhutan (established in June 2003) and Sherubtse College, which shares close relationships with University of Delhi in India. Many Indian teachers work at Sherubtse College. A lot of Bhutanese students study at India at their own expenses.

As for national defence and security, in July 1960 the Indian army dispatched the first Indian Military Training Team commander and some 10 officers to Bhutan. In May 1961, the Indian army sent a training team to Bhutan on scouting missions. So far the training team has set up 1 military academy and 2 hospitals in Bhutan in addition to its base. Bhutan is safe under India's protective umbrella as India is responsible for Bhutan's security, provides training for Bhutan's security troops, covers all of Bhutan's military expenses, and offers military equipment to Bhutan.

Bhutan and India have also joined hands in clearing anti-government organizations in India. There is a 380-kilometer border between Bhutan and Assam and West Bengal in India. Indian rebel troops have occupied southern borders of Bhutan for a long time, causing a headache for India and Bhutan. There are tens of various anti-government armed forces in northeast India, some have existed for half a century, and some are in their teens. These armed forces resort to the use of force to pursue greater extent of autonomy and even independence in their regions.

The India government tried to solve the problem with negotiations, with little progress. The three largest anti-government forces in India are United Liberation Front of Asom (ULFA), National Democratic Front of Bodos (NDFB), and Kamtapur Liberation Organization (KLO), all declared illegal by the India government. The ULFA, founded in 1979, is the largest of the three, and pursues independence of Assam just like the NDFB, whereas the KLO are basically people of the Kamtapur tribe seeking to establish their own homes in West Bengal.

The ULFA survived large-scale attack from Indian troops in 1990s and some of its members went on to team up with nearby anti-government forces to set up a base in southern Bhutan. According to statistics, these rebel groups have set up 19 or 20 bases in Bhutan.

They use the strategies of attack and retreat, crossing the India-Bhutan border and attacking targets in India, causing a serious headache for the India government. For 6 years, the Bhutan government has repeatedly asked the two anti-government forces to leave Bhutan and even held talks with them, but has been able to find a peaceful resolution.

Continuing pressure from the India government made Bhutan send troops in December 2003 to clear out the rebel forces, destroying some 30 bases and subjecting more than a hundred Bhutanese citizens who assisted the rebel groups to legal punishment. The rebel groups scattered everywhere and sought assistance from other countries, and were turned down by China. India, fearing that the rebels would seek asylum in places like Bangladesh and Myanmar and that Pakistan would supply them with weapons and training, resorted to diplomatic channels to put pressure on these countries.

Bhutan's attack on rebels was well received by the India government, which immediately extended an invitation to the King of Bhutan to be the guest of honour in the Republic Day celebrations on January 26, 2005.40 Both India and Bhutan have their own worries for the moment. India fears that rebels would remain in Bhutan or scatter elsewhere and still pose threat to India's security. India also fears that Nepali refugees in Bhutan would join the rebels and make them stronger. Bhutan worries that Mao rebels in Nepal would join the Indian rebels. India and Bhutan constantly discuss their worries to think of ways to protect themselves from the rebels.

DPT AND INDO-BHUTAN RELATIONS

DPT's foreign policy direction hinged consistently on the unquestionable and inextinguishable reality that India would always be the cornerstone of Bhutan's foreign policy matrix. The DPT government, therefore, did everything possible to expand, deepen, elevate and secure Bhutan-India relations in the past five years. This was evident from the fact that Jigmi Y Thinley visited

India nine times in five years, more than any other Bhutanese leader before him, with the exception of Their Majesties. In fact, Jigmi Y Thinley's first overseas visit as prime minister of democratic Bhutan was to India, barely a month after assuming office. His last official overseas visit, when leaving office, was also to India, in February 2013.

Jigmi Y Thinley interacted with Indian leaders at all levels from a wide social and political spectrum during his tenure as prime minister. His visit to Bihar resulted in the granting of two acres of land by the Bihar government to Bhutan at Rajghir, Bodhgaya, to build a Bhutanese temple and guesthouse. He also met the chief minister of Andhra Pradesh, and was in Madhya Pradesh in the capacity of chief guest at a Buddhist University. He hosted the chief minister of Assam in Bhutan and met Mamata Banerjee, the West Bengal chief minister. Further, he was invited by the government of India to deliver the prestigious Hiren Mukherjee memorial address to the Lok Sabha. He was also the keynote speaker at PAN IIT congress of the prestigious IIT, besides meeting Indian corporate leaders twice in Mumbai and Kolkata. Similarly, other Bhutanese cabinet ministers met Indian leaders, including the prime minister, in India, as well as at every international fora outside of India.

The visit of Indian leaders to Bhutan was also unprecedented during the tenure of the DPT government. The Indian prime minister, Dr Manmohan Singh, came to Bhutan twice, first on a state visit and second for the 16th SAARC summit hosted for the first time in Bhutan. The opposition leader, Susma Swaraj, also visited Bhutan, besides parliamentarians and leaders from all political walks.

It looks highly implausible that, after such intense and friendly interactions between the two governments and nation states in the past five years, that India should harbour any doubt and suspicion at all of the royal government's commitment to Bhutan-India relations.

If it is indeed true that India is still offended by the routine, harmless and friendly overture extended by Bhutan under the DPT government to China, as it did to so many other countries and heads of government at the Rio Earth summit, and is choosing to implicate DPT (and consequently Bhutan) with culpability at such a crucial point in the elections, I must confess that I am totally baffled and confounded.

Politicisation and Brinkmanship

Bhutan-India relations came to the fore as an issue during the 90-day election period. In fact, it intensified as campaign fodder after the primary round of elections, which gave the DPT a clear advantage and majority over the other party. The appearance of two articles, subsequently in the Times of India, whipping up an old issue, came like a bolt out of the blue. Our friends in India, unwittingly ensnared in this game of political brinksmanship, must remember that such inadvertent, mercenary and gravely injurious attitudes and moves do not bode well at all for Bhutan-India friendship in the long run.

For the discerning Bhutanese, alarm bells should start ringing, given the timing of the withdrawal of subsidies and other very strange posturing from certain quarters and individuals here in the country. The interest groups are resorting to desperate pressure tactics to leverage New Delhi's influence in Bhutan to not only induce, but perhaps blatantly rig, the electoral outcome.

BILATERAL RELATIONS BETWEEN BHUTAN AND INDIA

Formal bilateral relations between Bhutan and India were established in January 1968 with the appointment of a special officer of the Government of India to Bhutan. The India House (Embassy of India in Bhutan) was inaugurated on May 14, 1968 and Resident Representatives were exchanged in 1971. Ambassadorial level relations began with the upgrading of residents to embassies in 1978.

Beginning with India, Bhutan began to diversify its relations in the international community, thereby projecting its status as an independent and sovereign nation. With India sponsoring Bhutan's application for UN membership in 1971, the leaders of the two countries demonstrated that Article 2 of the Indo-Bhutan Treaty was not a restricting factor in the exercise of Bhutan's foreign policy.

Background

For much of its history, Bhutan has preserved its isolation from the outside world, staying out of international organisations and maintaining few bilateral relations. Bhutan became a protectorate of British India after signing a treaty in 1910 allowing the British to "guide" its foreign affairs and defence. Bhutan was one of the first to recognise India's independence in 1947 and both nations fostered close relations, their importance augmented by the annexation of Tibet in 1950 by the People's Republic of China and its border disputes with both Bhutan and India, which saw close ties with Nepal and Bhutan to be central to its "Himalayan frontier" security policy. India shares a 605 kilometres (376 mi) border with Bhutan and is its largest trading partner, accounting for 98 percent of its exports and 90 percent of its imports.

1949 Treaty

On August 8, 1949 Bhutan and India signed the Treaty of Friendship, calling for peace between the two nations and non-interference in each other's internal affairs. However, Bhutan agreed to let India "guide" its foreign policy and both nations would consult each other closely on foreign and defence affairs. The treaty also established free trade and extradition protocols. The occupation of Tibet by Communist China brought both nations even closer.

In 1958, the then-Indian Prime Minister Jawaharlal Nehru visited Bhutan and reiterated India's support for Bhutan's independence and later declared in the Indian Parliament that any aggression against Bhutan would be seen as aggression against India.

Bhutan, however didn't consider itself as a protectorate country of India. In August 1959, there was a rumour in India political circle that China was seeking to 'liberate' Sikkim in 1975 and Bhutan. Nehru stated in the Lok Sabha that the defence of the territorial uprightness and frontiers of Bhutan was the responsibility of the Government of India. This statement was immediately objected by the Prime Minister of Bhutan, saying Bhutan is not a protectorate of India nor did the treaty involve national defence of any sort.

The period saw a major increase in India's economic, military and development aid to Bhutan, which had also embarked on a programme of modernisation to bolster its security. While India repeatedly reiterated its military support to Bhutan, the latter expressed concerns about India's ability to protect Bhutan against China while fighting a two-front war involving Pakistan. Despite good relations, India and Bhutan did not complete a detailed demarcation of their borders until the period between 1973 and 1984. Border demarcation talks with India generally resolved disagreements except for several small sectors, including the middle zone between Sarpang and Geylegphug and the eastern frontier with the Indian state of Arunachal Pradesh.

INDIA, BHUTAN: NO MORE UNEQUAL TREATIES

Long looked on by its smaller neighbours as a big brother or a bully, India appears to be moving toward an image makeover. New Delhi's decision to revise an unequal treaty with Bhutan will not only remove an irritant in its relations with that country but it also could remove the sting from criticism of India's "hegemonistic ambitions" in the region. India and Bhutan are revising the 1949 Treaty of Friendship and Cooperation, which has hitherto provided the framework for bilateral relations. India has a similar but less offensive treaty with another Himalayan neighbor, Nepal, which was signed in 1950. India and Bhutan have reviewed the 1949 treaty over several meetings during the past six months. A new treaty is likely to be signed in a few months when Bhutan's new king, Jigme Khesar Namgyal Wangchuk, visits India.

While details of the new treaty have not yet been revealed, India's Ministry of External Affairs has said that the changes in the 1949 treaty "reflect the contemporary nature" of India's relationship with Bhutan and aims at strengthening the ties in a "manner that is responsive to and serves each other's national interests through close cooperation". It will enable the "further intensification" of cooperation in hydropower, trade, commerce and human-resource development.

Relations between India and Bhutan have been warm. Bhutan is easily India's closest friend in the neighborhood. India is Bhutan's largest donor, accounting for almost 80% of its foreign assistance, and its largest trade partner. It has contributed generously to infrastructural development in Bhutan. Besides, India provides military training to the Bhutanese forces and maintains a permanent military training presence in Bhutan.

Whether in the United Nations or in the South Asian Association for Regional Cooperation (SAARC), Bhutan has stood by India. It has endorsed New Delhi's position on a nuclear-weapon-free zone in South Asia, the Comprehensive Test Ban Treaty, the 1998 nuclear tests at Pokhran, and so on. And it has acted to address India's security concerns.

In 2003, on India's urging, the Royal Bhutan Army launched military operations against anti-India insurgents such as the United Liberation Front of Assam that had set up bases on Bhutanese soil. This was in sharp contrast with the response of Bangladesh, which despite India's requests has simply denied the presence of anti-India insurgents on its territory.

Although India-Bhutan relations have been largely trouble-free, there is an irritant. Bhutan has not been comfortable with Article 2 of the 1949 treaty. It feels that its sovereignty is circumscribed by this provision. India sought to address this to some extent by supporting Bhutan's membership in the UN in 1971.

Under the 1949 treaty, India has a significant role in Bhutan's external relations. Article 2 requires Bhutan "to be guided by the advice of India" in the conduct of its external relations, and Article 6 allows Bhutan to import "arms, ammunition, machines, warlike material or stores" for its "strength and welfare" but with India's "assistance and approval". It is believed that the new treaty will allow Bhutan to pursue a more independent foreign policy. According to a report in the Indian Express, the language in Article 2 "will be replaced by 'language of friendly cooperation' that, in effect, will give a free hand to Thimpu in international affairs as long as it does not act against Indian interests". As for Article 6, it is likely that "the idea of prior Indian approval for every military purchase will be relaxed". It is likely that "Bhutan will not require any such approval in purchase of non-lethal military stores and equipment. There will be influence in the form of assistance in making all military purchases" but "this will be reflected in the revised treaty more in the form of advice than control".

An unequal relationship between two sovereign countries defined in a treaty is an outdated idea, and this appears to have prompted India to make the treaty more equal and contemporary.

Bhutan has been quietly raising the issue of revising the treaty with India for several years, and although India did realize that this was necessary, little was done about it. What has prompted New Delhi to act now is the fact that Bhutan is democratizing - it has a new constitution and the Bhutanese will elect representatives to Parliament in an election likely to be held next year - and that India needs to acknowledge Bhutan's full sovereignty formally. This appears to have provided momentum to the process of revising the treaty.

"India's obligation under the treaty to not interfere in Bhutan's domestic affairs suited the interests of the monarchy," a Bhutanese journalist told Asia Times Online on condition of anonymity. The kingdom pursued a studied policy of isolation and therefore was not particularly perturbed with having limited relations with the international community. That could now change.

China and Tibet were at the core of India's policy toward Bhutan. In 1949, when the treaty was signed, China had begun asserting control over Tibet. This was viewed with concern by India and Bhutan. India needed to ensure that Bhutan wouldn't fall under Chinese influence and Bhutan wanted India's protection. The Treaty of Friendship and Cooperation served the interests of both countries then.

But the geopolitical context in which the 1949 treaty was signed no longer exists. Today, India recognizes the Tibet Autonomous Region as a part of China, relations are normalizing with Beijing, and the two countries are working toward resolving their decades-long border dispute. Similarly, Bhutan has initiated talks with China to resolve its long-standing boundary dispute, and both countries signed an agreement for the maintenance of peace and tranquility along the Sino-Bhutanese border in 1998.

Analysts in Delhi feel that Article 2 has become irrelevant. "Article 2 has not been invoked for decades," Smruti Pattanaik, research fellow at the Delhi-based Institute for Defense Studies and Analyses, told Asia Times Online. While Thimpu has stood by New Delhi on several foreign-policy issues, it has not hesitated to differ with Delhi either.

In 1978, for instance, Bhutan opened its first diplomatic mission outside India, in Bangladesh, without consulting Delhi. It openly differed with India on international forums as well. At the sixth summit of the Non-Aligned Movement in Havana in 1979, Bhutan, unlike India, condemned Vietnam's intervention in Cambodia. And when the Cambodian issue came up before the UN General Assembly, Bhutan voted in favour of seating the China/US-supported Democratic Kampuchea regime and against an Indian-proposed amendment that would have left the seat vacant.

While in practice Article 2 is not being implemented, its presence in the treaty has often been held up by India's critics as examples of its "hegemonic and expansionist ambitions". The allegation that India has unequal treaties with Bhutan and Nepal has been exploited by China and pro-Chinese elements in these countries to mobilize anti-India sentiment. It has provided China with ammunition to attack India for "bullying its smaller neighbours" to get them to toe its line.

So over time, Article 2 has become something of a burden for India, without providing any big benefits. Pattanaik said Article 2 is not required for India to retain influence in Bhutan. "There is no clash of interests in the foreign policies of the two countries," she said. Bhutan is dependent on India. Its geographic location - it is landlocked and surrounded by India on three sides - makes it dependent on India for access to the sea. Unlike Nepal, Bhutan has not been uneasy with India's influence over the country. Neither has it seen the need to use the China card to wring concessions out of India. A pro-China policy is not viable for Bhutan, as China is not in a position to sustain Bhutan economically in the long run. Supply lines into Bhutan favour India and not China.

"India will not be conceding much by doing away with Article 2," Pattanaik said. On the contrary, "India has much to gain," the Bhutanese journalist said. "It will be seen as a country that respects the sovereignty of its neighbours."

India is waking up to the fact that its "primacy in the neighborhood could be ensured by leveraging its geographic, economic and cultural strengths and not by waving crumbling pieces of paper", said an editorial in the Indian Express. This is prompting the rethink on its approach to its neighbours. There are reports that changes in the 1950 Treaty of Peace and Friendship with Nepal are in the pipeline as well. Earlier the political parties and now the Maoists in Nepal are demanding the abrogation of that treaty, and while India will not go that far to meet their demands, it is likely that Nepal too will see a change in its equation with India.

India's neighbours are intimidated by its size, and its economic and military power. And India has not been particularly gentle in dealing with its sovereignty-sensitive smaller neighbours.

India is still far away from being the gentle giant the neighbours want it to be. However, a revised treaty will go some way in assuaging its Indo-phobic neighbours. New Delhi's new willingness to rewrite treaties to correct the imbalance in the equation with some of them is a step in the right direction.

HISTORICAL PERSPECTIVE TO THE PROVISIONS OF THE TREATY

Reading and interpreting the treaty of 1949 between India and Bhutan in isolation to the relations and treaties which existed between Bhutan and British India will give an incomplete picture. In this context, the relevant provisions of two important treaties concluded between British India and Bhutan—the Treaty of Sinchula, 1865,[2] and the Treaty of Punakha, 1910[3] are looked into.

Article 1 of the Treaty of Sinchula reads, "There shall henceforth be perpetual peace and friendship between the British Government and the Government of Bhutoon." Article 4 goes into details of the reasons for the compensation paid by the British Government to Bhutan. It is in continuance of this Article that India, as spelt out in Article 3 of the 1949 Treaty, till date makes an annual payment of Rs. 5 lakh. Article 6 of the 1865 treaty spells out details on surrender of Bhutanese subjects accused of any crime and taking refuge in British dominions. The various crimes are then mentioned. It is the same for British subjects accused of crimes and taking refuge in Bhutan. Article 9 of the treaty refers to provisions of free trade and commerce between the two governments. Article 8 is very important and it refers to the British government's arbitration in matters of differences which Bhutan might have with the Rajahs of Sikkim and Cooch Behar, and that the British government's decision would be abided by. Article 2 of the 1949 Treaty should be read in the background of Article 8 of the Treaty of 1865.

The Treaty of Punakha of 1910 has only two Articles. One deals with increasing the amount of the annual allowance paid to the Government of Bhutan by the British Government. The other deals with revising Article 8 of the 1865 Treaty. The revised Article reads, "The British Government undertakes to exercise no interference in the internal administration of Bhutan. On its part, the Bhutanese Government agrees to be guided by the advice of the British Government in regard to its external relations. In the event of disputes with, or causes of complaint against, the Maharajas of Sikkim and Cooch Behar, such matters will be referred for arbitration to the British government which will settle them in such manner as justice may require and insist upon the observance of its decisions by the Maharaja named." Article 2 of the 1949 Treaty should be read along with this provision of the 1910 Treaty. It throws light on the continuity of arrangements as existed between Bhutan and British India. It is thus important to note that all the provisions of the 1949 Treaty were not being negotiated for the first time.

At this stage, it is important to mention the circumstances under which the British sought to include Article 8 in the treaty of 1910 by which Bhutan agreed to be guided by the advice of the British government in regard to its external relations. The 1865 Treaty enabled the British government to negotiate the disputes of Bhutan with regard to Sikkim and Cooch Behar. However, with the Chinese forward policy towards Tibet and other Himalayan states, the British became concerned. The Chinese representative in Lhasa sought to liken the union of China, Tibet, Nepal, Bhutan and Sikkim to the blending of the five principal colours which would produce an excellent political model like a beautiful design. The British realised that it was essential to prevent China from encroaching on Bhutan if they wanted peace on the frontier. The British were keen on maintaining Nepal, Bhutan and Sikkim as buffer states. Bhutan however, remained vulnerable to Chinese influence in as much as China claimed suzerainty over Bhutan. It was in such circumstances that it was proposed that in view of the great importance of the British interests at stake, it was necessary for the Government of India to persuade Bhutan to place its foreign relations under British control. For, going by the clauses of the treaty of 1865, the British could not prevent Bhutan from receiving Chinese agents. In return, it was suggested that the British should abstain from interfering in the internal administration of the country. The Treaty of 1910, thus, was an attempt by the British to checkmate China's ambition to either impose its authority on, or interfere in, Bhutan. Through this, Bhutan was maintained as a buffer state. The clause was thus prompted by the circumstances and postures advocated by China.

It is appropriate to note here that the British did not want to control Bhutan. One of the very first British missions to Bhutan advised against it in terms of the inhospitable terrain under which it would be difficult to hold the conquest. The British aim was primarily to find a route to trade with Tibet through Bhutan. Later, there was some controversy over the possession of the fertile and economically valuable duars of Assam and Bengal which was settled through the 1865 Treaty. Most important, even after the 1910 Treaty was signed, (following which Bhutan's external relations were placed under British India) the British Indian government maintained that there was no departure in its policy of non interference in the states bordering the frontiers of India and the obligations would not go beyond what was stated in the letter of the treaty.

Working of the Treaty of 1949

The major provision which has to be examined is Article 2 of the treaty of 1949. When the controversy regarding Sino-Bhutan boundary arose, Nehru wrote to the Chinese, "Under the treaty relationship with Bhutan, the government of India are the only competent authority to take matters concerning Bhutan's external relations, and, infact, we have taken up with your government a number of matters on behalf of the Bhutan government." However since 1984, the government of India has not objected to Bhutan and China having direct bilateral negotiations regarding the border dispute on the northern side of the border. More than ten rounds have been held so far and their differences seem to have narrowed down. One of the factors enabling this was the move towards normalisation of relations between India and China.

Similarly, as Bhutan expands its relations with the outside world, it is interesting to note that the strict implementation of the 1949 Treaty does not take place. In 1971, Bhutan was the second country after India to recognise Bangladesh. The decision was in the interest of the Indian government. However, the important point is not the issue of recognition of Bangladesh by Bhutan but the fact that Bhutan took an independent foreign policy decision—which it could do again on any other issue.

One of the bilateral foreign policy problems presently facing Bhutan is its negotiations with the Nepalese government on the refugee issue. Bhutan's interactions with Nepal surely come under the realm of Bhutan's external relations. India's position, in spite of all that is written in the 1949 Treaty, has been that it will not interfere in the bilateral matter of the two countries.

It is not being indicated that India should go in for strict implementation of the Article 2 of the 1949 Treaty and thereby restrict the space Bhutan has to independently conduct its foreign relations. In the present circumstances neither is this feasible nor desirable. The changing regional and international environment and Bhutan's own desire to assert its independent sovereign status have resulted in not only a flexible interpretation of Article 2 of the Treaty of 1949 but also, in India assisting Bhutan to have an independent identity in the international forum. In fact over time, the treaty has been amended in spirit though not in letter. An important question, which follows, is whether this duality will stand against India's security interests. It will not be unwise to conclude that if a situation emerges in the near future whereby China makes moves with reference to Bhutan which are inimical to India's security, the position of India will not be that it is a bilateral issue between China and Bhutan. Would it be possible for India to then selectively apply Article 2 of the treaty with reference to a particular country or to a particular situation?

It is important to emphasise that the aim of Article 2 of the Treaty is not to bind Bhutan but to ensure India's security interests. At present India and Bhutan share a cordial relationship and the Bhutanese presently do not have any complaints over the provisions of the treaty. However, there have been occasions when there was controversy over its provisions, especially regarding the interpretation of the word 'guidance'. Thus, in a situation where Article 2 is not strictly implemented, it is being suggested that India should seek an assurance that issues concerning security of India will be respected by Bhutan. This will ensure that future changes in either the regional or international environment will not adversely affect India's security interests.

Bhutan's Interests

For Bhutan, its relations with India have been beneficial on three specific fronts: the domestic, international and economic.

DOMESTIC AFFAIRS: NON INTERFERENCE BY INDIA

Even in the period of British India, there was no interference by it in the internal political struggle and civil war that was taking place in Bhutan. The monarchy as we know it today was established only in 1907. British India, by recognising it, gave additional legitimacy to the monarchy and contributed to stability. Later, in 1910, the Treaty of Punakha, by incorporating the clause that there would be no interference in the internal affairs of Bhutan, ensured the primacy of the new regime. This continued after the withdrawal of the British from India. With a democratic India as its neighbour, it was feared that monarchy in Bhutan could face problems. However, this was not to be. Presently, even as Bhutan is witnessing a movement for change and democracy from certain quarters, India has continued to adhere to the clause of non interference in its internal affairs. It seems to believe that whatever changes take place, should be from within and not from outside. In the past Bhutan had fears that following Sikkim's incorporation into India, it too would be affected. But India assured it that its territorial integrity would be respected. Bhutan also feared that like in Sikkim where the minorities were overtaken by the Nepali population, in Bhutan too the Nepalese would overtake the locals. Bhutan's problems at present revolve around the concept of "Greater Nepal." To this is linked the problem of refugees from southern Bhutan who are of Nepalese origin. There are a large number of Nepalese in India and the movement for Gorkhaland and the consequent autonomous council have made Bhutan concerned about its people of Nepalese origin and their intentions. India's official position of non-interference has ensured Bhutan a free hand to deal with its centrifugal tendencies in a manner as it feels is right.

International Relations: Coming out of Isolation

Bhutan has followed a policy of isolation from the beginning—it did not trust the British too. Following the threat from China, it was the aim of the British that Bhutan should come out of its isolation. It was slightly successful but the consequent World War II and later the British withdrawal in 1947 sent it into isolation again. To begin with, Bhutan was suspicious of independent India's intentions after the Chinese occupation of Tibet in 1950. However, following the Chinese action of 1958-59 it slowly realised that it needed to come out of isolation for its own survival. During this time when its territorial integrity was in danger, India ensured it security though there was no provision in the treaty of 1949 for the defence of Bhutan by India. Since then, Bhutan has tried to assert its sovereign existence at every forum.

India has made it clear that Bhutan's quest for an international role does not contradict with the provision of Article 2 of the 1949 Treaty. Its international journey began with becoming a member of the Colombo Plan in 1963. Bhutan's membership of the Colombo Plan was sponsored by India. Bhutan said that its admission to the Colombo Plan had considerable bearing on its sovereign and modern status and registered its first entry into a regional group of sovereign states. As a result of its membership, Bhutan received technical assistance from Japan, Australia, India, Canada, New Zealand and England. Later, in 1969, Bhutan's entry into the Universal Postal Union was sponsored by India. In 1971, Bhutan was admitted to the United Nations with the full assistance of India. In 1972 Bhutan became a member of Economic and Social Council for Asia and Pacific (ESCAP). The process thus continued and in 1985, Bhutan became a member of the South Asian Association for Regional Cooperation (SAARC), providing it another forum to expand and conduct its foreign relations and this time more effectively since SAARC is a grouping of only seven countries.

After Bhutan became a member of the UN, it was opined by many that India had renounced its right to look after Bhutan's foreign relations which it had been enjoined to do under the Treaty of 1949. Surely India would have been aware that an independent international role and strict implementation of the 1949 Treaty would be contradictory. However, an independent Bhutan recognised by the international community ensured that its territorial integrity could not be easily violated and that Bhutan remained a buffer state. Further, in the changing regional and international context had India not taken into consideration the aspirations of Bhutan, some other country would have. Such a move would have been detrimental to India's long term interests. Presently, Bhutan has diplomatic and non diplomatic relations with many countries.

BHUTAN ELECTIONS: A CASE OF INDIA'S DIPLOMATIC BANKRUPTCY!

The recently concluded second general election in Bhutan on July 13 has once again exposed the bankruptcy of India's foreign policy. This election saw the defeat of ruling incumbent Druk Phuensum Tshogpa (DPT) at the hands of main opposition party Peoples' Democratic Party (PDP), which secured 35 votes against 12 votes of DPT. It must be noted that in the National Assembly's primary election held on May 31, DPT got 33 votes as compared to 12 of PDP. The other two parties that took part in primary election namely Druk Namdruk Tshogpa (DNT) and Druk Chirwang Tshogpa(DCT) got two and none respectively. As per Bhutan's constitution, the final election is held between winner and runner-up of primary elections. It is very striking to note as to what happened within just one and a half month from May 31 to July 13 that DPT lost its electoral base and finally lost to PDP.

In fact, the Government of India had stopped subsidizing kerosene and cooking gas for Bhutan in the first week of July. It is interesting to know that this sanction did not originate from financial constraints or whatsoever of the Indian Oil Corporation rather directed by the external affairs ministry of GOI. Actually, Indian government was unhappy with DPT leader and Bhutanese Prime Minister Jigme Y. Thinley because it held that Thinley was arbitrarily running his foreign affairs. On the other hand, supporters of Thinley argued that regardless of being neighbor to a big country and receiving economic support from it, any sovereign nation does not lose its universal right to decide its foreign affairs. It is to be reminded that although there was a provision in the Indo-Bhutan Friendship Treaty of 1949 that Bhutan would run its foreign policy on India's advice, but the renewed treaty of 2007 had omitted the clause after which Bhutan became independent to shape its foreign policy at its own end. It is a different scenario altogether that still there are many official and unofficial arrangements that ensure whoever is in power there will have to abide by the interests of India while shaping Bhutan's internal and external policies. Prime Minister Thinley was obviously well aware of this so he did nothing during his tenure that could possibly thwart India's security concerns.

Then what is the reason behind India's resentment? The conundrum is rooted in an international convention held last year in Brazil's Rio de Janeiro where Bhutan's PM Thinley had an informal chat with the then Chinese Premier. China is Bhutan's immediate neighbor other than India despite this was the first meeting between both heads of governments. India's stance towards Bhutan changed in this backdrop when external affairs officials started talking off the record that Bhutan was now getting out of control. Since Bhutan's all ten five-year plans till date have been supported by India and many hydel projects too are dependent on India's aid (benefitting India only), so it was indigestible for India to see Bhutan getting close with China. It was not just the meeting of leaders but procurement of 15 Chinese buses by Bhutan in particular that invited India's ire.

The issue is not confined to relations with China alone. India never wants Bhutan to foster relations with any country. Bhutan had diplomatic relations with 22 countries until 2008 that flourished in Thinley's regime and number increased to 53. Bhutan has no diplomatic relation with China until date but India is wary of the possibility in future as Bhutan-China border dispute is largely sorted out now. Indian government is aware of Chinese plan to lay rail line up to Chumbi Valley located at the interjection of India (Sikkim)-Bhutan-China (Tibet) and the very day this project is completed; Bhutan will become free from the obligation that arises due to its three-sided land locked territory from India. This rail line project is inevitable as China is pressing hard on it. India would have accepted this situation in advance and framed its strategy accordingly but this is sheer bankruptcy of its diplomacy that the country on which it has spent billions so far is now being pushed to a politically amphibious state.

Apart from cutting subsidy on oil and gas to Bhutan, India has also announced nonpayment of excise duty refund and scrapping subsidy on power generated from Chukha hydel project. India has argued that due to economic reasons it has scrapped subsidy in its various sectors too, but people of Bhutan are not easily convinced with this logic. They know that amounts saved by cutting subsidy in a country of more than a billion and Bhutan, that has a mere 6-7 lac population, are not comparable. This is insignificant for India. Bhutanese people have perceived this as an arm twisting tactics of Indian establishment and India through its move just on the eve of elections has reached out with the message that they will have to face more sanctions if they vote back Thinley's party DPT to power. In response to resenting Bhutanese people, external affairs ministry of India had assured that the issue would be resolved through bilateral talks with the new government. This was a clear indication of regime change in Bhutan and its citizens did no mistake to read this in true context.

The reaction to India's move in Bhutan cannot be termed as healthy and positive in the bilateral relations. Indian establishment will have to pay a price for this eventually. Wangcha Sangye, a popular blogger of Bhutan wrote in his blog: "National interests of Bhutan have to rise over and above the politics of always playing the Indian tune. We are not just good neighbors of India. We are a good and reliable friend of India. But Bhutan and Bhutanese are sovereignty unto our self. Therefore Bhutan's paramount national interests and affairs just cannot be only pleasing India. We have to please ourselves too!" He made scathing comments in the same blog further, "Why do Indian media and politicians want to castrate Bhutan for the most harmless relationship effort with China? Just the other day, I heard a rumour of a bureaucrat of India chastising Bhutanese leadership of being "dishonest". What the hell is that suppose to mean? Which national leaders and governments bare its soul to another nation? We are not paid sex workers that benefactors need to know when our eyelashes and asses move and in which direction". Wangcha Sangye has expressed the sentiments of Bhutanese people through his blog. After the elections I talked to one of my acquaintances in Phuentsholing (Bhutan) who is a supporter of DPT. He told me that he too had voted in favour of PDP on July 13 because he was assured that if DPT returns to power, India will not roll back subsidy cuts. He said that there was a further indication that India may stop aiding five-year plans too.

It must be recalled that more than one lakh Bhutanese people were ousted from the southern part of this country in 1990-91 when they had demanded democracy. India was hand in gloves with Bhutanese king in this act. It has took some time for Bhutanese citizens and left out Lhotsampas (Bhutanese people of Nepalese origin) in southern part to heal their wounds when they are again exposed to the tragic subsidy cut and anti-Thinley politics of India. PDP's victory has although instilled a sense of satisfaction in India's establishment and an interim assurance to the Bhutanese people that they will not be pauperized any more, but its consequences will prove to be unpleasant in the long run. India's foreign policy makers will have to rethink over its mentality towards neighbors and realize the need to rectify it at the outset.

BHUTAN'S ECONOMIC CONCERNS AND INDIA

Bhutan is not only a landlocked country but also extremely backward. Having decided to come out of isolationism, India helped it by completely financing the first two five- year plans. Presently, the Indian government is involved in many projects, which include hydropower plants, cement plants, roads, etc. 40 per cent of the external revenue that Bhutan gets is presently from the sale of electricity to India. In this sense, Bhutan has benefited immensely from assistance by India. Most important, of the total aid given by India to other developing countries in 1996-97, the share of Bhutan was 52 per cent, which amounts to Rs. 181 crore. There is a free trade regime between India and Bhutan not requiring even customs posts on the Indian side of the border. Being a landlocked country, India provides it with about 13 transit routes. Presently, Bhutan is very keen on sub-regional cooperation through the growth quadrangle which encompasses Bangladesh, Nepal and the north eastern parts of India. It is emphasising on the economic content in its relations with the SAARC member countries.

The China Factor

The China factor has been very important in defining the nature of relationship between India and Bhutan. In fact, it is this which gives Bhutan the geostrategic importance with respect to Indian interests. It is interesting to note that to begin with, the British were primarily interested in Bhutan for facilitating a trade route to access Tibet, that is to say, the aims were purely economic in nature. It was only later when China started laying claims to the territory of Bhutan that the clause enabling British India to guide the foreign relations of Bhutan was incorporated in the Treaty of 1910. Later, independent India too included this clause in the Treaty of 1949. The Chinese occupation of Tibet and later the uprisings in Tibet following the Chinese action there, made Bhutan think seriously about coming out of its isolationist policy. This later led to the close involvement of India in Bhutan's economic development. In 1958, China had not only claimed Indian territory, its maps also showed 200 sq miles of Bhutanese territory as part of Tibet. It was at this defining moment that Nehru said in the Parliament that any attack on Bhutan would be considered an attack on India. Later, India's defeat against China in the 1962 War, made Bhutan skeptical about the capability of India to look after its defence. But confidence was restored following the Indian victory in 1971. The process of normalisation of relations between India and China, made it possible for Bhutan to have direct bilateral talks with China on the boundary question, thus, providing Bhutan an extra space to conduct its foreign policy.

It is seen that the attitude of China towards Tibet has played a major role in shaping Bhutan's attitude towards India. Bhutan has many historical links with Tibet. The experience of the Tibetan refugees has made it apprehensive of developing close ties with China. In fact, the desire of Bhutan to gain recognition in the international arena has a lot to do with the attitude of China. The fear that Bhutan will go into China's fold seems unlikely with regard to the current state of beneficial relations Bhutan has with India and its past experience with China. Bhutan's experience with China has not been all smooth sailing and, in fact Bhutan itself follows a restrictive policy with regard to its interaction with China. The then Foreign Minister Tsering said in an interview that Bhutan had "correct relations" with Beijing. He added that there was not much trade or economic interaction. Bhutan was conducting negotiations with China on the 500-km-long border and the area under dispute was small, according to the minister.

India's Interests

Bhutan has immense security imperatives for India. A stable, independent Bhutan is essential for it to be an effective buffer state. India does not have any imperial or colonial agenda while dealing with Bhutan. Prime Minister Nehru said in 1958 in the most categorical terms that though Bhutan is a small country, it should remain independent in choosing its own way of life. This policy enunciated by Nehru was continued by the succeeding governments in India, which has played an active role in Bhutan getting the international recognition that it deserves. While initially the economic aid given by India can be said to have been influenced by security concerns in enabling Bhutan to have the essential infrastructure, in later years this has not been so. It presently follows a policy of mutual benefit from the projects which are being undertaken in Bhutan. The market for these projects will be India and in this manner it also ensures the development of the northeast part of India. While Bhutan is a small country and its wants are limited, with time they are sure to grow. Any amount of Indian aid would then not be able to meet the required needs. However, through the approach being presently followed, India ensures the sustainable development of Bhutan. The 336MW Chukha Hydel project ensures power supply to parts of West Bengal and Assam. This one project provides nearly 40 per cent of Bhutan's national revenue. The

1020MW Tala project is under way and once it is commissioned, the revenue Bhutan can earn will be substantial. On the Indian side, with such projects the power shortage problem will be partially resolved.

The goodwill India is able to generate through its activities are likely to ensure that whatever changes might come in the future in the political structures in Bhutan, the attitude towards it will not change. Bhutan will see it in its own interest to be friendly with India for it is beneficial to it economically and in the international arena.

India's major concerns with Bhutan presently are those relating to the disturbed situation in the northeast. It is reported that insurgents have established camps in the border areas of Bhutan, and without Bhutan's help, it will not be possible to combat the insurgency. India and Bhutan have concluded an extradition agreement in 1996. Though the 1949 Treaty mentions extradition, the present agreement is aimed at simplifying the procedure and making it more effective to deal with cross border terrorism and organised crime. Bhutan is not in any way assisting these insurgents, but its police forces are limited to meet such contingencies. Important questions thus arise about implementation of the extradition treaty. India is spending crores of rupees on combating insurgency in the North East. By setting camps in Bhutan, these insurgents are able to escape from the Indian authorities. In days to come the problem may assume serious dimensions. There is also the danger that if Bhutan were to take stern action against them, then the militants would disturb the peace and harmony there. There are as yet no confirmed reports that the two governments have taken a joint action or conducted joint raids against the hideouts of these insurgents, but both are closely cooperating and this issue remains on the top of the agenda.

BHUTAN AND THE INCEPTION OF INDO-BHUTANESE RELATIONS

Although a concrete knowledge of prehistoric Bhutan is yet to emerge through archaeological studies, stone tools and weapons, remnants of large stone structures, and other artifacts provide evidence of civilization as early as 2000 B.C. Historians have theorised about the state of Lhomon (southern darkness) or Monyul (dark land, a reference to the Monpa aborigines of Bhutan), possibly a part of Tibet that was then beyond the purview of Buddhist teachings. Monyul is thought to have existed between 500 B.C. and 600 A.D. The names Lhomon Tsendenjong (southern Mon sandalwood country) and Lhomon Khashi (southern Mon country of four approaches), found in ancient Bhutanese and Tibetan chronicles, may also have credence, and have been used by some Bhutanese scholars when referring to their homeland. Variations of the Sanskrit words Bhota-ant (end of Bhot, an Indian name for Tibet) or Bhu-uttan (meaning highlands) have been suggested by historians as origins of the name Bhutan, which came into common foreign use in the late nineteenth century and was used in Bhutan only in English-language official correspondence. The traditional name of the country since the seventeenth century has been Drukyul—country of the Drukpa, or the Land of the Thunder Dragon.

The introduction of Buddhism seemed to have had occurred in the seventh century, when Tibetan king Srongtsen Gampo, a convert to Buddhism, ordered the construction of two Buddhist temples, at Bumthang in central Bhutan and at Kyichu in the Paro Valley. Buddhism replaced, but did not eliminate the Bon religious practices that had also been prevalent in Tibet until the late sixth century. Instead, Buddhism absorbed Bon and its believers. In 747 A.D., a Buddhist saint, Padmasambhava (known in Bhutan as Guru Rinpoche and sometimes referred to as the Second Buddha), came to Bhutan from India. According to tradition, he founded the Nyingmapa sect—also known as the Red Hat sect—of Mahayana Buddhism, which became for a time the dominant religion of Bhutan. Following this event, Indian influence played a temporary role until increasing Tibetan migrations brought in new cultural and religious contributions. Apart from such shared cultural and religious heritage, there were other areas of interaction which developed during the British rule in India, which included several Anglo-Bhutanese skirmishes and battles that were consequently followed by treaties and agreements. It was during this period of interaction with the British, that trade between Bhutanese and Indians was also recorded to have taken place for the first time (1873).

The Chinese invasion of Tibet (1910-12) and subsequent claims made on Bhutan resulted in the signing of the Treaty of Punakha in 1910 with British India. Although this treaty served to expel any claims that China might have tried to make, it did not define Bhutan's status technically or legally; for the Bhutanese, this was a source of uncertainty over its relations with India at the time that the British rule was nearing an end. After India's independence in 1947, standstill agreements with Sikkim, Nepal and Tibet were signed to continue existing relations until new agreements were made. Bhutan's status as a country with respect to India became clearer following Prime Minister Jawaharlal Nehru's invitation to participate in the Asian Relations Conference in 1947.

4

India's Relation with Maldives

Bilateral relations between the Republic of India and the Republic of Maldives have been friendly and close in strategic, economic and military cooperation. India contributed to maintaining security on the island nation and has forged an alliance with respect to its strategic interests in the Indian Ocean.

The Maldives is located south of India's Lakshadweep Islands in the Indian Ocean and approximately 700 kilometres from Sri Lanka. Both nations established diplomatic relations after the independence of Maldives from British rule in 1966.

Since then, India and Maldives have developed close strategic, military, economic and cultural relations.

India has supported Maldives' policy of keeping regional issues and struggles away from itself, and the latter has seen friendship with India as a source of aid as well as a counter-balance to Sri Lanka, which is in proximity to the island nation and its largest trading partner.

India enjoys a considerable influence over Maldives' foreign policy and provides extensive security co-operation especially after the Operation Cactus in 1988 during which India repelled Tamil mercenaries who invaded the country. As founder member in 1985 of the South Asian Association for Regional Cooperation, SAARC, which brings together Afghanistan, Bangladesh, Bhutan, India, Maldives, Nepal, Pakistan and Sri Lanka, the country plays a very active role in SAARC. The Maldives has taken the lead in calling for a South Asian Free Trade Agreement, the formulation of a Social Charter, the initiation of informal political consultations in SAARC forums, the lobbying for greater action on environmental issues, the proposal of numerous human rights measures such as the regional convention on child rights and for setting up a SAARC Human Rights Resource Centre. The Maldives is also an advocate of greater international profile for SAARC such as through formulating common positions at the UN. But the Maldives claims the Indian-administered territory of Minicoy as part of its country, that is inhabited by Muslims.

India is starting the process to bring the island country into India's security grid. The move comes after the moderate Islamic nation approached New Delhi earlier this year over fears that one of its island resorts could be taken over by terrorists given its lack of military assets and surveillance capabilities.

India is also signing an agreement later this year which includes following things:

- India will permanently base two helicopters in the country to enhance its surveillance capabilities and ability to respond swiftly to threats. One helicopter from the Coast Guard is likely to be handed over during Antony's visit while another from the Navy will be cleared for transfer shortly.
- Maldives has coastal radars on only two of its 26 atolls. India will help set up radars on all 26 for seamless coverage of approaching vessels and aircraft.
- The coastal radar chain in Maldives will be networked with the Indian coastal radar system. India has already undertaken a project to install radars along its entire coastline. The radar chains of the two countries will be interlinked and a central control room in India's Coastal Command will get a seamless radar picture.
- The Indian Coast Guard (ICG) will carry out regular Dornier sorties over the island nation to look out for suspicious movements or vessels. The Southern Naval Command will overlook the inclusion of Maldives into the Indian security grid.
- Military teams from Maldives will visit the tri-services Andaman Nicobar Command (ANC) to observe how India manages security and surveillance of the critical island chain.

Development of Bilateral Relations

India and Maldives officially and amicably decided their maritime boundary in 1976, although a minor diplomatic incident occurred in 1982 when the brother of the President of Maldives Maumoon Abdul Gayoom declared that the neighbouring Minicoy Island that belonged to India were a part of Maldives; Maldivies quickly and officially denied that it was laying claim to the island. India and Maldives signed a comprehensive trade agreement in 1981.

Both nations are founding members of the South Asian Association for Regional Cooperation (SAARC), the South Asian Economic Union and signatories to the South Asia Free Trade Agreement. Indian and Maldivian leaders have maintained high-level contacts and consultations on regional issues.

Operation Cactus

In November 1988 speedboats carrying 80 armed militants of the People's Liberation Organisation of Tamil Eelam landed in Maldives and along with allies who had infiltrated the country, began taking over the government. The plot, planned in Sri Lanka by the Tamil nationalist group was believed to be an attempt by a Maldivian businessman and politician opposed to the regime of the President of Maldives Maumoon Abdul Gayoom to gain control while the PLOTE sought a safe haven and base for its activities.

The militants took control of the airport in Male, the national capital, but failed to capture the President of Maldives Maumoon Abdul Gayoom, who had fled and asked for military aid from India on November 3. The then-Indian Prime Minister Rajiv Gandhi ordered 1,600 troops to aid the Maldivian government. In a military operation codenamed "Operation Cactus," Indian forces arrived within 12 hours of the request for aid being made, squashed the coup attempt and achieved full control of the country within hours. 19 PLOTE militants were killed and 1 Indian soldier wounded.

India's intervention was endorsed by other nations such as the United States, Soviet Union, Great Britain and its neighbours Nepal and Bangladesh. Its speedy and decisive victory and the restoration of the Maldivian government brought both nations even closer in friendship and cooperation. In wake of internal security crises and tensions with Sri Lanka, Maldives saw its relationship with India as a source of future security.

Commercial Relations

Since the success of Operation Cactus, the relations between India and Maldives have expanded significantly. India has provided extensive economic aid and has participated in bilateral programs for the development of infrastructure, health, civil aviation, telecommunications and labour resources. It established the Indira Gandhi Memorial Hospital in Male, the capital of Maldives, expanded telecommunications and air links and increased scholarships for Maldivian students. While India's exports to Maldives during 2006 were worth Rs. 384 crores, imports were worth less than Rs. 6 crores. The State Bank of India has contributed more than USD 500 million to aid the economic expansion of Maldives. India and Maldives have announced plans to jointly work to expand fisheries and tuna processing.

Military Relations

On 7 March 2005 Defence Attaché's Office (DAO) was established in the High commission of the Republic of Maldives in India by making Lt.Colonel Abdulla Shamaal as first defence attaché. This was the first Defence Attaché's office set up abroad. Given, that defence relations is a major component of the Indo-Maldives bilateral relations and both counties have a long record of strengthening their defence ties through a wide range of activities, such as Military Joint Exercises, exchange of visits of senior officers of the Armed forces, training of large number of defence services personnel from the Maldives at Indian defence establishments, provision of military aid, and intelligence and information sharing, the necessity for a DAO was felt.

Hence, the DAO was instituted to further strengthen and consolidate the already existing bilateral defence relations in a mutually beneficial manner. As a result, the DAO functions as the primary mechanism integrated in the resident Mission of the Republic of Maldives in New Delhi, India to guide direct and coordinate defence ties between the two countries.

On April 2006 Indian Navy gifted a Trinkat Class Fast Attack Craft of 46m length to Maldives National Defence Force's Coast Guard. India start the process to bring the island country into India's security grid. The move comes after the moderate Islamic nation approached New Delhi earlier this year over fears that one of its island resorts could be taken over by terrorists given its lack of military assets and surveillance capabilities. India is also signing an agreement later this year which includes following things.

- India will permanently base two helicopters in the country to enhance its surveillance capabilities and ability to respond swiftly to threats. One helicopter from the Coast Guard is likely to be handed over during Antony's visit while another from the Navy will be cleared for transfer shortly.
- Maldives has coastal radars on only two of its 26 atolls. India will help set up radars on all 26 for seamless coverage of approaching vessels and aircraft.
- The coastal radar chain in Maldives will be networked with the Indian coastal radar system. India has already undertaken a project to install radars along its entire coastline. The radar chains of the two countries will be interlinked and a central control room in India's Coastal Command will get a seamless radar picture.

- The Indian Coast Guard (ICG) will carry out regular Dornier sorties over the island nation to look out for suspicious movements or vessels. The Southern Naval Command will overlook the inclusion of Maldives into the Indian security grid.
- Military teams from Maldives will visit the tri-services Andaman Nicobar Command (ANC) to observe how India manages security and surveillance of the critical island chain.

Background

Maldives is located south of India's Lakshadweep Islands in the Indian Ocean. Both nations established diplomatic relations after the independence of Maldives from British rule in 1966. Since then, India and Maldives have developed close strategic, military, economic and cultural relations. India has supported Maldives' policy of keeping regional issues and struggles away from itself, and the latter has seen friendship with India as a source of aid as well as a counterbalance to Sri Lanka, which is in proximity to the island nation and its largest trading partner.

Development of bilateral relations

India and Maldives officially and amicably decided their maritime boundary in 1976, although a minor diplomatic incident occurred in 1982 when the brother of the President of Maldives Maumoon Abdul Gayoom declared that the neighbouringMinicoy Island that belonged to India were a part of Maldives; Maldives quickly and officially denied that it was laying claim to the island. India and Maldives signed a comprehensive trade agreement in 1981. Both nations are founding members of the South Asian Association for Regional Cooperation (SAARC), the South Asian Economic Union and signatories to theSouth Asia Free Trade Agreement. Indian and Maldivian leaders have maintained high-level contacts and consultations on regional issues.

Operation Cactus

In November 1988 speedboats carrying 80 armed militants of the People's Liberation Organisation of Tamil Eelam landed in Maldives and along with allies who had infiltrated the country, began taking over the government. The plot, planned in Sri Lanka by the Tamil nationalist group was believed to be an attempt by a Maldivian businessman and politician opposed to the regime of the President of Maldives Maumoon Abdul Gayoom to gain control while the PLOTE sought a safe haven and base for its activities.

The militants took control of the airport in Male, the national capital, but failed to capture the President of Maldives Maumoon Abdul Gayoom, who had fled and asked for military aid from India on 3 November. The then-Indian Prime Minister Rajiv Gandhi ordered 1,600 troops to aid the Maldivian government. In a military operation codenamed "Operation Cactus," Indian forces arrived within 12 hours of the request for aid being made, squashed the coup attempt and achieved full control of the country within hours. 19 PLOTE militants were killed and 1 Indian soldier wounded.

India's intervention was endorsed by other nations such as the United States, Soviet Union, Great Britain and its neighbours Nepal and Bangladesh. President Reagan called India's action, a valuable contribution to regional stability'. Margaret Thatcher reportedly commented: 'Thank God for India: President Gayoom's government has been saved. We could not have assembled and dispatched a force from here in good time to help him'. But the Sri Lankan Island newspaper commented, 'It would be ostrich-like to ignore the fear of smaller nations in South Asia about current developments providing opportunities for what has been described as the spread of Indian hegemonism.'

Its speedy and decisive victory and the restoration of the Maldivian government brought both nations even closer in friendship and cooperation. In wake of internal security crises and tensions with Sri Lanka, Maldives saw its relationship with India as a source of future security.

Commercial relations

Since the success of Operation Cactus, the relations between India and Maldives have expanded significantly. India has provided extensive economic aid and has participated in bilateral programs for the development of infrastructure, health, civil aviation, telecommunications and labour resources. It established the Indira Gandhi Memorial Hospital in Male, the capital of Maldives, expanded telecommunications and air links and increased scholarships for Maldivian students. While India's exports to Maldives during 2006 were worth Rs. 3.84 billion, imports were worth less than Rs. 60 million. The State Bank of India has contributed more than US$500 million to aid the economic expansion of Maldives. India and Maldives have announced plans to jointly work to expand fisheries and tuna processing.

Military relations

India started the process to bring the island country into India's security grid. The move comes after the moderate Islamic nation approached New

Delhi earlier in 2009, over fears that one of its island resorts could be taken over by terrorists given its lack of military assets and surveillance capabilities.

India has also signed an agreement which includes following things.

- India will permanently base two helicopters in the country to enhance its surveillance capabilities and ability to respond swiftly to threats.
- Maldives has coastal radars on only two of its 26 atolls. India will help set up radars on all 26 for seamless coverage of approaching vessels and aircraft.
- The coastal radar chain in Maldives will be networked with the Indian coastal radar system. India has already undertaken a project to install radars along its entire coastline. The radar chains of the two countries will be interlinked and a central control room in India's Coastal Command will get a seamless radar picture.
- The Indian Coast Guard (ICG) will carry out regular Dornier sorties over the island nation to look out for suspicious movements or vessels. The Southern Naval Command will overlook the inclusion of Maldives into the Indian security grid.
- Military teams from Maldives will visit the tri-services Andaman Nicobar Command (ANC) to observe how India manages security and surveillance of the critical island chain.

Aftermath of GMR - Maldives Airport Row

Bilateral relations between the two countries hit an all time low after the GMR row. Indian government froze its US$25 million aid to the island nation. Construction of a national police academy in Maldives has also been put on the back burner besides other infrastructure commitments that India had made to Maldives earlier. The ties between the two countries strained after the cancellation of the GMR airport contract, the largest single Indian investment in the island nation, but the real reason for New Delhi's anguish is said to be the anti-India sentiments being aired by some parties in President Mohamed Waheed's coalition.

Drinking-water crisis in Male

In the wake of a drinking water crisis in Male on 4 December 2014, following collapse of the island's only water treatment plant, Maldives urged India for immediate help. India came to rescue by sending its heavy lift transporters like C-17 Globemaster III, Il-76 carrying bottled water. The navy also sent her ships like INS Sukanya, INS Deepak and others which can produce fresh water using their onboard desalination plants. The humanitarian relief efforts by the Indian side was widely appreciated in Male across all sections of people even the Vice-President of Maldives thanked the Indian ambassador for swift action.

2015 arrest of ex-President Nasheed

Maldives' first democratically elected President from 2008 to 2012 Mohammed Nasheed, was arrested on 22 February 2015 on terror charges. India and US expressed concern over Nasheed's arrest and manhandling. Indian PM Modi was to also visit Maldives in the second week of March as a part four nation visit to Indian Ocean neighbours. But, he later omitted Maldives from his tour.

POLITICAL TURBULENCE AND STRAIN IN BILATERAL RELATIONS

Maldives has undergone considerable political turbulence in 2012-13. The presidential election held on September 7, 2013 was annulled by the Supreme Court over allegation of voting irregularities. The court also cancelled the second round planned on September 28, because none of the candidates could poll more than 50 per cent of the votes. In the annulled election former President Mohamed Nasheed of Maldivian Democratic Party (MDP) had secured 45.45 per cent, while Abdullah Yameen of the Progressive Party of Maldives (PPM) came second with 25.35 per cent of the votes.

In the first round of election held subsequently on November 9, 2013, Nasheed won about 47 per cent of votes leaving behind his nearest rival Abdulla Yameen at 30 per cent.

However, in the second round of election, Abdulla Yameen, getting the support of other opposition parties, managed to get 51.39 per cent, compared to 48.61 percent for Nasheed. The turnaround in Yameen's fortunes happened as all opponents of Nasheed joined hands to isolate and defeat him.

It is interesting that Nasheed accepted his defeat graciously despite the narrow margin of his loss. Hopefully, this will help bring political stability in the country. Soon after his election the new President said that his priority was to stabilize *rupiah* and create jobs.

During 2012-13, India-Maldives relations suffered considerably. The Maldivian Government terminated the Indian company GMR contract of the Male airport on allegations of irregularity in awarding the project.

The former President Nasheed had to take shelter in the Indian embassy in 2013 due to violent protests on the streets of Male. The bilateral relations touched a new low in February 2013. It is in this context that Mr Yameen's visit to India becomes important.

President Yameen's Visit

During the visit, Mr Yameen was effusive in praising India. He said, "In every hour of national distress, be it a foreign terrorist coup attempt as with the 1988 mercenary attack or a natural catastrophe such as the 2004 Asian Tsunami, India helped us wholeheartedly and generously in restoring normalcy to the lives of our people." For India, Maldives' location in the Indian Ocean and close to its southern tip makes it a strategically significant country. The report of increasing Chinese presence in the Maldives is a matter of anxiety for India. Mr Yameen's visit was aimed at reassuring India that his country recognises India's importance for Maldivian stability and would take India's security concerns on board.

During the visit, Mr Yameen sought India's help in putting the Maldivian economy on track. He specifically asked for India's assistance in skill building and training of personnel.

KEY AGREEMENTS TO BOOST COOPERATION

Trade and Investment, Connectivity

The 1981 trade agreement between the two countries provides for export of essential commodities and bilateral trade has grown to Rs.700 crores. India imports scrap metals from Maldives while its exports include agriculture and poultry produce, sugar, fruits, vegetables, spices, rice, flour (atta), textiles, drugs and medicines, a variety of engineering and industrial products, sand and aggregate, cement for building, etc. In June 2011, India released three-year quota for export of essential commodities like Stone Aggregates, Rice, Wheat Flour, Sugar, Dal, Onion, Potato and Eggs from India to Maldives.

Table-: India-Maldives Trade Figures (in Rupees Crore)

Year	*Total Exports to Maldives*	*Total Imports from Maldives*	*Total Trade*
2007-08	360.55	16.69	377.24
2008-09	590.28	17.93	608.21
2009-10	378.49	17.07	395.57
2010-11	455.54	145.43	600.97
2011-12	597.78	92.04	689.82
2012-13	666.21	40.48	706.69

During President Yameen's visit, further attention was paid to strengthen bilateral trade and investment. The Indian Prime Minister highlighted the key agreements and decisions based on the joint statement. These include the facilitation of trade credit to the Maldives to the amount of 25 million dollars, the relaxation of restriction on export of stone aggregates, the favourable disposition of India for the Maldives request to import petroleum from India, and the supply of other essential commodities.

India and Maldives have also agreed to enhance connectivity, set up a joint consultative commission, promote investments, and step up security cooperation between the two countries. President Yameen acknowledged that Indian supplies of petroleum product would help Maldives to reduce its debt burden and the visa regime would be simplified to promote people to people contacts.

Security

Security cooperation is a highly significant dimension of bilateral cooperation. The joint statement recognises that "security interests of both the countries are interlinked". Within the institutional framework of security cooperation, India and Maldives have agreed to enhance anti-terrorism cooperation and intensify cooperation in the areas of training and capacity building of the Maldives National Defence Force and the Maldives Police Service.

Cooperation in Indian Ocean

A notable feature of the joint declaration is that it recognises India-Maldivian cooperation not only in the context of South Asia but also in the context of the Indian Ocean. Importantly, Maldives is willing to acknowledge India's role in regional integration.

The Maldivian President urged India to play a leadership role in strengthening SAARC. The declaration says, "The two leaders shared the confidence that cooperation at the bilateral, sub-regional and regional levels will enable the two countries to realise their developmental aspirations, and contribute to peace, prosperity and security in the Indian Ocean Region and South Asia".

Further, they agreed to "strengthen cooperation to enhance maritime safety and security in the Indian Ocean Region through joint patrolling and aerial and maritime surveillance, exchange of information, capacity building and the development of an effective legal framework against piracy." This is a welcome framework for bilateral cooperation but should also be seen in the context of the ongoing trilateral India-Sri Lanka-Maldives talks on regional security. Interestingly this is a first trilateral security cooperation of its kind for India. The security dialogue at sub-regional cooperation, which was agreed to, must continue.

New Opportunities for Consolidation of Relations

The visit has opened up an opportunity for the consolidation of relationship. The two leaderships must take the process forward and address each other's concerns. The Maldivian President should walk the talk and try to resolve the contentious GMR issue quickly to help restore investors' confidence in his country. He should also reassure India of the reports of growing Chinese presence in the country.

India on its part should help Maldives in building its economy and addressing the needs of its manpower development. India should also provide developmental assistance to Maldives the way it has done for Bhutan.

The Framework agreement of November 2011 and 2014 joint declaration provide the ground for deepening of the ties. The two sides should work out a comprehensive plan of developmental partnerships.

No doubt there are many factors of instability operating in Maldives. Internal politics in Maldives has been volatile lately.

A stable democracy in Maldives is in India's interest. It is fortunate that the results of the November 2013 elections were accepted by all concerned.

India needs to remain engaged with all sections of the society and its approach should be people-centric. India should share its democratic experiences to strengthen Maldives fledgling institutions of democracy. People-to-people contacts must be strengthened.

A regular bilateral security dialogue amongst the officials of both sides should be instituted to expand the scope of security cooperation. This should be supplemented by Track-II and Track-1.5 dialogues. India can help build think tanks in the country. A deeper and comprehensive engagement with Maldives as with the other neighbours is vital for India.

Any hesitation in dealing with its neighbours will only invite external powers to step in making a difficult situation even more complex. With the visit of the newly elected president, India has made a good beginning in its relations with Maldives and this should be truly sustained.

5

India's Relation with Nepal

Nepal has been wracked by a Maoist insurgency for the last five or six years. India has remained a passive bystander witnessing the growing erosion of Nepal's state power. Other than giving some military materiel for counter insurgency operations, no weighty measures have been taken.

India has not recognized the gravity of a Maoist take-over of Nepal as American analysts have done in depth. As per American analysts, the strategic implications of a Maoist take-over of Nepal are:

- Nepal becomes a total client state of China. A Maoist Nepal under Chinese tutelage would be a serious disruptive factor for US global strategies in the region.
- Maoist-insurgents ruled Nepal would inextricably get dragged into Islamic terrorist organizations linkages, besides China's policies towards the Islamic world.

India needs to realise the gravity of the strategic implications, specific to India, namely:

- A China-aligned Nepal, removes an important buffer state between India and China. India would have to militarily man the India-Nepal border in strength, which may eat up two to three infantry divisions.
- A China-aligned Nepal adds to the existing China-client states in South Asia i.e. Pakistan and Bangladesh. It would be a very unholy trinity with not only the Western and Eastern flanks of India under China's influence, but the Northern flank too added.
- For the majority peoples of India, the only Hindu kingdom in the world would slide down ignobly into a Chinese-Islamic coalition in South Asia.

India must therefore, immediately, cast away its existing reluctance and inhibitions to act firmly, even militarily, to prevent a Maoist take-over of

Nepal. Fortunately in Nepal's current Maoist-threatened environment, convergence of security interests exist between the United States and India. India must therefore jointly work with the United States to protect the sovereignty of the Nepalese state against a Maoist takeover.

It was so stated by US Assistant Secretary of State, Christiana Rocca during her recent visit to New Delhi: " Working in tandem, our governments can help Nepal defeat the Maoists threat and re-establish democratic institutions responsive to the needs of the people".

India must therefore act forcefully and unapologetically in Nepal forthwith to secure her national interests. It would be a convincing demonstration of what this paper espouses: " India will intervene forcefully to secure her national interests in the region".

In recent years, the increasing dominance of Maoism in Nepal's domestic politics, along with the strengthening economic and political influence of China, has led the Nepalese government to gradually distance itself from India. Nepal has also become a haven for terrorists and separatists operating in India: the recent arrests of two high profile terrorists – Abdul Karim Tunda and Mohammed Ahmed Sidibappa – have brought the India-Nepal border into sharp focus. India has been seeking Nepal's cooperation in managing the border through several bilateral mechanisms. However due to domestic political turmoil, lack of political will and a resource crunch, Nepal has been unable to effectively cooperate with India. But that could change if Nepal sees increasing political stability in 2014.

India-Nepal relations have been formed and shaped by their geographical contiguity and socio-cultural identities which has influenced their historical past. The historical linkages emanating from the racial, religious and linguistic affinities were possible because of the 1,750-km- long open border which made communication easier and possible. The crossing of the border by the people has not only influenced each other's history, culture and tradition but also had an impact on the political, economic and strategic relations between the two countries.

The geo-strategic location of Nepal between India and China has also shaped its relations with its neighbours. The high peaks and rough terrain towards the north made communication and people's movement and habitation difficult, if not impossible, towards the Tibet region of China. This is not to say that Nepal did not have historical political linkages with its northern neighbour. However, the presence of imperialist China and Russia in the north led British India to consider Nepal has a buffer state and integrate Nepal into British India's security parameters.

Independent India also could not ignore the geo-strategic importance of Nepal and considered it as a buffer between itself and Communist China. It was not only the ideological differences with China that alarmed India but also the Chinese efforts to undermine India's security interests by undertaking road construction projects in Terai area which is contiguous to the plains of India.

In fact, soon after Communist China's expansion towards Tibet, India entered into the Treaty of Peace and Friendship with Nepal in 1950 which defined the political, economic and strategic relations between the two countries. The Chinese expansion towards Tibet had perturbed Nepal as it not only exposed China's historical claims of maintaining the Himalayan state as its feudatory but also Nepal's vulnerability in containing any armed aggression from the north. Hence, Nepal agreed to enter into treaty arrangements with India.

However, too much dependence brings forth to the small state fear of being incorporated or turned into an ally of the dominant state. The open border between India and Nepal had created ideological and political linkages between the two countries much to the chagrin of the monarch. For instance, the Nepali National Congress, a protagonist of democracy and a socialistic society, had links with the Indian National Congress even before the independence of India. Landlocked Nepal utilised its geographical location to its advantage by undertaking strategies of distancing with India, neutrality or non-alignment with its neighbours, to preserve its own interest. Such as Nepal developed diplomatic relations with China in 1960 under King Mahendra's rule and tried to assert its independence and sovereignty.

The internal political dynamics in Nepal also influenced the making of its foreign policy with India. There have been frequent changes in the political system in Nepal from the rule of Ranas to the monarchy to the Panchayat democracy and constitutional democracy and in every political change the ruler has looked towards those out of power with suspicion. Such as when King Mahendra faced opposition from pro-democracy political parties like the Nepali Congress and Communists, he apprehended Indian support to them. To strengthen the monarchy, King Mahendra tried to diversify relations with extra-regional countries and tried to maintain a distance from India. Similarly, King Birendra tried to maintain a distance from India which was alleged by Nepal to be supporting the pro-democracy and anti-monarchy Congress rebels, by proposing to be a Zone of Peace in the region. Despite the Government of India's assurances on various occasions, Nepal remained unconvinced. One reason could be that certain political idealogues in India, like the socialists, supported the cause of the Nepali Congress. Even during the agitation against the monarchy in 1989, the socialists like Chandrashekhar and Communist leaders from India were present in Kathmandu to extend their support to the democrats. However, they have to be differentiated from the official stand taken by the Government of India.

The Cold War politics also affected India-Nepal relations. The impact of Sino-Soviet differences alongwith the growing Sino-US rapprochement in the international politics percolated down to South Asia where the Sino-India differences drew India and the Soviet Union closer. Nepal also made use of the Sino-India differences and followed the policy of distancing from India to reap advantages from the global and regional actors. For example, in 1961, King Mahendra signed an agreement on the road construction from Kathmandu to Kodari with China in 1961. The agreement came at a time when the monarchy had dissolved the Parliamentary democracy, a move not favoured by India, and Nepal needed to allay any fears of outside support to democracy for which nothing could have been better than to use China whose relations with India had fallen to the lowest.

Since then the ground realities have changed. The Cold War has come to an end with the disintegration of the Soviet Union in 1989 and the worldwide resurgence of democratic forces. The Chinese policy makers have done a rethinking on their policies after the disintegration of the Soviet Union. China has tried to create its own "Socialist Market Economy" and has opened its doors to foreign investors in order to globalise its economy.

In this task it will not be favourable for it to have any irritant impeding its growth. Hence, China responded favourably to the Indian desire to improve their relationship. Indian Prime Minister Rajiv Gandhi visited China in 1989, the first ever visit by an Indian Prime Minister.

Three agreements were signed, on cultural exchange, air service between the two countries, and on science and technology. This opened up diplomatic visits between the two countries. During his visit to India in November 1996, the Chinese President, Ziang Zemin, said that "though we still have some outstanding problems left over from history, I can say for sure that our common interests far outweigh our differences, as neither of us poses a threat to the other." Emphasis has been laid on economic cooperation though a Joint Working Group has been set up to resolve the border issue. In the latest round of border talks on August 5, 1997, both the sides agreed to identify an interim border and accelerate the pace of demilitarisation of the eastern border. There has been an attitudinal change in India and China commensurating with the global trend where all the countries cooperate with one another keeping aside their differences and disputes.

In the meantime, Nepal was also undergoing rapid political changes. Invigorated by the worldwide movements for democracy, the democratic forces in Nepal worked with added vigour to overthrow the Panchayat regime. In 1990, King Birendra accepted the popular demand for greater participation of the people's representation and multi-party democracy was established in Nepal. A democratic government of Prime Minister K.P. Bhattarai consisting of the Nepali Congress and the Communist Party of Nepal-United Marxist Leninist [CPN(UML)] took control of power. The democratic government had the responsibility to steer the country towards the radically changed world polity devoid of clear-cut Cold War politics and define foreign policy in the region where the security situation is threatened from within.

The Growing Ties

The multi-party democracy in Nepal infused new hopes of normalising relations between the two countries who had become aware of the post-Cold War world order where emphasis was laid on economic relations.

The first requirement to forge closer ties was by normalising trade relations which had nosedived following the expiry of the treaty of trade and transit in 1989 and the subsequent closure of the border except for two points at Raxaul and Jogbani. The interim government of K.P. Bhattarai declared it would improve trade relations with India on a priority basis. The Nepalese perspective was favourably responded to by India. In fact, the then Foreign Minister of India, I.K. Gujral, declared India's readiness to "accommodate the economic aspirations of the Nepalese people."

During K.P. Bhattarai's visit to India in 1989, the trade relations with India were resumed. The trade embargo was removed and the bilateral relations were restored to the situation prevailing on April 1, 1987. The date was significant because it annulled the "work permit system" restricting Indians from seeking employment in Nepal.

Emphasis was given on developing economic relations between the two countries with areas identified for joint cooperation. The Joint Communique signed on the occasion declared that the countries would cooperate on "industrial and human resource development, for harnessing of waters of the common rivers for the benefit of the two peoples and for the protection and management of the environment." However, instead of creating an environment of trust and confidence, the media and the Opposition parties criticised the term "common rivers" considering it as the surrender and compromise of

Nepal's sovereign rights over water resources. The two Prime Ministers gave assurances to each other that all the bilateral disputes would be settled peacefully and pledged "territorial integrity, non-use of force and non-interference in each other's internal affairs." They agreed to be sensitive to each other's security and agreed not to allow activities in their territory inimical to the interest of each other. They agreed to "have prior consultations with a view to reaching mutual agreement on such defence related matters which, in the view of either country, could pose a threat to its security." These assurances were not something novel and are contained in the Treaty of Peace and Friendship (1950). Article V of the treaty allows Nepal to import arms, equipment or war-like material from or through the Indian territory for its security provided the imports are done with the prior consultation of the latter. The letter exchanged along with the treaty substantiated the security provision contained in the treaty and said that "neither government shall tolerate any threat to the security of the other by a foreign aggressor. To deal with any such threat the two governments shall consult with each other and devise effective counter-measures." However, reiteration by both the countries was important in the background of Nepal granting road construction deals to China in the Terai or importing arms from China, for instance, in 1989, which was against the spirit of the 1950 Treaty. In fact, the last consignment of arms coming from China was deferred by Nepal as a goodwill gesture towards India. The interim government showed its sincerity to develop friendly, unique and brotherly relations with India and even dropped the Zone of Peace proposal from the Constitution as was propounded by King Birendra in 1974.

The friendly gestures made by the interim government were significant as it consisted of the Nepali Congress and the CPN (UML), the two forces committed to the cause of democracy who also had historical linkage with India. Also the relations developed between Nepal and India acted as a guideline for the future governments.

The Nepalese Prime Minister's visit was reciprocated by the Indian Prime Minister, Chandrashekhar, on February 13-15, 1991. Chandrashekhar had been in close association with the Nepali Congress and had extended his vocal support to the pro-democracy movement in Nepal. He had attended the meeting organised by the Nepali Congress on January 18, 1990, to chart a future course of action to restore democracy in Nepal. Hence, Chandrashekhar's visit raised lots of expectations from Nepal. He accepted the Joint Communique signed in 1990 as the basis for India's relations with Nepal. It was decided that India would restore the Jayanagar-Janakpuri-Bizalur railway line. Under its aid programme India agree to open three more entry points at Nepalganj,

Gauriphaula and Banbasa for third country nationals on the Indo-Nepal border. Discussions were held on harnessing of water resources, restoration of registration facilities for vehicles owned by Indian residents, removal of impediments to ensure free movement of Indian currency from Nepal to India and removal of discriminations against the Indian teachers working in Nepal. Both the countries agreed to set up a High Level Task Force to identify areas of economic cooperation and propose its recommendations to the two Prime Ministers. Accordingly, the High Level Task Force was set up in 1991.

Nepal had its first general election in 1991 in accordance with the new Constitution formulated by the interim government. People voted the Nepali Congress to power which had a long history of fighting for people's rights and multi-party democracy. Girija Prasad Koirala became the Prime Minister of Nepal. He gave primacy to developing relations with the neighbouring countries.

His visit to India, his first ever visit abroad as Prime Minister, from December 5 to 10, 1991, was not only fruitful in defining relations with India but was also successful in concluding two separate treaties on trade and transit for five and seven years respectively. India also reduced the domestic content and labour requirement on Nepalese goods from 65 per cent to 50 per cent to provide duty free access to India. The agreement to control unauthorised trade was also extended for five years. The signatories committed themselves to ensure the interests of each other by not allowing illegal trade, narcotic and psychotropic substances and agreed to exchange information on such related matters.

A Memorandum of Understanding was signed for cooperation in developing agricultural yield through cooperation in science and technology, research, processing and agro-based industries. As a measure towards closer trust and confidence, the B.P. Koirala Foundation was set up to promote exchange of views on education, culture, science and technology.

In fact, India agreed to improve and simplify the rules for export of goods from Nepal during Prime Minister P.V. Narasimha Rao's visit to Nepal in October 1992. India agreed to extend stand by credit facility to Nepal from (IC) Rs.35 crore to Rs.50 crore. The term of the agreement was extended from one to three years during which period the interest rate of 7 per cent per annum was levied. Nepal's private vehicles were allowed to move from its border to Calcutta and Haldia ports and back provided the vehicles were authorised by the Nepal Transit and Warehousing Company Ltd or Nepal Transport Corporation. This was agreed to facilitate Nepal's exports to India. Movement of vehicles from Nepal to Nepal via Indian territory was allowed without any bond or cash deposit. Nepal was also allowed to import goods from India in convertible currency.

Taking the discussion further on cooperation in harnessing of water resources, both the sides agreed on a time-frame for investigations, preparation of project reports on Karnali, Pancheshwar, Sapta-Kosi, Budhi Gandaki, Kamala and Bagmati projects. Priority was given to work on the Pancheshwar and Budhi Gandaki projects. On the Tanakpur Barrage, it was accepted that the area remains under the sovereign control of Nepal. However, the barrage project does not make any consumptive use of water. India agreed to supply 150 cusecs of water to irrigate 4,000 to 5,000 hectares of land and would supply 20 million units of power, free of cost to Nepal. It was also agreed to either renovate or replace the missing boundary pillars at Tanakpur Barrage by May 1993.

India showed keen interest to accelerate the pace of economic development in Nepal which was necessary to consolidate the democratic aspirations of the people who had expected overnight change in their status quo. Lack of employment opportunities could create frustration and disappointment amongst the people who expected miracles from their representatives.

The improvement in the relations resulted in the increased industrial production which increased by 19.26 per cent for the year 1990-91 whereas the rate of growth in the last fiscal year was estimated to 4.4 per cent. The first volume of trade between the two countries increased from NRs 5,273.6 million in 1988-89 to NRs 9,473.6 million in 1990-91.

Another matter of concern which needed special attention of the two countries was the use of the open border by subversive elements against Indian security interests. Prime Minister Koirala has assured India of Nepal's total cooperation in curbing terrorism from its soil against India, it being a threat to Nepal's security also. The Nepalese Prime Minister was keen to include Indian participation in any negotiations with Bhutan on the issue of refugees which was turned down by India as it considered the issue to be affecting the relations between Nepal and Bhutan which had to be resolved by both the parties bilaterally.

The significant change in the political relationship between India and Nepal was the frankness in negotiations and discussions which was virtually absent during the monarchy which looked towards democratic India with suspicion. However, the change of the political system from monarchy to multi-party democracy in Nepal did not bring forth changes in its political culture. For instance, the erstwhile monarchy and the Panchayat regime had used anti-India slogans to counter any opposition at home and stabilise their power by heightening the passions of the people. After the change of the political system, those not in power used similar tactics to criticise the government in power. The Nepali Congress is considered to be pro-India and the Opposition utilised this label to criticise the government and involved India's name to give authenticity to their charges. The perfect case was of Tanakpur. The Opposition considered Tanakpur as a sellout to India. They claimed that India had constructed the 577 metres of the bund in the Nepali territory without the government's approval. Koirala blamed the Opposition for instigating anti-India feeling in Nepal straining the upward movement in their relations. He said, "We have not compromised our sovereignty with India."

The Tanakpur issue brought into prominence the fears and apprehensions of Nepal of not being given "mutual benefit" on earlier agreements on the Kosi and Gandak. Since the matter was of national importance, they expected it to be discussed at home before taking it for bilateral discussion with India. Also recognising the sensitivity of the issue which could be related to the sovereignty of the country, the Tanakpur agreement was politicised by the political parties in Nepal for their own political gains. However, its impact on India-Nepal relations cannot be ignored. The politicisation of any project slows down the progress in the development of the project as happened in the Tanakpur Barrage where the work had come to a standstill. Much time was consumed in taking the matter to the Supreme Court of Nepal and the Parliament. However, Nepal did learn a lesson of taking a consensual approach before taking the issue on water resource or any matter of national importance with India as was done in the Mahakali Agreement in 1995.

Domestic compulsions pressurised Koirala to resign and mid-term elections were held in November 1994. Man Mohan Adhikari heading the CPN (UML) formed the government. Adhikari also opened his diplomatic initiatives by visiting India in April 1995. In a Press conference he said, "I would like to review all aspects of relations as well as changes in the trade and transit agreements with India. This is in view of the changes taking place in international relations as well as in South Asia." He had reservations on the 1950 Treaty and wanted some changes in it, specifically on clauses related to security issues. However, in the same vein, he said, "Nepal was totally in support of India's security concerns." He reassured India that the Nepalese territory would not be used for anti-India activities.17 To keep a vigil on the cross-border movement, a technical committee was set up to discuss the issue. The Adhikari government was eager for Indian investment in the hydro-power sector. However, its tenure was shortlived. The government was ousted from power through a no-confidence motion and the Nepali Congress with the support of the Rashtriya Prajatantra Party and Nepal Sadbhavana Party came to power under the leadership of Sher Bahadur Deuba.

The major achievement of the Deuba government lies in taking a consensus approach in signing a Treaty on Integrated Development of the Mahakali Basin in February 1997 in New Delhi. The treaty envisages construction of the 2,000 MW Pancheshwar power project within eight years. Both governments agreed to workout an umbrella for the sale of power to each other and encourage Indian investment in the hydro-power sector in Nepal as a part of an action plan to further strengthen bilateral economic cooperation. The treaty had put to rest the controversy which had been raised after the signing of the Tanakpur agreement. Nepal's share of water was increased from 150 cusecs and 20 million units of power to 300 cusecs of water in the dry season and 1,000 cusecs of water in the monsoons besides 70 million units of power. Another agreement was signed on the construction of 22 bridges on the Kohalpur-Mahakali sector of the east-west highway.

At home Deuba received an unexpected reaction from the left parties towards the treaty which had otherwise received public support. The CPN (UML), which was initially satisfied with the treaty, along with other left parties expressed dissatisfaction over it. It blamed Deuba for tampering with the treaty which was initiated in Nepal and for signing a new version in New Delhi. Defending the treaty, Deuba called the allegation "baseless and fictitious and is an excellent attempt to mislead people." Despite the furore and criticism, the parties ratified it in the Parliament on September 11, 1996, with certain modifications.

Nepal had learnt certain lessons from the earlier agreement on Tanakpur Barrage. Not to repeat the furore at home, the government had taken a national consensus with all the parties on the subject. Thus, at the time of ratification in the Parliament, the Opposition had no moral right to reject it. More so because it was the CPN(UML) which had initially proposed the Mahakali Treaty during Prime Minister Adhikari's visit to India in April 1995.

Prime Minister Deuba also spoke about modification of the Treaty of Peace and Friendship, especially, the clauses related to the security concerns and said that his government will pursue the same policy on security related matters as was followed by the previous government. Expressing Nepal's concern towards India's security issues, Deuba said that "Nepal will never pose a security threat to India." In fact, both the countries were determined to fight terrorism and reiterated their commitment not to allow any activities on their territory prejudicial to the security interests of the other. Subsequently, a Joint Working Group was set up in August 1996 during the visit of P.C. Lohani, the Foreign Minister of Nepal, to India. The Group is expected to give suggestions on the ways and means to monitor the open border in order to check the movement of undesirable subversive elements inimical to the security of both states.

A major turning point in the relationship was felt when I.K. Gujral became the Prime Minister of India. He gave a thrust on maintaining bilateral relations with the neighbouring countries in the spirit of non-reciprocity and non-interference in the internal affairs. India being dominant in size had to show magnanimity towards its smaller neighbours. One magnanimous gesture shown by India was to allow Nepal to use Phulbari as a transit point to get access to Bangladesh. India had been denying the transit point to Nepal because of its proximity to the Siliguri corridor which is sensitive to India's security concerns. However, Gujral showed trust and confidence in the country's neighbour by allowing it to use the Phulbari-Banglabandh transit route.

During Gujral's visit to Nepal in June 1997, a power agreement was signed to encourage private and semi-government investment in Nepal. After the Mahakali Agreement this was a significant development because the countries could meet any shortage in power from Pancheshwar.

Also, both the countries had freedom to enter into an agreement with a third party to generate resources for exploiting power. India is aware that the excess power can be utilised by its power deficient areas. Letters were exchanged on developing the Raxaul-Sirsiya rail link and supply of medical equipment to a hospital in Kathmandu from India. A Memorandum of Understanding was signed on civil aviation which allows private airlines to operate between the two countries in the light of growing business and tourism; Bangalore and Lucknow airports are open for the flights arriving from Nepal.

There has been an element of "mutual benefit" and "non-reciprocity" in India's relations with Nepal as envisaged in the Mahakali Treaty. India and Nepal relations hitherto defined in terms of geo-politics had to accord primacy to economic cooperation in the light of the changing global economic environment.

The main thrust of the economic cooperation has been on four areas: trade and transit relations, sharing of water resources, Indian aided projects and joint ventures. In fact, the countries have moved ahead from bilateralism and are looking towards multilateralism.

In December 1996, Nepal submitted an approach paper on sub-regional cooperation within the South Asian Association for Regional Cooperation (SAARC) parameters which suggests creation of growth polygons between Nepal, Bhutan, Bangladesh and India in the fields of transit, multimodal transport, irrigation, energy, environment, tourism, trade and investment.

INDEPENDENT POLITICAL HISTORY

1950-1970

In the 1950s, Nepal welcomed close relations with India, but as the number of Nepalese living and working in India increased and the involvement of India in Nepal's economy deepened in the 1960s and after, so too did Nepalese discomfort with the special relationship.

Tensions came to a head in the mid-1970s, when Nepal pressed for substantial amendments in its favour in the trade and transit treaty and openly criticized India's 1975 annexation of Sikkim which was considered as part of Greater Nepal. In 1975 King Birendra Bir Bikram Shah Dev proposed that Nepal be recognized internationally as a zone of peace; he received support from China and Pakistan.

In New Delhi's view, if the king's proposal did not contradict the 1950 treaty and was merely an extension of nonalignment, it was unnecessary; if it was a repudiation of the special relationship, it represented a possible threat to India's security and could not be endorsed. In 1984 Nepal repeated the proposal, but there was no reaction from India. Nepal continually promoted the proposal in international forums, with Chinese support; by 1990 it had won the support of 112 countries.

1970-1980

In 1978 India agreed to separate trade and transit treaties, satisfying a long-term Nepalese demand. In 1988, when the two treaties were up for renewal, Nepal's refusal to accommodate India's wishes on the transit treaty caused India to call for a single trade and transit treaty. Thereafter, Nepal took a hard-line position that led to a serious crisis in India-Nepal relations. After two extensions, the two treaties expired on March 23, 1989, resulting in a virtual Indian economic blockade of Nepal that lasted until late April 1990. Although economic issues were a major factor in the two countries' confrontation, Indian dissatisfaction with Nepal's 1988 acquisition of Chinese weaponry played an important role. treaty and letters exchanged in 1959 and 1965, which included Nepal in India's security zone and precluded arms purchases without India's approval. India linked security with economic relations and insisted on reviewing India-Nepal relations as a whole. Nepal had to back down after worsening economic conditions led to a change in Nepal's political system, in which the king was forced to institute a parliamentary democracy. The new government sought quick restoration of amicable relations with India.

1990s

The special security relationship between New Delhi and Kathmandu was reestablished during the June 1990 New Delhi meeting of Nepal's prime minister Krishna Prasad Bhattarai and Indian prime minister V.P. Singh. During the December 1991 visit to India by Nepalese prime minister Girija Prasad Koirala, the two countries signed new, separate trade and transit treaties and other economic agreements designed to accord Nepal additional economic benefits.

Indian-Nepali relations appeared to be undergoing still more reassessment when Nepal's prime minister Man Mohan Adhikary visited New Delhi in April 1995 and insisted on a major review of the 1950 peace and friendship treaty. In the face of benign statements by his Indian hosts relating to the treaty, Adhikary sought greater economic independence for his landlocked nation while simultaneously striving to improve ties with China.

21st Century

In 2005, after King Gyanendra took over, Nepalese relations with India soured. However, after the restoration of democracy, in 2008, Prachanda, the Prime Minister of Nepal, visited India, in September 2008. He spoke about a new dawn, in the bilateral relations, between the two countries. He said, "I am going back to Nepal as a satisfied person. I will tell Nepali citizens back home that a new era has dawned. Time has come to effect a revolutionary change in bilateral relations. On behalf of the new government, I assure you that we are committed to make a fresh start." He met Indian Prime minister, Manmohan Singh, and Foreign Minister, Pranab Mukherjee. He asked India to help Nepal frame a new constitution, and to invest in Nepal's infrastructure, and its tourism industry.

In 2008, Indo-Nepali ties got a further boost with an agreement to resume water talks after a 4 year hiatus. The Nepalese Water Resources Secretary Shanker Prasad Koirala said the Nepal-India Joint Committee on Water Resources meet decided to start the reconstruction of breached Kosi embankment after the water level goes down. During the Nepal PM's visit to New Delhi in September the two Prime Ministers expressed satisfaction at the age-old close, cordial and extensive relationships between their states and expressed their support and cooperation to further consolidate the relationship. The two issued a 22-point statement highlighting the need to review, adjust and update the 1950 Treaty of Peace and Friendship, amongst other agreements. India would also provide a credit line of up to 150 crore rupees to Nepal to ensure uninterrupted supplies of petroleum products, as well as lift bans on the export of rice, wheat, maize, sugar and sucrose for quantities agreed to with Nepal. India would also provide 20 crore as immediate flood relief.

In return, Nepal will take measures for the "promotion of investor friendly, enabling business environment to encourage Indian...investments in Nepal." Furthermore, a three-tier mechanism at the level of ministerial, secretary and technical levels will be built to push forward discussions on the development of water resources between the two sides. Politically, India acknowledged a willingness to promote efforts towards peace in Nepal. Indian External affairs minister Pranab Mukherjee promised the Nepali Prime Minister Prachanda that he would "extend all possible help for peace and development."

In 2008, the Bollywood film *Chandni Chowk to China* was banned in Nepal, because of a scene suggesting the Gautama Buddha was born in India. Some protesters called for commercial boycott of all Indian films.

INDIA-NEPAL RELATIONS

India-Nepal relationship is shaped by the centuries old social-cultural, historical and geographic linkages. Extensive people-to-people contacts permeate all aspects of the lives of the people of India and Nepal and transcend borders and governments. Welfare of the people of the two countries is interlinked and developments in one country invariably have an impact on the other. Few other sovereign states in the world can take pride in a relationship as wide-ranging and multi-faceted as that shared between India and Nepal.

Beginning with the 12-Point Understanding reached between the Seven Party Alliance (SPA) and the Maoists in Delhi in November 2005. Government of India welcomed the roadmap laid down by the historic Comprehensive Peace Agreement of November 2006 towards political stabilization in Nepal through peaceful reconciliation and inclusive democratic processes, India has consistently responded with a sense of urgency to the needs of the people and Government of Nepal in ensuring the success of the peace process and institutionalization of multi-party democracy through the framing of a new

Constitution by a duly elected Constituent Assembly. India was the first country to welcome the restoration of democracy in Nepal. India has also provided material assistance to strengthen the government machinery in Nepal and for successful CA elections. Overall, over Rs.170 crores of assistance in the form of supply and equipment has been extended as part of India's support to the peace process in Nepal in response to requests from the Government of Nepal.

The visit of Prime Minister Hon'ble Mr. G.P. Koirala to India one month after the restoration of multi-party democracy in Nepal saw India extend a comprehensive package of assistance to help Nepal tide over immediate financial needs and support peace, democracy and stability. A comprehensive economic package worth Rs.1000 crores was announced during the visit. A soft credit line of USD 100 million for infrastructure development projects was extended, and outstanding dues on defence purchases worth NRs. 1.6 billion waived. Government of India also agreed to doubling the number of GOI scholarships for Nepalese students and to supply of 25,000 metric tons of fertilizers to Nepal at subsidized prices.

Prime Minister Hon'ble Pushpa Kamal Dahal 'Prachanda' paid an official visit to India from 14-17 September 2008, and met President, Vice President, Prime Minister, and External Affairs Minister as well as Chairperson of UPA and the Leader of Opposition. A Joint Press Statement was issued at the conclusion of the visit, reiterating the special features of the bilateral relationship and committing both sides to work towards further improving relations. India agreed to implement the Naumure hydro-electric project on Rapti river besides the Rs. 20 crores assistance for Kosi breach relief. Credit of up to Rs 150 crores was also provided to GON to ensure uninterrupted supplies of petroleum products. We have also permitted export of 10,000 tonnes of wheat and 15,000 tonnes of rice to Nepal, along with lifting of ban on other food items. PM Prachanda visited India again from November 12-14, 2008 to attend the BIMSTEC Summit.

The Foreign Minister of Nepal Hon'ble Mrs. Sujata Koirala visited India from 5-10 August 2009 where she held fruitful discussions with their counterparts. Foreign Secretary of India visited Nepal on 14-15 September 2009 to exchange views on the future course of cooperation between the two countries.

Prime Minister Hon'ble Mr. Madhav Kumar Nepal paid an official visit to India from August 18 – 22, 2009 at the invitation of the Prime Minister of India. The two leaders had also met earlier on the sidelines of the XVth NAM Summit in Sherm-el-Sheikh, Egypt.

The two Prime Ministers expressed their satisfaction on the age-old, close, cordial and multifaceted relations between Nepal and India and agreed to expand them further. India expressed full support for the ongoing peace process and the efforts to bring about economic transformation in Nepal. The two Governments decided to reinvigorate bilateral relations by ensuring effectiveness of all established institutional mechanisms.

The two sides also agreed to enhance bilateral trade on a sustainable basis. To facilitate Nepalese foreign trade, India agreed to utilization of Vishakhapatanam port for movement of transit traffic to and from Nepal. A MoU was signed for continuation of Indian grant assistant for "Goiter Control Programme" in Nepal.

Nepal assured India that it will not allow its territory to be used for any activity against India and India also gave the same assurance to Nepal. A number of projects with Government of India assistance with a total outlay of over Rs. 1600 Crores were agreed upon including, construction of National Police Academy in Nepal, construction of poly-technique at Hetauda, construction of two integrated check-posts, construction of 660 kilometres of roads in the Terai region, construction of two cross-border rail-lines and continuing provision of Indian faculty to B.P. Koirala Institute of Health Sciences, Dharan.

The two Governments also agreed to take up preventive measures and consultations to address the problem of inundation to border areas between Nepal and India. The Government of India also agreed, in principle, to double the number of scholarships offered to Nepalese students and to increase the number of slots offered for training of Nepalese Government officials.

The two sides also agreed to facilitate increased Indian public and private sector involvement to harness Nepalese hydro-power potential. It was also decided to cooperate bilaterally in areas such as culture, science and technology, tourism and sports and to facilitate contact and cooperation among the parliamentarians of the two countries.

The Minister of External Affairs of India (EAM), H.E. Mr. S.M. Krishna paid an official visit to Nepal from January 15 – 17, 2010 at the invitation of Hon'ble Deputy Prime Minister and Minister of Foreign Affairs of Nepal Ms. Sujata Koirala. During his visit, EAM called on Rt. Hon. Dr. Ram Baran Yadav, President of Nepal and Rt. Hon'ble Mr. Madhav Kumar Nepal, Prime Minister of Nepal. He conveyed to them the greetings of the Indian leadership and reiterated that India attaches the highest priority to its relations with Nepal.

EAM also called on Rt. Hon'ble Mr. Subas Chandra Nembang, Chairman of the Constituent Assembly and held an interactive discussion with

Parliamentarians representing the different political parties in the Constituent Assembly.

He also met senior political leaders representing various political parties of Nepal. During his visit, EAM held official talks with the Deputy Prime Minister and Minister for Foreign Affairs of Nepal on all aspects of bilateral relations and issues of mutual interest. The two Ministers expressed their satisfaction regarding the age-old, multifaceted relations that exist between Nepal and India and agreed to expand these further.

They also reviewed the implementation of the decisions taken during the official visit of the Prime Minister of Nepal, Rt. Hon. Madhav Kumar Nepal to India from 18 – 22 August 2009. A total of four MoUs for various projects to be conducted with Government of India's assistance were signed that included (i) MoU for construction of Terai roads with an estimated cost of IRs. 805 Crores; (ii) MoU for construction of a Science Learning Centre at an estimated cost of IRs 16.6 Crores; (iii) MoU between Nepal Stock Exchange Limited (NEPSE) and Central Depository Services (India) Ltd. (CDSIL), India at an estimated cost of IRs. 9.2 Crores; and (iv) MoUs for electrification of five different VDCs in Nepal at a total cost of IRs. 6.3 Crores.

In keeping with the tradition of regular high-level exchange of visits between India and Nepal, President, Hon'ble Dr. Ram Baran Yadav, first President of Nepal, paid a state visit to India from 15-18 February 2010 at the invitation of our President. He was accompanied by Mr. Sharat Singh Bhandari, Minister for Tourism and Civil Aviation and a high-level official delegation. During the visit he met the President. The Vice President, the Prime Minister, Minister of Finance, External Affairs Minister, Minister for Home Affairs, the Chairperson of UPA and the Leader of Opposition and the Foreign Secretary called upon the visiting President. He also visited Haridwar and met a cross section of political leaders in India. During the visit of President of Nepal to India (15-18 February 2010) four MoUs/agreements were signed in the presence of the President of Nepal and our Prime Minister. These included (i) Air Services Agreement between India and Nepal; (ii) MoU for extension of railway lines to five cross border points along the India Nepal border; (iii) MoU on establishment of Nepal-Bharat Maitree Polytechnique at Hetauda and (iv) MoU on establishment of Nepal Bharat Maitri Sabhagraha in Birgunj. In response to Nepal's request for supply of food items, our Prime Minister announced that India will supply 50,000 metric tones of wheat, 25,000 metric tones of rice and 10,000 metric tones of pulses to Nepal. Our willingness to supply an additional 200 thousand metric tones of wheat, if required, was also conveyed. To facilitate economic and infrastructure development in Nepal,

Prime Minister also announced the extension of a new concessional Line of Credit for US $ 250 million.

India remains steadfast in its commitment to extend assistance for Nepal's economic development and political stabilization. India's support continues to be in accordance with the wishes and priorities of the people and Government of Nepal. India Nepal Economic Cooperation stands to be further strengthened with the ushering in of a new era of hope and peace in Nepal.

BORDER CULTURES - IDENTITY, BELONGING AND SEPARATION

There are different perspectives on the border and on India, some people feel close to India, for some it seems to be a threat. This led to an impression of internal differentiation, which will be discussed in the following. Nationality has different meanings for different parts of the border area's population, there are different constructions of identity, history and ethnic boundaries. As I have written 'the construction of', we understand identity as fluid, changing images of self and external reference and description. Identity must not be homogeneous, but can overlap in one person or group. "To insist on an identity is also to insist on certain rights and to be denied an identity implicates a denial of rights" (Sökefeld 2001: 34), so identity can be used as a strategy, even different identities can be used in different situations for the own benefit. It can be constructed out of self-sameness as well as of sameness in difference from 'the Other'. Even though identity can be used in an essential way, for example by speaking of 'the people', 'we are' 'or we were since ever', etc., we think of identity as a constructed part of human culture, which is used to separate oneself from others. To enclose the quite broad concept of identity, which can relate to many attributes, such as gender, class, profession, etc., we have to define two types of identity construction, which are nationality and ethnicity and seem to be of greatest importance in the following. As we defined identity in a constructivist way, we understand nationality and ethnicity as constructed concepts of human beings for creating an internal *We* against an external *Other* In the tradition of most scholars, dealing with a constructivist understanding of ethnicity, we have to quote Frederik Barth, on whom this perspective on ethnicity is grounded:

When defined as an ascriptive and exclusive group, the nature of continuity of ethnic groups is clear: it depends on the maintenance of a boundary. The cultural features that signal the boundary may change, and the cultural characteristics of the members may likewise be transformed, indeed, even the organizational form of the group may change – yet the fact of continuing dichotomization between members and outsiders allows us to specify the nature of continuity, and investigate the changing cultural form and content. [...] The critical focus of investigation from this point of view becomes the ethnic *boundary* that defines the group, not the cultural stuff that it encloses.

In this sense, ethnic groups are no given cultural entities, which can be differentiated by its essential cultural features. It is the ethnic group as a social organization, which produces difference by using cultural features for defining members and outsiders. Not the *objective* cultural differences mark different ethnic groups, but the ones which are of subjective relevance for members or outsiders, for internal or external description. (Ibid.) As these cultural features are changeable and differ in their in- and exclusiveness, Individuals can shift their ethnic identity or stress different aspects of their identity in different situations. "Many people change their ethnic identity only if they can profit by doing so." (Roosens 1989: 13) The formation of different groups by making boundaries of cultural features, like religion, food habits, rituals, shared history etc. is the foundation of ethnic groups and ethnic identity. Especially in the border area it is interesting, if ethnic boundaries correspond to the national border, or if a transcendence of border by ethnic groups is to be observed. It is the question of whether ethnic identity can be integrated into national identity concepts or if they confront and contradict. As the state border is the boundary for national identity, the border area could be the best place to deconstruct concepts of nation and nationality. Nationality is understood here similar to the concept of ethnicity, but deeply related to the nation state, whereas ethnicity can be understood as independent from state and territory.

As the history, especially of migration and belonging, seems to be important for the construction of identity in the border area, I have to give some basic information on Terai's history of settlement. In Nepal's history there are two important phases of populating the Terai, which is often described as being covered by dense jungle with only few population because of malaria before the 1950s: "After the unification of Nepal (1768-1845) encouraged Indian people to settle in the Tarai regions of Nepal [...] During 1960 this 'Indiasation policy' was followed by the 'Paharisation policy'." (Buggeland 1999: 97f.) So there seemed to be two waves of people moving to the Terai, one from India, the other from the hills. Besides people from hills or from India, the Terai is populated by Tharus, which are called to be the indigenous Terain people. As borders shifted, it is quite difficult to say, who is Nepalese and who is not, who belongs to the land and who migrated when and from where. But regarding different types of identity constructions in the border area, descriptions and tales of being of Nepalese *origin* are very importance. This must not relate on historical facts, but on tales of history, which are used to legitimize land ownership and the right for national and regional participation or for denying these for another group.

The Madheshis, the Muslims and the Tharus. These three groups give different insights in identity constructions, as the first differentiates itself from others through region and race, the second through religion and the third through ethnicity. Of special interest is the relation between the Madheshis and the other two, as at first being Madheshi included Muslims and Tharus, but because of different reasons parts of both groups separated from and refused being Madheshi.

Being Madheshi – History of Exclusion and Discrimination

Madhesh is an alternative word for the Terai, the southern plain area of Nepal. So first of all *Madheshi* is the term for people, who are living in the Terai. This includes a separation of the country in different regions and in different people:

"As from the very beginning, this region is quite separate, that is low land, here after hilly land, that is called Pahar, after that in the north, Himalayan province" (Madheshi Forum, Biratnagar) and "in Nepal there are two groups, one is Pahari, one is Madheshi." (Ex Coal-Businessman, Muslim Neighbourhood in Biratnagar). The distinction of Nepal into Pahar, the hills and Madhesh, the plain land is the basis for the construction of one Madheshi identity. But the division in Paharis and Madheshis is not only a regional one, it also has political and social, even racial implications: "People who are having the Madheshi face, they are Madheshi. And people who are having the Pahari face, they are Pahari" (Butcher 1, Muslim Neighbourhood, Biratnagar).

The term Madheshi became popular in Nepal with the rising of the Madheshi movement, the fighting of Madheshis for equal rights. The following excerpt of an interview with a Madheshi activist will give a short overview of the movement, its reasons and results:

[...], the main purpose of Madhesh movement was almost about 50% population of Nepal they are from the Terai. [...] They are from that origin. And about half population they are from the hill. But when the Prithvi Narayan Sha unified Nepal, he was hill Brahmin. So he (interests?) his own ethnic groups, his own caste. And that caused that in all of the structures, the mechanisms of the government is those hilly people (???) the opportunities. And in one way [...] Terai was internally colonized. [...], so 2 years ago there was a movement from the Madheshi people under the leadership of Upendra Yadav, who is now foreign minister and deputy prime minister. And all the

Madheshis they marched on the road for their rights. They protested against the government [...] about 58 people were killed during that movement and many people about 10.000 people were wounded, 20.000 people were arrested, about. [...] After that the government had to surrender and accept the identity of the Madheshis and then the scenario changed and there was election of constituent assembly. In that election luckily the Madheshi regional party got some of the major seats, major wing.

As we worked on Madheshis as one important group for border areas politics and identity, we used to ask myself, through which kind of linkages besides the region the people would be connected. Who are the people, who call themselves or are called Madheshi. The linkage is neither religion, as the majority of Madheshis are Hindus, but Muslims are also included, nor language, because Hindi is used as *lingua franca*, but there are at least three major dialects in the Terai. Madheshis are not one ethnic group, as "In Terai different caste and ethnic groups are living here, [...] the Tharu, (???), Muslim, (Cha?), they all are Madheshis." (Butcher 1, Muslim Neighbourhood, Biratnagar) Nevertheless, Hindi language and strong relations to India are important linkages, especially against the hill population, which is connected through the national language Nepali. The main important aspect of the construction of being Madheshi seems to be difference. Madheshi identity is constructed against the Paharis. In the above quoted statement, there are some aspects which seem to be very important for Madheshi's identity construction and exemplify the boundary making between Madheshis and Paharis. Madheshis in Terai form about 50% of Nepal's population, the other 50% are the Paharis of the hills. Paharis are dominant in participation in government and administration, Madheshis are excluded. The Madheshi movement was created against the Pahari dominated government. The basic issue of being Madheshi is being different from the Paharis in region and race, which is connected with social exclusion, being dominated and deprived. Many people told me, that Madheshis are deprived, that they cannot participate in government, administration and army, that they have disadvantages, because Nepal's official language Nepali is only their third tongue. So Madheshis are feeling discriminated:

And there is discrimination policy. [...] All the people from the hill area have come here, and they are doing all the facilities giving by the government. And all the officers are belonging to that community. There are no fair dealing with Madheshi people. This is why we are going backward. In respect of money, income, and in other respect also, in education, in social standing, in (local?) standard, in every respect we are going backward. We have got not participatory in the government from the very beginning. Being Madheshi includes the self-description of regional belonging, because of their history in Terai, the sharing of Hindi language, the discrimination from the hill population and a foreign description of being Indian-based and non-Nepali. So Madheshi identity is made up of self and external descriptions of racial differences and historical origin and of a history of exploitation and discrimination. From an external perspective, Madheshis are often described as migrants from India:

They come from India. Normally, there is no Madheshi Nepal. There is only Terai. They call themselves Terai people. [...] There is no Madhesh. They call this plain of Nepal, plain area, this is Terai, not Madhesh. And those people who call themselves Madheshis, they are from India.

They get married always in Indian side. They have big relation, family relation in Indian side, lot of their family members live in India. That proofs, they are Indian. [...] But Madheshi, they have maximum relation in that side. Their relation in Nepal, their relation in India, Indian side they have a big relation rather than in Nepalese side.

From a Madheshi perspective, history is narrated in an antagonistic way. In several interviews people claimed being of Nepalese origin, that Madheshis lived in the Terai since time immemorial and Madheshi-India relations have their beginnings in times before Nepal's unification:

Another thing is, before the unification of this country this state, this zone and Indian side some state zone, they were one country. Later on, unification divided this place. So you cannot blame that Madheshi people marry there and have relationship. This is not a relationship established a few years ago. This has been generations, this has been before the unification of Nepal.

I feel proud to say, I am Nepalese. But we have noticed is that the people who are living in hills area and they are called the Pahari, they just scold us. They abuse us, like saying they have migrated from India, they are not Nepalese. They are Indians. [...] if we have right to equality, why we are separated, why we are discriminated? Same rights are exercising by the Pahari people, why not Madheshi people? Yeah, we are the son of Nepal, I am Nepali, I have got citizenship, I have got birth certificate. So from this I'm Nepali. Why the Pahari people are not [...] accepting, that they are also Nepali. They are scolding us, they are abusing, using the wrong word, Madheshi migrated from India, you are Indian. So we will continue our protesting program until we get our right.

Both statements articulate an ambiguous relation to the Nepalese state. On the one hand there is the internal separation and exclusion of Madheshis, on the other hand the emphasizing of being of Nepalese origin and the demand of participation. Differences are accentuated as an argument for taking part. In the case of the Madheshis, the combination of difference and exclusion led to the formation of a political movement, which was quite successful, as the Madheshi Forum became the fourth biggest party in the Constituent Assembly and part of the government. The demand of an autonomous Madhesh within Nepal is still discussed in the parliament, as in the process of democratization a new type of federalism is planned to be implemented. But as the Terain population is quite heterogeneous, there are separation tendencies inside the Madheshis, especially after the success of the movement. In interviews with Muslims and Tharus I could observe some divergent demands and unwillingness to call oneself a Madheshi. Regarding latest news from Nepal, these demands got their way into the public discourse.

Being Muslim – Demanding Religious Rights

Being a Muslim in Nepal means being the marginalized of the marginalized, especially in Biratnagar. The census of 2001 estimates 4.2% Muslims in Nepal, new estimations differ from 3.5% to 7%. Most Muslims live in the Terai and many Muslims I talked to in the Muslim neighbourhood in Biratnagar were involved in or supported the Madheshi movement, as they shared the feelings of being deprived and discriminated by the hill population. But even within the Madheshis, Muslims felt excluded because of religion:

And Muslim was more one of the group of Madheshi, within Madheshi group. Because Madheshi means that is geographical defined. The people living in Terai, having their own culture, tradition and language. [...]. And during that Muslim community also comes [...]. Muslim is one of the most disadvantageous, most excluded group in Nepal. These people are excluded in two ways, one way they are excluded from the state mechanism. Another way they are excluded in the society, Madheshi society. [...] This was a Hindu kingdom before the republic been here. So obviously Hindus have more rights.

As Nepal was ruled by Hindu kings from the hills since the unification, Muslims claim to be deprived from their rights of participation in Nepal, as being part of the discriminated Madheshi group and within this group being excluded because of religion. When the Madheshi movement seemed to have some success, the Madheshi Forum became fourth biggest party in the Constituent Assembly, the time was right for special Muslim demands:

This is not a part of Madhesh movement, most of the demands were fulfil by the present government during the Madhesh movement. What were the demands by the Muslim community. The demands are fulfil. But some are left. So right now they have to unite together and just for that left demands Muslims have to confront and fight with the government.

The achievements of Madheshis bear benefits for the whole region, but as Muslims claim to have further religious needs, it seems quite opportunistic to shift from regional to religious identity. This politic of difference is quite similar to the politics of Madheshi movement. As the Madheshis emphasize the difference between them and the Paharis, connected with exclusion and deprivation, Muslims can focus on the difference between themselves and Hindus and create a new distinction within the Madheshis.

In many interviews with Muslims in Biratnagar, people at first pointed on the exclusion because of being Madheshi and later on explained, that Muslims have some extra-needs because of their religion. These needs are special religious holidays, political participation, special development projects and governmental acceptance of religious education:

So we are Muslims, we have also our own language, own lifestyle. So we are also asking the Muslim religious right with government. So what is our demand [...], in Hindu's festivals, they have got their long holidays, but we are also asking our holidays in our festivals, like eat, [Bakhrit?], [Bakharam?] and [Sabebarat?]. So we are asking the holidays, that you gives us.

In whole situation in the nation. means that, their social life, their financial life, their educational life, their participate in all activities in government of Nepal. They are very low percentage. So that Muslim want more. And NEED more. Some reservation need for Muslim in Nepal. Because he's so backward in Nepal. And they are very poor and uneducational.

[...] we Muslim community send our children to Madarsa, religious school, where the Muslim children, , religious teachers are working there. They are getting the salary through the collection with the people. Not through the government. But this is also one problem.

Kind of problem is that, these Madarsas were not recognized by the government. The children, those who receive the education from these Madarsas, they were not handed over the certificate and they were, lack of opportunities later. They were deprived of the opportunities, because of their identity.

These interview excerpts show the making of a Muslim identity with special Muslim needs. The history of exclusion and deprivation is similar to Madheshi's history, but the basis of difference is different. The boundary between Madheshi and Pahari is made of region and race, whereas here the distinction is drawn basically on religion. The research in the Muslim neighbourhood in Biratnagar has shown the fluent character of building up one's identity. People can shift the focus, on which dimension of identity they relate, if it is important to call oneself Madheshi, Muslim or Nepalese. Different dimensions of identity can overlap, like the national, regional and religious in the case of Muslims:

First my nationality is Nepal, because I born here, Nepal country, second Madhesh is a part of Nepal, so I am Madheshi, and third I born in Muslim, so I'm Muslim. So I would like to connect this all things. [...]

Is there one of this three things which is the most important thing for you?

First thing is that, first I am Muslim and second is that I born in Nepal. So I would like to give importance to Muslims. Because I am Muslim. Second to my country, Nepal and third Madhesh.

The population of the Muslim Neighbourhood in Biratnagar, in which I did one week of intense research, is marginalized and deprived. The quarter is situated directly at the border side, many people depend on illegal border trade, infrastructure is bad, with rough streets and bad sewage system. But it is a question of whether the situation is worse than for other groups in Terai or in whole Nepal. Making boundaries for creating themselves as a marginalized group might be a strategy to legitimize the demand for special rights. But before concluding we will present another type of identity construction by separating in the name being indigenous.

Being Tharu – Being Indigenous and of Nepalese Origin

When we was talking to different people about the meaning of being Madheshi and the Madheshi movement, we got to know that there would be one group in the Terai which separated from the movement, the Tharus.

Unfortunately this was in my last days of research, so I could only only do one short trip to some Tharu villages near Biratnagar. So I could only fetch a few impressions by this visit, but even though these are worth mentioning, because they can bring in a new perspective and dimension into this illustration of border cultures.

Tharus are regarded as indigenous people of Nepal: "But main citizen of Nepal was, is Tharu. They have not migrated from other any country. So what we have seen, they are spread all over the nation" (Butcher 1, Muslim Neighbourhood in Biratnagar).

This description of being indigenous and of Nepalese origin is the main important aspect in the construction of Tharu identity against Madheshi, from an external as well as from an internal perspective. Tharus I interviewed emphasized the history of being the original Terain population, while others, especially the Madheshis, *only* immigrated:

That is different thing between Madheshi and Tharu. They get married always in Indian side. They have big relation, family relation in Indian side, lot of their family members live in India. That proofs, they are Indian. But we are local people of Nepal, very old community of Nepal and we don't have any relation in Indian side. But Madheshi, they have maximum relation in that side. Their relation in Nepal, their relation in India, Indian side they have a big relation rather than in Nepalese side.

Those people who call Madheshi themselves, they are not Nepalese. They are from India, they are Indian people. We are Terain people. Nepalese tribals. Nowadays some people are live in Terai from India, they call themselve Madheshi. they have already in India, but our community only in Morang and Sunsari, only two districts. They get lot of support from India side. There is nobody to support us. They are [dominate/colonize?] us. They call us also Madheshi, but we are not Madheshi. We are Terain people, we are Tharu.

Besides this, the Tharus I talked to related to the "difference occasions, different culture, different dresses, different language, they have their own language, woman dress." (Tharu Farmer, Tharu Village near Biratnagar).

Similar to Madheshis and Muslims, the stressing on difference is combined with a history of economic and social exclusion and the need for change and development:

Tharu community is a little bit backward. [...] Tharu are not modernized, they are a little bit back, rather than other communities. Even in economic sector, even in social, even in education, in these sectors, Tharu is a little bit

backward, rather than other communities of Nepal.

-What should be improved, what do you think?

Main thing is education. [...] For to develop the education level of our community, we need money. We make, little bit change our economic condition for education. (Tharu NC Member, Tharu Village near Biratnagar)

Another similarity between Tharus and Muslims is the tendency to separate from the Madheshi movement, in which they were involved in the beginning:

Sometimes after, we are involved in Madheshi Forum, this is another matter, but nowadays, we are completely separate [...] This time, when we involve, because some of other people call us forum. We are, that time we are also angry with them. And [that was a little bit differences?], we involved in Madheshi forum. But after that, we feel that Madheshi normally came from India, they are Indian based people. But we are not Indian based people, we are Nepal origin. [...] We don't have to involve in that Indian political party, Madheshi Forum. So they feel, we are Nepalese, they are not Nepalese. This is the main cause we separated.

In this statement, the basis for separation of Tharus from the Madheshis is articulated. The separation of Tharu identity against Madheshi is not only about ethnic identity, nationality, being Nepalese becomes important as well. As the national border is more or less deconstructed and transcended by Madheshi identity, here it is of great importance for defining and separating who is of Nepalese origin and who is not. This accentuation of nationality is related with the economic condition of Tharus. The villages I visited were mainly inhabited by rice farmers. "Nowadays rice is quite cheap in India. Due to open border, this reason and the Indian side rice price is quite less. So it's a big threat for them, because they are not getting a good price for their rice." (Tharu Farmer, Tharu Village near Biratnagar). Neither socially nor economically do Tharus benefit from Nepal-India relations and the open border, so emphasizing Nepalese nationality might be advantageous for them.

The structures of all three types of identity construction are quite similar. The first thing is to draw a distinction to constitute one group separated from the others. Then all the people I talked to claimed, that their group is backward and excluded, which is followed by a demand for special rights, like quotas or special development programs. By focussing on difference, they create inner inclusion, which strengthens demands for special rights:

Tharus is also struggling and in democracy, it's a natural thing, we also have to fight for our right to save our culture, to save our community, to build up our community, for development of community. Tharus also have right to make their voice loud, to raise their problems. It's the process of democracy. It's not big things, it's natural things. (Tharu NC Member, Tharu Village near Biratnagar)

Nepal's development into a democratic republic gives the potential for identity politics. Basics for establishing an identity group for enforcing particular rights seems to be at first any sort of difference, like region and race in case of the Madheshis, religion for the Muslims or belonging for Tharus. Besides this a history of deprivation and exclusion is necessary for strengthen inclusion and legitimizing the demands. Separation policy seems to be useful for achieving participation in Nepal. "If you shout, they will give, if you not shout, they will not give" (Tharu Activist, Town near Biratnagar).

An important issue for the groups is the creation of a national or regional history. Even though an exact history of the Terai is not accessible for ancient times,1 both Tharus and Madheshis, and within Madheshis the Muslims, claim to inhabit this region since time immemorial, even before the unification of Nepal. This legitimises the demand for participation within the Nepalese state. On the other hand blaming Madheshis of being Indian and non-Nepalese is used to exclude them and strengthen the own position.

Madheshi's relation to Nepal is quite special, because on the one hand they emphasize being Nepalese because of their history of inhabitance in the Terai, on the other they deconstruct being Nepalese within Nepal's borders, because they relate to times, when there was no border and people had their social relations without being separated by the nation states of Nepal and India.

CHANGING PARADIGMS IN INDIA-NEPAL RELATIONS

Today Nepal stands at the crossroads amidst the swiftly changing political tracts and it becomes a scarce to found a closer understanding over the core issues among all the political parties. Such political opportunism truly missing the plight of democracy besides pulling down the national priorities in crucial matters; indeed it's an outcome of internal political strife instead from an imposed international pressure. Stability is very crucial for India in the case of Nepal where India hasn't any option except to see a sovereign Nepal; concerned authority in India's External Affairs Ministry has been consistently showing similar concern and landed all possible support to assist in Nepal's integration. Through an honest introspection it's easily revealed that India never resolute any action in past against the national interest of Nepal, further India never obstruct the formation of any democratic government even including the Maoist government and send their foreign secretary just three days before the government formation.

India-Nepal relations are so strong that it's very hard to shape in mere words because these two neighbouring nation has a history of deep ties and shared concern from ancient times. Quality of relationship between these two countries shouldn't be seen in terms of treaty; having faith in each other's role any dispute can be solved and consensus could be formed between these two friendly nations. Indeed there are no reasons among the peoples of the both side of border to involved in any sort of hate campaign against each other; any development in this regard would be ended with an impractical and unviable consequences. So, it must realized that that interest of India wouldn't affect the any move of peace process in Nepal; it's need of hour to end the causes of political insecurity among the diasporas on the both side of borders.

State of Nepal's internal security possessed as much concern as her own existential safety for India, so any anti Indian move will jeopardize the friendly terms and left alarming ramifications for both the country. India's concern over the presence of ISI's agents inside the territory of Nepal must be seen in genuine light by the Nepalese government since it could be highly disturbing in long term for Nepal's own sake as well. Indian government is very serious towards tackling the terrorist network with wrenched resoluteness and would keep affirming on Nepalese government to check their activities from their sovereign territory.

With more meticulous action some unfortunate developments may be easily avoided; that would required a consensus based approach in top notch Nepalese political circle and within their civil society towards the India's plight for security. India never felt any sort of discontents with the democratic proceedings in Nepal; of course Maoist should stay and play active role within their national political framework. Indian government would remains very keen for strengthening of democracy in Nepal and issues like human rights would be a key priority for them with putting finest efforts to see it in universal way beyond the geographical boundaries. In recent past Gorkha's role in Indian Arm Forces has gained some critical applauds from a reactionary section in Nepal which is quite unfortunate and is an effort to dampen the historic and marvelous symbolic ties between these two friendly nation.

The word consensus has been largely misused in Nepal consequently ultra nationalism in Nepal largely seen in the context of anti-Indian sentiment; a very lucid approach would be needed from Nepalese side over such relentless unfortunate developments. In international affairs domain Nepal needs to play more matured role and must develop a sense of its own best interest; mutual integrated relationship with India paves way for safe passages of trust between them which is quite symmetric to the actual requirements and should remain a foremost concern for both the countries to keep intact these flame of spirits; any constructive solution of joint interest would be emerged from mutual effort instead through isolatory stances.

In changing circumstances it's quite essential for both the countries to make immediate revisions in bilateral treaties and shaping them as per the suitability of present time. Infrastructures are major issues that needs to look on in such active manner since perennial floods is a major impediment for socio-economic structure of Terain region in Nepal and entire north Bihar. A radical shift in policy towards the existing infrastructure of water management is the first step that required to be taken by the governments of both countries. Water management possessed very crucial and strategic place in the sphere of India-Nepal relations as their catchments are very productive for the vast agricultural areas as well an alternative source of energy; projects like Pancheswar, Saptakosi, Naumure etc. needs rational handling as they are immensely crucial for the sake of both countries energy requirements. Border management is another issue that needs more regulated treatment though it should remain open as even before because prevalence of open border is the biggest asset of India-Nepal relation and it has potential to be framed as an ideal border of south Asia. Indeed open border plays utmost significance in the lives of population adjacent to border; since time immemorial they have been sharing the ties of Roti (Bread) and Beti (Matrimonial ties) which even creates complexities of identity.

In present state Nepal is coping with the difficulties of constitution making besides having to win the trust of peoples in democratic institution which shown severe fluctuation in immediate past. In this situation grooming of an idea of ethnic federalism and other major issues wouldn't be less than a fatal as handling of such major issues depends upon the state of stability which is completely out of seen in present circumstances. Terain's plight and refugee's problems are some other rudimentary issues that need proper concern and action from the governments of both the side as law and order situation is a matter that requires the co-operation of other side due to geographical nature and open borders. In decade long civil war like situation, the Terai region faced adverse setbacks and witnessed the losses of human lives, infrastructure, ecology, law and order etc. Even in last few months toll of losses in Terai is quite frightening, almost 1200 peoples has been killed and more than 3600 were abducted; situation is still very grim inside the Terai region and peoples have some distraught feeling as they used to feel during the bloody strife phase. Glorifications of Terain Armed groups are caused by the political affiliations and patronage that's making situation worse in any effort to contain and disband their growing role; catchments areas of North Bihar or Mithilanchal region becomes a hideout place for these groups in the absence of a specified and clear set of mechanism on joint level; a strategic move in this regard is immediately required.

Till today Nepal is missing the actual taste of democracy and whatever has been represented on the name of democracy that never touched the ground of actual aspiration of its citizen. Maoists short stint in government couldn't materialized their own professed goals instead they turn up to attack on religious identities, authoritarianism, non-pluralism, against right of property besides showing very immature stand on Nepalese Armed Force chief Rukmangad Kotwal; such bad conflict management with Arm force deciphered the feeble understanding of realpolitik in Maoist camp.

Before that incident Nepali Army has history of passive presence and following the civil supremacy which was very conducive with the expectation of Nepalese intelligentsias. But now stands humiliated, Nepalese Army becomes more powerful and strategic which may played crucial roles in further phage of development. India too witnessed some implications after this incident as the role of India felt prominent by a section of reactionaries in Nepalese politics; former Prime Minister Prachanda's remarks as "Promped by Prabhu" to present Prime Minister Madhav Kumar Nepal was clearly referred towards the India which was completely unjustifiable. India maintains silence over such rambling propositions even the Indian side never downbeat with the growing Chinese influence in Maoists rule and regarded it just as lacking immune system. India has utmost concern with Nepalese state of affairs in similar manner; Nepal too has immense benefits from a stronger India, so despite some ups and down in events it would be compatible to remains in same strong bond of sharing forever' Brotherhood always remains a great idea as in such set of relationship every member has some specific roles to play irrespective of identities like big brother and small brother; being sanguine for same must in case of India-Nepal relations.

MAOISTS RHETORIC ON INDIA-NEPAL RELATIONS

India's External Affairs Minister SM Krishna will undertake a three-day official visit to Kathmandu from January 15, 2010. According to the Indian Embassy in Kathmandu, at least five memorandums of understanding will be signed during Krishna's visit. The possible MoUs include construction of a National Police Academy at Panauti in Kavre district, Indian assistance for the Nepal Stock Exchange, construction of roads in the Terai, establishment of a science learning centre and a solar electrification project. Krishna will also take up issues related to Indian security and counterfeit currency issues.

Though the visit is timely and significant, uncertainties over the future of the peace process continue due to differences between the political parties on contentious issues like federalism, rehabilitation of Maoist combatants, and the nature of Constitution.

The UCPN-Maoist leader Prachanda has accused the ruling parties of being puppets of the Indian ruling class, accused the Indian establishment of intervening in Nepal's internal affairs and trying to derail the peace process.

He also said that the UCPN-Maoist should hold direct talks with New Delhi since the ruling parties are guided by remote control and talks with them to establish civilian supremacy have been failing.

The Maoists have made elaborate arrangements to express displeasure during Krishna's visit. Recently, they declared the fourth phase of their nationwide agitation demanding restoration of civilian supremacy and formation of a Maoist-led national government. As part of the fourth round of protest programmes, senior party leaders will visit those locations along the open border with India where India has reportedly occupied Nepal's territories. The Maoists will organise mass rallies at several bordering regions 'encroached' by India and torch the copies of the various treaties with India. They will hold demonstrations outside the Indian Embassy and Singha Durbar on January 19.

Krishna's visit is taking place at a time when the Maoist sponsored anti-India feeling is at an all time high in Nepal. Maoists have been consistently branding the 1950 treaty as unequal, raising issues such as illegal encroachment and the recruitment of Nepalse Gurkhas into the Indian Army. But none of these demands are genuine and valid. The Maoists, in fact, do not want to resolve these issues since these give them huge political dividends to retain public support. Pushpa Kamal Dahal alias Prachanda, during his nine month tenure as prime minister, did not take any steps to withdraw from the 1950 treaty though clause 10 of the agreement cleanly mentions that the "Treaty shall remain in force until it is terminated by either party by giving one year's notice." The issue figured prominently during his visit to New Delhi in September 2008. On this occasion, Prachanda had agreed with India's Prime Minister to "review, adjust and update" the 1950 Treaty of Peace and Friendship and other agreements, while giving due recognition to the special features of the bilateral relationship. Why did Prachanda not use clause 10 of the treaty and agreed to review the same during his visit?

Regarding the Gurkha recruitment issue, Pracahnda preferred to remain tightlipped during his visit to India. On the eve of the visit, Deepak Bahadur Gurung, chairman of the Nepal Ex-Servicemen's Association, warned that his organisation would start a new 'People's War' if the Maoist government stopped the recruitment. Most importantly, Maoists' argument about Gurkaha recruitment being colonial is illogical because Gurkha Nepalese have been joining the Indian Army purely on a voluntary basis. This is not forced recruitment or conscription by the Indian Army.

Given the geographical dynamics in the border region, "encroachment" is more a natural phenomenon than man-made. Rivers flowing from Nepal to India frequently shift their course during the monsoons. As a result, certain portions of the border region either come to Nepal or to India depending on the shifting of the river course. Since farmers from both countries find that part of the land fertile, they encroach upon it for agricultural purposes. In fact, Prachanda during his last visit to India acknowledged the problem of inundation in the border areas and agreed to take up necessary work for its effective prevention on the basis of bilateral consultation. Both countries have already (unofficially) agreed that 98 per cent of the border is demarcated except two disputed areas in Kalapani and Susta. India's former external affairs minister Pranab Mukhrjee during his official visit to Kathmandu in November 2008 talked about it before the media. Interestingly, then the Maoist-led government in Kathmandu did not contradict his view on border demarcation. The issue rose to prominence again only after Prachanda's resignation. The Maoists have accused encroachment of Nepalese territory by Indian security forces in the Dang district.

The problem is not only with the Maoists. India has consistently given space to the Maoists to take advantage of the faultlines in India-Nepal relations. Till date, India has hardly clarified its stand on these controversial bilateral issues in a public forum. All discussions have taken place only at the official level, which have been tampered with and then highlighted by the pro-Maoist or Royalist Nepalese media. One such faultline is the absence of high-level political engagements from the Indian side while Nepal is passing through political turbulence.

In the last 13 years, seven Prime Ministers of Nepal have visited India in return for one Prime Ministerial visit from India to Nepal. Prime Minister I. K. Gujaral visited Kathmandu in June 1997. The political imbalance in the relationship has been gradually eroding India's traditional leverages in Nepal. If the vacuum continues, other countries including China may consolidate in near future. Another major faultline is unnecessary statements from various agencies of India about internal developments in Nepal. Third, India has a very good relationship with many leaders of Nepal cutting across party lines. But it is yet to introduce a comprehensive policy towards Nepal.

INDIA'S OPTIONS IN NEPAL

1. Stability in Nepal is extremely important for India. It has to acknowledge that the present political stalemate is an internal matter of Nepal and encourage the stakeholders to hammer out their differences. India should strike a neutral stance and play the role of an honest negotiator to bring the various factions together.

2. Existing controversial treaties, border disputes, encroachment issues and the Indian Embassy's alleged support to certain groups in the Terai region and personal level support to Nepali Congress leaders are major irritants in India-Nepal relations. These issues have been generating huge anti-India feelings and thus need immediate attention. This will help prevent the growing Chinese role in Nepal. India needs to come out with a clear policy on these issues and express positive views to resolve them.
3. India should focus more on socio-economic and development programmes. India's assistance to Nepal should be enhanced and directed towards projects which benefit the Nepalese people directly.
4. Hydro-projects and dams situated on the Indo-Nepal border should be maintained and managed by the Union Government under the Ministry of External affairs.
5. Border crossing should be mechanized. People crossing the border should be treated with dignity.
6. India should realize that the monarchy is gone for ever although the pro-monarchy sentiment remains. India needs to acknowledge the emergence of new forces in Nepal and learn to deal with them.
7. India should enhance and upgrade co-operation with Nepalese agencies to patrol and manage the border.

Anti-India feeling is a permanent phenomenon in India's neighbourhood including in Nepal. India should not deterred by these activities. This visit is a golden opportunity for India to reactivate its relationship and reassure both the ruling and opposition parties about India's positive contribution to the peace process. During the visit, India should come out with some official statements that India is interested more in people to people relations and the prosperity of Nepal. If possible, India should seriously engage and talk to the Maoists. They may have their own ideology which may not be comfortable to India. But there is no harm in talking to them and learn about their concerns. Similarly, India should make its concerns in Nepal clear to the Maoists. It should clarify through actions and declare that India has no intention to interfere in Nepal, that it respects Nepal's sovereignty and that it is ready to work with any dispensation in Nepal for furthering mutual security and economic concerns.

INVESTMENT POLICIES IN NEPAL AND INDIA

The Constitution of the Kingdom of Nepal 1990 refers to that " The State shall, for the purposes of national development, pursue a policy of taking measures necessary for the attraction of foreign capital and technology, while at the same time promoting indigenous investment Constitution of the Kingdom of Nepal, 1990: 19)". The Tenth Plan, 2002-07 has the objective to develop Nepal as an attractive and reliable investment center at international perspective. The Plan states that procedures to attract foreign investment will be made simple, comprehensive and transparent through administrative and legal reforms. Also the Plan will review Foreign Investment and Transfer of Technology Act 1992; Industrial Enterprises Act 1992; existing labour policy and Labour Act 1992 and make investment-friendly.

The Tenth Plan has the policy to provide facilities and infrastructure services to investors from one window; procedures will be simplified to repatriate investment made by the investors; in no case facilities and incentives provided to attract FDI in Nepal will be less than what is available in the neighbouring countries; Labour Act will be made more flexible; on the basis of feasibility studies and identification of areas of comparative advantages information will be provided to investors to promote investment in Nepal; and the Royal Nepalese Embassies abroad will be urged to promote foreign investment in Nepal through mobilizing investors in respective countries (Tenth Plan, 2002: 79-80). Since 1990 Nepal has adhered to the policy of liberalization in trade and investment regime.

Statutory Provisions

The Foreign Investment and Technology Transfer Act (FITTA) 1992 govern the entry of FDI in Nepal. FDI is permitted in all industries in Nepal except for those reserved exclusively for national investors and statutory state monopolies. Foreign individuals are not permitted to own land but resident companies may do so even if foreign owned.

Foreign ownership of commercial banks is limited to 66 percent. Foreign investment is allowed in the areas except specified in the "negative list". These include: (a) sensitive industries related to national security; cottage industries; personal services of a kind that would normally be performed by self employed people; and real estate business. In these areas amendments would be possible only through parliament, and (b) retail business; travel agency; cigarette, tobacco and alcohol production other than for export; a range of small tourist related activities, including tourist lodging but not hotels; some small scale farming; and consultancy services. In these areas government has the authority for amendments, if it is necessary.

Inclusion of consultancy services in the negative list is strange, which explicitly includes management, accounting, engineering and legal services.

International accounting and law firms, and other professionals are not allowed to practice for an establishment in Nepal. In case of business in Nepal wishes to engage such services from an offshore provider, which falls within the jurisdiction of "transfer of technology", requires government approval. These features add up to a protectionist regime wherein it would be difficult for foreign investors to access "brand" international services or head office services (UNCTAD, 2003). The other items included in the negative list are not so unusual. However, FDI in Nepal is restrained to 32 public enterprises due to existing negative list.

Privatization is one of the cornerstones of liberal economic policy followed by Nepal after 1990. As per Privatization Act 1994 the Government has either privatized or liquidated a total of 23 public enterprises by the end of FY 2002/03 (Economic Survey, FY 2002/03). Of the total public enterprises, four are of statutory monopolies. These are: (a) Nepal Oil Corporation (monopoly on the import of refined petroleum fuels), (b) Nepal Drinking Water Corporation, (c) Nepal Telecommunication Corporation, and (d) Nepal Electricity Authority. The Government has recently announced to privatize, dissolve or liquidate 9 public enterprises during FY 2003/04. The Budget for current FY refers to that "the companies wholly owned by Nepalese entrepreneurs or with 50 percent foreign equity participation and registered in Nepal will be allowed to import and deal in petroleum products" (Budget Speech, 2003). This is the manifestation of flexibility over the existing provisions that would help attract FDI to Nepal.

"Within the ambit of these corporations some private investment, including FDI potentially, is possible. Private investors may operate value-added network services in telecommunications and the industry regulator is separate from the Nepal Telecommunications Corporation. Private investment is encouraged in electricity generation, whilst the Nepal Electricity Authority retains a monopoly of domestic transmission and distribution. Also water reticulation and sanitation are municipal services but it may be possible to contract out these services to private operators" (UNCTAD, 2003).

6

India's Relation with Pakistan

Pakistan has emerged as a "rogue nuclear state" however much the United States may like to paint it white. It has proliferated uranium enrichment technology to North Korea and Iran too (estimative analysis) and thereby jeopardizing vital United States strategic interests in East Asia and the Middle East. This is taking place with the assistance of and bidding of China. India should not therefore depend on or expect United States and China to restrain Pakistan's disruptive policies in South Asia. In relation to bringing Pakistan to heel in South Asia, India's foreign policies concerning Pakistan must incorporate the following ingredients:

- Pakistan's proxy war against India needs to be carried back into Pakistan. Self-determination movements in Sindh, Baluchistan, Pashtunistan and Northern Areas need to be exploited. India's oft-quoted 'pro-active policies' must be put into effect here.
- Pakistan based terrorist organizations must be struck the way the Israel strikes back at its opponents.
- India's foreign policies and military policies lack the essential ingredient of "Psychological Warfare" and allied operations.
- Pakistan Army's stranglehold over the Pakistani nation-state and thwarting the emergence of democracy and pluralism in Pakistan needs to be vigorously exposed as part of the above operation.
- India must impose an arms-race on Pakistan the pace of which Pakistan can ill-afford economically and nor can its external patrons subsidise.
- In relation to Pakistan, India must make it clear to the other South Asian countries, that they have to choose between India and Pakistan in South Asia. "Either you are with us, or against us" and if their choice is "against us" they should be prepared to face the consequences of their choice.

Some may like to argue that the above are not realistic steps and that India does not have the capabilities to do so. This author would like to maintain, that it is within India's means to do so seeing India's preponderant power attributes. All that India needs is to give a 'shaped-charge' focus to these factors and re-order its priorities in its foreign policies.

As a starter, let India change its stand in relations to the conditions it stipulates for resumption of dialogue with Pakistan. India's strong-man, Deputy PM Advani's constant refrain is that unless Pakistan returns the persons in the "list of 20" no dialogue can take place.

This is not an advisable stand as it reduces India to the level of trading far more important considerations in its approaches towards Pakistan than the extradition of 20 street-side hoodlums.

India's conditions for resumption of dialogue with Pakistan need to rest on far more important considerations, namely that:

- India will enter into dialogue with Pakistan only when a democratically elected government comes into power, through elections supervised by international observers.
- India will not enter into dialogue with Pakistan based on Pakistani imposed pre-conditions of Kashmir and the rest.
- India should maintain that Kashmir is not an issue historically nor is it now. Kashmir's accession to India is non-negotiable as per the unanimous resolution of the Special Session of the Indian Parliament.
- India will enter into a dialogue with Pakistan only when it begins to respect the sanctity of the Line of Actual Control (LAC) in Jammu and Kashmir-a point endorsed by the United States through President Clinton's statement.

Social Relations

Cultural Links

India and Pakistan, to some degree have similar cultures, cuisines and languages which underpin the historical ties between the two. Pakistani singers, musicians, comedians and entertainers have enjoyed widespread popularity in India, with many achieving overnight fame in the Indian filming industry Bollywood.

Likewise, Indian music and films are very popular in Pakistan. Being located in the northernmost region of the South Asia, Pakistan's culture is somewhat similar to that of North India. The Punjab region was split into Punjab, Pakistan and Punjab, India following the independence and partition of the two countries in 1947. The Punjabi people are today the largest ethnic group in Pakistan and also an important ethnic group of northern India. The founder of the Sikhism religion was born in the modern-day Pakistani Punjab province, in the city of Nankana Sahib. Each year, millions of Indian Sikh pilgrims cross over to visit holy Sikh sites in Nankana Sahib.

The Sindhi people are the native ethnic group of the Pakistani province of Sindh. Many Hindu Sindhis migrated to India in 1947, making the country home to a sizable Sindhi community. In addition, the millions of Muslims who migrated from India to the newly-created Pakistan during independence came to be known as the Muhajir people; they are settled predominantly in Karachi and still maintain family links in India.

Relations between Pakistan and India have also resumed through platforms such as media and communications. Aman ki Asha is a joint venture and campaign between *The Times of India* and the *Jang Group* calling for mutual peace and development of diplomatic and cultural relations.

Geographic Links

The Indo-Pakistani border is the official international boundary that demarcates the Indian states of Punjab,Rajasthan and Gujarat from the Pakistani provinces of Punjab and Sindh. The Wagah border is the only road crossing between India and Pakistan and lies on the famous Grand Trunk Road, connecting Lahore, Pakistan withAmritsar, India. Each evening, the Wagah border ceremony takes place at the Wagah border in which the flags are lowered and guards on both sides make a pompous military display and exchange handshakes.

Linguistic Ties

Hindustani is the linga franca of North India and Pakistan, as well as the national language of both countries, under the name Hindi and Urdu, respectively. Standard Urdu is mutually intelligible with Standard Hindi. Both languages share the same Indic base and are all but indistinguishable in phonology and grammar. Most linguists consider them to be two standardized forms of a same language; when speaking colloquially, a speaker of Urdu has no trouble understanding a speaker of Hindi.

Apart from Hindustani, India and Pakistan also share a distribution of the Punjabi language (written in the Gurmukhiscript in Indian Punjab, and the Shahmukhi script in Pakistani Punjab), Kashmiri language and Sindhi language.

Matrimonial Ties

Some Indian and Pakistani people marry across the border, particularly with present generation of relatives who had migrated from India at the time of partition.

In April 2010 a high profile Pakistani cricketer, Shoaib Malik married the Indian tennis star Sania Mirza. The wedding received much media attention and was said to transfix both India and Pakistan.

Sporting Ties

Cricket and hockey matches between the two (as well as other sports to a lesser degree such as those of the SAARC games) have often been political in nature. During theSoviet invasion of Afghanistan General Zia-ul Haq traveled to India for a bout of "cricket diplomacy" to keep India from supporting the Soviets by opening another front. Pervez Musharaff also tried to do the same more than a decade later but to no avail.

In tennis, Rohan Bopanna of India and Aisam-ul-Haq Qureshi of Pakistan have formed a successful duo and have been dubbed as the "Indo-Pak Express."

Diasporic Relations

The large size of the Indian diaspora and Pakistani diaspora in many different countries throughout the world has created strong diasporic relations. British Indians and British Pakistanis, the largest and second-largest ethnic minorities living in the United Kingdom respectively, are said to have friendly relations with one another. It is quite common for a "Little India" and a "Little Pakistan" to co-exist in South Asian ethnic enclaves in overseas countries.

There are various cities such as Birmingham, Blackburn andManchester where British Indians and British Pakistanis live alongside each other in peace and harmony. Both Indians and Pakistanis living in the UK fit under the category ofBritish Asian. The UK is also home to the Pakistan & India friendship forum. In the United States, Indians and Pakistanis are classified under the South Asian Americancategory and share many cultural traits. The British MEP Saj Karim is of Pakistani origin. He is a member of the European Parliament Friends of India Group, Karim was also responsible for opening up Europe to free trade with India. He narrowly escaped the Mumbai attacks at Hotel Taj in November 2008. Despite the atrocity, Mr Karim does not wish the remaining killer Ajmal Kasab to be sentenced to death. He said: "I believe he had a fair and transparent trial and I support the guilty verdict. "But I am not a supporter of capital punishment. I believe he should be given a life sentence, but that life should mean life."

Trade Links

Trade across direct routes has been curtailed formally, so the bulk of India-Pakistan trade is routed through Dubai. Re-evaluation

The insurgents who initially started their movement as a pro-Kashmiri independence movement, have gone through a lot of change in their ideology. Most of the insurgents portray their struggle as a religious one. Indian analysts allege that by supporting these insurgents, Pakistan is trying to wage a proxy war against India while Pakistan claims that it regards most of these insurgentgroups as "freedom fighters" rather than terrorists

Internationally known to be the most deadly theatre of conflict, nearly 10 million people, including Muslims, Hindus, and Buddhists, have been fighting a daily battle for survival. The *cross-border firing* between India and Pakistan, and the terrorist attacks combined have taken its toll on the Kashmiris, who have suffered poor living standards and an erosion of human rights.

HISTORY OF INDO-PAKISTANI WAR OF 1947

After rumours that the Maharaja supported the annexation of Kashmir by India, militant Muslim revolutionaries from western Kashmir and Pakistani tribesmen made rapid advances into the Baramulla sector. Maharaja Hari Singh of Kashmir asked the government of India to intervene. However, India and Pakistan had signed an agreement of non-intervention. Although tribal fighters from Pakistan had entered Jammu and Kashmir, there was no iron-clad legal evidence to unequivocally prove that Pakistan was officially involved. It would have been illegal for India to unilaterally intervene in an open, official capacity unless Jammu and Kashmir officially joined the Union of India, at which point it would be possible to send in its forces and occupy the remaining parts.

The Maharaja desperately needed military assistance when the Pakistani tribals reached the outskirts of Srinagar. Before their arrival into Srinagar, India argued that the Maharaja must complete negotiations for ceding Jammu and Kashmir to India in exchange for receiving military aid. The agreement which ceded Jammu and Kashmir to India was signed by the Maharaja and Lord Mountbatten of Burma. In Jammu and Kashmir, National Conference volunteers worked with the Indian Army to drive out the Pakistanis.

The resulting war over Kashmir, the First Kashmir War, lasted until 1948, when India moved the issue to the UN Security Council. Sheikh Abdullah was not in favour of India seeking UN intervention because he was sure the Indian Army could free the entire State of invaders. The UN had previously passed resolutions for setting up monitoring of the conflict in Kashmir. Following the set-up of the United Nations Military Observer Group in India and Pakistan (UNCIP), the UN Security Council passed Resolution 47 on 21 April 1948.

The resolution imposed an immediate cease-fire and called on the Government of Pakistan 'to secure the withdrawal from the state of Jammu and Kashmir of tribesmen and Pakistani nationals not normally resident therein who have entered the state for the purpose of fighting.' It also asked Government of India to reduce its forces to the minimum strength, after which the circumstances for holding a plebiscite should be put into effect 'on the question of Accession of the state to India or Pakistan.' However, both India and Pakistan failed to arrive at a Truce agreement due to differences in interpretation of the procedure for and extent of demilitarisation one of them being whether the Azad Kashmiri army is to be disbanded during the truce stage or the Plebiscite stage.

In November 1948, The Indian and Pakistani governments agreed to hold the plebiscite, but Pakistan did not withdraw its troops from Kashmir, thus violating the conditions for holding the plebiscite. In addition, the Indian Government distanced itself from its commitment to hold a plebiscite. India proposed that Pakistan withdraw all its troops first, calling it a precondition for a plebiscite. Pakistan rejected on the grounds that the Kashmiris may not vote freely given the presence of Indian army and Sheikh Abdullah's friendship with the Indian Prime Minister, Jawaharlal Nehru. However, Pakistan proposed simultaneous withdrawal of all troops followed by a plebiscite under international auspices, which India rejected. Hence Pakistan didn't withdraw its forces unilaterally In addition, the Indian Government distanced itself from its commitment to hold a plebiscite. Over the next several years, the UN Security Council passed four new resolutions, revising the terms of Resolution 47 to include a synchronous withdrawal of both Indian and Pakistani troops from the region, per the recommendations of General Andrew McNaughton. To this end, UN arbitrators put forward 11 different proposals for the demilitarization of the region.

Sino-Indian War

In 1962, troops from the People's Republic of China and India clashed in territory claimed by both. China won a swift victory in the war, resulting in the Chinese annexation of the region called Aksai Chin, which has continued since then. Another smaller area, the Trans-Karakoram, was demarcated as the Line of Control (LOC) between China and Pakistan, although some of the territory on the Chinese side is claimed by India to be part of Kashmir. The line that separates India from China in this region is known as the "Line of Actual Control".

1965 and 1971 Wars

In 1965 and 1971, heavy fighting broke out again between India and Pakistan. The Indo-Pakistani War of 1971 resulted in the defeat of Pakistan and the Pakistani military's surrender in East Pakistan, leading to the creation of Bangladesh. The Simla Agreement was signed in 1972 between India and Pakistan. By this treaty, both countries agreed to settle all issues by peaceful means using mutual discussion in the framework of the UN Charter.

THE INTRUSIONS IN KASHMIR - OPERATION GIBRALTAR - AUGUST 1965

It is clear from Pakistani published sources that in mid May,six weeks before signing the formal cease fire in London, President Ayub Khan was given a military presentation on Operation Gibraltar. During the presentation, at his behest, the assault on Akhnoor was included in Operation Grand Slam. He accorded approval for Operation Gibraltar to be launched. In end July, he addressed the Force Commanders of Operation Gibraltar. The first infiltration across the Cease Fire Line (CFL) started on 1 August over a 700 kilometer front from Kargil to Chhamb. The Indians as well as the local Kashmiris were taken by surprise.

Operation Gibraltar commenced on 5 August. Sixty companies of Pakistani armed personnel in disguise, armed with modern weapons and explosives, infiltrated across the cease fire line to blow up strategic bridges, raid supply dumps, kill VIP's and cause arson. On 5 August itself, some infiltrators were apprehended.

In his foreword to Air Marshal Asghar Khan's book 'The First Round', Mr Altaf Gauhar, then Pakistan's Secretary of Information and Broadcasting states: (Page xii)

"The truth is that the first four volunteers who were captured by the Indians described the whole plan in a broadcast on All India Radio on 8 August 1965, nearly a month before India crossed the international boundary".

On hearing these broadcasts, Pakistan realised that their secret plan was now open knowledge.

Mr C P Srivastava's memoirs state:

"It was only on 8 August 1965 that more detailed information about extensive infiltration by armed men from Pakistan was provided to Prime

Minister Shastri. He immediately summoned a meeting of the Emergency Committee of the Cabinet. The Chief of Army Staff attended this meeting. He assured the Prime Minister that the Army and the police were in control of the situation, the raiders were being rounded up but further sabotage could still occur by the raiders not yet captured. The Prime Minister asked the Chief of Army Staff to take whatever action he considered necessary to prevent new infiltrations."

"On 9 August, as per its pre-arranged plan, Pakistan announced a rebellion in Kashmir and the heroic exploits of the freedom fighters who were helping them. It also reported receiving a broadcast, by a secret radio station calling itself as the 'Voice of Kashmir', of the setting up of a Revolutionary Council to take over all authority in Kashmir. Within days however, it became clear to the world that this was a propaganda hoax. Soon even Pakistani newspapers ceased further propaganda. By 11 August, the Pakistan Army realised that Operation Gibraltar had flopped. From 15 August onwards, the Pakistan Army stepped up its violation of the cease fire line on the Srinagar - Leh road".

Mr PVR Rao, the Defence Secretary in 1965, stated in his 1972 USI Lecture:

"The firm decision that the Army should cross the Cease Fire Line to root out the infiltrator's bases and, in case Pakistan regular forces intervened, our forces should be free to retaliate at any suitable place of their choice was taken on the night of the 13th August by the Prime Minister, when the Defence Minister and certain officials, including the Chief of the Army Staff were present. These decisions were taken on the request of the Chief of the Army Staff that to check infiltration, the infiltrators' bases should be destroyed and in any fight between regular forces, the Services should not be restricted. Shri Lal Bahadur Shastri was anxious to avoid any extension of the conflict but was determined that measures to liquidate infiltrators should be pursued vigorously. The Prime Minister gave expression publicly to the decision taken at his speech from the Red Fort on the 15th August, when he declared that ``resort to the sword will be met with the sword'. And even as the speech was being made, our troops occupied certain posts across the Cease Fire Line near Kargil and, in the following days, occupied various places across the Cease Fire Line, including Haji Pir and destroyed the infiltrators' hideouts. After giving the broad directive on the 13th August, the Prime Minister did not concern himself with the details of the operations. He left all operational decisions to be supervised by the Defence Minister, but I used to report to the Prime Minister at his residence every evening the progress of the operations".

In Naval Headquarters in Delhi, the situation had become quite vexed. With all the operational ships of the Indian Fleet away in the East, the resources available in Bombay were meagre. The frigate TALWAR, which had been carrying out essential maintenance was hurriedly boxed up and sent for investigating the presence of possible enemy vessels in the Kori Creek, a few miles southwest of the Indo Pakistan border in the Gulf of Kutch.Her first patrol was for 5 days from 12 to 16 August, then again from 24th to 28 August. No encounter occurred.

From the East, the Flag Officer Commanding the Indian Fleet (FOCIF), Rear Admiral B A Samson, reading of the increasing tension in Kashmir, rang up the Chief of the Naval Staff (CNS), Vice Admiral Soman, on more than one occasion and suggested that the Fleet return to Bombay. He was told that the Fleet should adhere to its programme of visiting the Andamans and Calcutta.

THE SUBSEQUENT KASHMIR WAR (SEPTEMBER 1965)

Pakistan became frustrated with India's increasing attempts to integrate Kashmir into its fold. Embolded by a presumed victory against India in the Rann of Kutch in April 1965, Pakistan made plans for "Operation Gibraltar" to recover Kashmir. As it did in 1947, it first sent Pakistani guerrillas into the Valley in August 1965 hoping that the Kashmiri Muslims would rise in rebellion against India. Instead, the guerrillas were apprehended and handed over to the Indian authorities. The situation worsened rapidly. On September 1, when Indian troops crossed the international border, Pakistan launched an attack on Jammu. In response, India launched a series of attacks through the state of Punjab toward Lahore, Pakistan, and battled the Pakistani army. As the clashes continued, the UN Security Council, supported by the United States, Britain, and the USSR, called for an immediate cease-fire, which India and Pakistan accepted on September 6. Although the war was brief, it was a bitter one. Neither country was a winner. In January of 1966, at the invitation of Soviet Premier Alexsei Kosygin, both Shastri and Khan met in the city of Tashkent (Republic of Uzbesistan) and signed the agreement known as the Tashkent Declaration. On January 10, the agreement was formalized and the hostilities ended followed by the withdrawal of the Indo-Pakistani forces to the previous cease-fire lines. Shastri died of a heart attack in Tashkent right Pakistan fought a third war over Bangladesh's Independence in which the Kashmir dispute was only a peripheral issue.

On July 2, 1972, Mrs. Gandhi signed the Simla agreement with Mr. Zulfikar Ali Bhutto, the first President and later Prime Minister of Pakistan who had succeeded the military dictator General Yahya Khan in 1971. Under this agreement, India and Pakistan, among others, committed themselves to "settling their differences through bilateral negotiations or by any other peaceful means mutually agreed upon between them," and that the "basic issues and causes which bedeviled the relations between the two countries for the last 25 years shall be resolved by peaceful means."

They also agreed that in "Jammu and Kashmir, the Line of Control (LOC) resulting from the cease-fire of December 17, 1971, shall be respected by both sides without prejudice to the recognized position of either side." The agreement became the basis for the renewal of official relations between the two countries both at political and economic levels, thus ending any role for either the UN or outside powers including the US. On July 24, 1973, they both signed another agreement in New Delhi agreeing to repatriate all POW's except for 195 who were held to be tried but were later released without trial.

While it demanded a plebiscite in the Indian-part of Kashmir, Pakistan unilaterally detached Gilgit Agency and Baltistan from Azad Kashmir in 1974, and integrated them into Pakistan. This move ignored the UN Security Council's longstanding resolutions in the same fashion that India did when it had integrated Kashmir into her union in 1956. Pakistan and India also renewed diplomatic recognitions in 1976.

In 1968, following the end of the third Indo-Pakistani war, India released Sheikh Abdullah and his colleague, Mirza Afzal Beg, from jail unconditionally. Abdullah became reconciled to accepting Kashmir's accession to India as final. For example, on March 10, 1972, in an interview with *The Times* (London), he said, "our dispute with the government of India is not accession but it is the quantum of autonomy" for Kashmir.

In June of the same year, the state government headed by Side Mir Passim lifted the ban on Abdullah's entry into Kashmir as he dropped the demand for a plebiscite. Beginning in 1974, he and Beg joined India in a series of negotiations. The negotiations between Mrs. Gandhi's special representative G. Parthasarathi and Beg resulted in a six-point accord called the Kashmir Accord signed by Abdullah on February 12, 1975.

Abdullah agreed to Kashmir's status as a part of India while being allowed to enjoy special provisions for the state under Article 370. On February 25, 1975, Abdullah became the Chief Minister of the state replacing Qasim of the Congress Party. In July 1975, his party, the National Conference finally came into existence again. He governed the state until he died on September 21, 1982. His son, Dr. Farooq Abdullah, succeeded him.

But Farooq joined by the influential Cleric Maulvi Farooq of the Awami Action Committee demanded autonomy, the kind that had been promised in the 1952 Delhi Agreement to his father. During the 1983 legislative elections despite Mrs. Gandhi's anger and her manipulation of the elections, he stressed this theme and won the election. Upset by his demand for autonomy, Mrs. Gandhi intervened in the domestic politics of the state and dismissed Abdullah's government in 1984, by engineering defections from his party led by his brother-in-law, G. M. Shah. She brought the state under central control (Presidential violence increased under his leadership, in the Valley and Jammu, between Muslims and Hindus allegedly encouraged by him, he was dismissed in 1986.

In the same year, in a surprisingly *volte face*, perhaps, as a matter of expediency, Abdullah signed a deal with Mr. Rajiv Gandhi, the new Prime Minister, who had succeeded his mother following her assassination in June 1984. In June 1986, a coalition of National Conference and Congress was formed. This coalition won a landslide victory in the March 1987 elections but it did not help Abdullah to keep power for long. The election of 1990 resulted in Abdullah downfall following the outbreak of a Muslim uprising in 1989.

SUBMARINE AND ANTI SUBMARINE OPERATIONS IN SEPTEMBER 1965

The Story of the Pakistan Navy States:

"Just after the Dwarka attack on night 7/8 September, the Pakistan submarine GHAZI had been patrolling off the Saurashtra coast. She tracked 4 to 5 escorts on passage from Bombay proceeding up the coast but did not attack them as her orders were to attack only heavy ships."

While on return passage to Bombay from the East coast, BEAS picked up a submarine contact at 1230 on 9 September about 45 miles south of Bombay. She carried out an urgent attack, followed by a deliberate attack half an hour later. Thereafter contact was lost. GHAZI makes no mention of this attack.

On 11 September, there were intensive anti submarine air patrols off Bombay. One Alize aircraft flew over GHAZI while she was snorkeling but failed to detect her. GHAZI returned to Karachi thereafter to rectify her defective electronic counter measures equipment and resumed patrol on 15 September.

Between 7 and 10 September, the Indian Fleet was in Bombay. When GHAZI was in Karachi from 12 to 14 September to effect repairs, the Indian

Fleet was operating off the Saurashtra coast. When GHAZI resumed patrol on 15 September, the Indian Fleet was in Bombay from 14 to 17 September, in between sorties.

On 17 September, FOCIF sent out five escorts for an anti submarine search in the southern approaches to Bombay. They searched an area of 5000 square miles between 17 and 23 September. Several sonar contacts were picked up. On two occasions, 21 and 23 September, contacts were attacked for several hours. GHAZI makes no mention of these two attacks. Presumably she was nowhere near.

GHAZI's 'Record of Service', retrieved from the sunken hull in 1972, indicates that "In 1965, while on war patrol off the port of Bombay, GHAZI encountered three frigates. She fired four torpedoes and scored three hits on the British Type 41 frigate INS BRAHMAPUTRA".

The Story of the Pakistan Navy' mentions that:

"Off Bombay, on 22 September, GHAZI gained a firm contact. After tracking the zig-zagging contact all day, GHAZI fired four torpedoes at an ' A A frigate ' in the evening. After one and a half minutes, the first torpedo was heard to hit, followed five seconds later by another hit. GHAZI's sonar reported patterns of explosions being fired. After this attack, GHAZI returned to Karachi on 23 September where the Captain was decorated for having sunk the Indian Navy's anti aircraft frigate INS BRAHMAPUTRA".

After the cease fire, FOCIF invited the foreign naval attaches from New Delhi on board the BRAHMAPUTRA in Bombay to remove any doubts that the ship was afloat and fighting fit.

Overall, the above account provides a glimpse of the complexity of submarine and anti submarine warfare and the difficulties of predicting, with any degree of certainty, the outcome of submarine and anti submarine operations in the North Arabian Sea.

Other Minor Incidents

There were two other incidents which to this day remain unexplained:

(a) On 11 September an unidentified aircraft was reported over Visakhapatnam. Fire was opened by the ack ack guns of the Naval Coast Battery. The History of the Pakistan Air Force makes no mention of any attack on Visakhapatnam on 11 September.

(b) On 15 September, unidentified aircraft were reported over Cochin. Fire was opened by the ships patrolling off Cochin and by the Naval Battery located at the harbour entrance. Some shells fell into the populated areas adjoining Ernakulam. Some shells, which fell into the water near the harbour entrance were mistaken for air dropped mines. A minesweeper was rushed from Goa to Cochin to sweep the mines - no mines were found. A Seahawk aircraft got airborne from Cochin airfield to intercept the aircraft - no encounter occurred. The History of the Pakistan Air Force makes no mention of any attack on Cochin on 15 September. A post war analysis suggested that the jet aircraft could have been from a British or American aircraft carrier task force which might have been operating in the area. The reminiscences of some participants at Cochin indicate that there were no echoes of any aircraft on the scans of the warning radars being manned in the ND School.

Analysis of the Reasons for Not Using the Navy Offensively

In considering the reasons why the Navy did not achieve anything significant, several basic questions arise. Was there any flaw in the higher direction of war? After the Rann of Kutch incident, why was the Fleet sent to the Bay of Bengal? When the intrusions started in Kashmir in early August, why wasn't the Fleet immediately recalled to the West Coast? Given the constraints imposed by the Government, could the Navy have done better than it did?

The Higher Direction of War

There were two aspects of the higher direction of war in 1965 which created confusion. The first was the Government's genuine and sincere belief that in modern warfare, it was meaningful to engage in warlike activity without formally declaring war. The second was that once the Government had decided to counter hostile acts by Pakistan, it was reasonable that activity be selectively confined to only one or two of the Armed Forces. As regards the first aspect, the extracts quoted above from Mr PVR Rao, the Defence Secretary in 1965, the memoirs of Mr C P Srivastava, the Private Secretary to Prime Minister Shastri in 1965, the recollections of Mr L K Jha, the Principal Secretary to Prime Minister Shastri in 1965 make it clear that the Government was determined not to enlarge the scope of the conflict beyond the minimum required to safeguard its position in Kashmir and to prevent any escalation of the conflict beyond this objective. It will also appear from the extracts given below that the Chief of the Army Staff, who was the de facto Chairman of the Chiefs of Staff Committee, excluded the Navy from participation in the contingency plan in case Pakistan attacked Kashmir. In the 1971 National Security Lecture of the United Services Institution of India, General Chaudhuri stated:

"Now that both Mr Bhutto and Air Marshal Asghar Khan have publicly claimed that they were responsible for planning and instigating Pakistan's attack on India in 1965, I think I could interpolate here a footnote from history. In 1964, when we were revising military plans to defend ourselves in case of an attack from our neighbor, the troops available on the Western Front were roughly equivalent to those of Pakistan. Our rapid expansion had meant some dilution. In the limited advance which must form the fulcrum of any defensive plan, we were faced with three alternatives. The first one was the occupation of some unguarded territory. This seemed unproductive and non -permanent. The second was the occupation of and probably substantial destruction to a big city. For this there were insufficient troops. Anybody who has studied the capture of a big town, will realise how expensive this operation is in manpower. The resistance put up by beleaguered Berlin in 1945, defended only by the remnants of a defeated army, against overwhelming odds, is a good example of what I mean. In dealing with this alternative, there was also the political view that any substantial destruction of a major population and historical centre, would leave a raw wound between two neighbors, delaying unduly the eventual aim of living in amity together. The third alternative was the destruction of equipment, cheaply obtained but if destroyed, expensive in every way to replace. This third alternative seemed the correct choice. I would submit that we were successful in the pattern we adopted and the ensuing heavy economic and political disturbances in Pakistan, certainly contributed to the downfall of the Ayub Government and perhaps to the democratisation now pending.

"Incidentally, Pakistan's own plan for 1965 was based on first getting us to panic and move down heavy reinforcements from the main Punjab theatre to Kutch. Once they had got us there, then the so called raiders would have gone into Kashmir, supported by the Pakistan regular army capturing the key point of Akhnur. Though the first part of the Pakistani plan misfired, the originators were so intrigued with the ingenuity of the second part, that they put it into action anyway. Operations by emotion are always incorrect and the second part also failed. It was on the 5th May 1965 that the larger pattern of Pakistan's intentions to seize Kashmir before we got too strong became apparent, though the actual details of how they would do it were not clear at that time, for the initiative lay, as it always does, with the aggressor.

"Previous to 1965, it had always been said by our political leaders that any attack by Pakistan against Kashmir would be construed as an attack against India. Consequently India would then be at liberty to attack Pakistan in order to improve her own defences. This statement of policy, however, was never incorporated into any military plan. The explanation for this omission was that a decision would only be taken at the time and the military would then be duly informed. Despite the public political statement, the military were always in great doubt as to whether at the appropriate time any such permission would really be given. They were also aware that if a positive decision was made at this late stage, then it would be most difficult, if not impossible, to finalise the operational plans, make the necessary concentration of units - always a long and complicated business - brief the commanders at all levels fully about the tactical picture and then launch a successful operation. The troops were fully convinced that at this last moment, the Government could have a drastic change of mind and militarily the final result might then be a fiasco.

"After the 5th May 1965, when it appeared that an attack on Kashmir or India later that year was a distinct possibility, the first matter that needed clearance was this ability to retaliate. In my discussions with both the Prime Minister and the Defence Minister after the pros and cons had been fully discussed, the necessary sanction was obtained. Consequently, we had plenty of time to work out the appropriate moves. The day Pakistan moved her regular troops,infantry and armour into the Jammu sector, I was in Kashmir.

As I was coming back in the plane to Delhi, the Director of Military Operations, who was in the aircraft with me, started writing out the required signals to go to the formations concerned. On landing, he went straight off to send them out and I immediately went to see the Defence Minister who formally confirmed my action. He then informed the Prime Minister and that evening the PM asked me to see him, discussed a few details and further approved the action taken. The PM might then have informed some of his close colleagues, but this was not my concern.

"As a number of other broad policy points connected with the operations had also been cleared in this same manner, I feel it is desirable to mention the mechanics by which these clearances were given. In 1965, somehow in a rather unconventional, unplanned way, a series of informal meetings started up between the PM, the DM, the PS to the PM and myself. A little later on, my very esteemed and valuable colleague, Air Marshal Arjan Singh, joined us, for obviously the Army and the Air Force were closely linked together in any defence role. The Naval Chief did not come, for the Navy's role did not look like being a very big one. At these meetings, there was a free interchange of views and the many implications of the various actions which might be taken in a variety of circumstances were discussed in detail. No formal notes were kept for very often it was only a clearing of minds. When however, a certain policy matter was accepted, it was noted and put up for clearance later in a more formal manner. During these meetings, it was intrinsically understood that I would keep my colleagues, and particularly the Naval Chief, informed of the more important decisions, that Mr L K Jha would similarly keep the appropriate members of the Civil Services informed and, of course, the PM and the DM would keep their political and Ministerial colleagues informed as they thought fit.

As Chief of Army Staff, I found these meetings extremely valuable, for not only was I quite sure of the parameters within which I could work but I was also well briefed on the possible political, domestic and economic implications. This saved a lot of time later in more formal discussions and also, when I was discussing plans for the future war with the PSO's and the Army Commanders, I was in a position to give them a good deal of background information which they, in their turn, found useful. These meetings with the PM and the Defence Minister also gave me the opportunity to put my view point directly to the two people who would ultimately play the largest part in making the final overall decisions.

"In this particular case, these informal, 'clear the air' meetings seemed to have worked very satisfactorily and advantageously. There were no personality clashes, while the small numbers concerned seemed to keep discussion down to essentials. Everyone present was fully aware of the security implications and so there were no leaks or fear of leaks.

An air of informality and, I might add, good humour allowed a great deal of freedom in speaking and thinking, while a mutual confidence was built up which was most important then and later. I am not saying that this particular method of discussion could have worked equally well or at all, with another group of people in the same position. But it does emphasise what I consider to be the second important point in organisation for defence. This is the need for a free interchange of views between the various sections of the decision making authorities concerned and then enough liberty given to each one to work within his own sphere with a minimum of interference."

In the 1972 National Security Lecture of the United Service Institution of India, Mr PVR Rao, who was the Defence Secretary from 1962 to 1966, stated:-

"After November 1962 the Defence Committee of the Cabinet was revamped into the Emergency Committee. But the major change was in the working of the Defence Ministers Committee. This Committee, less the Finance representative, met daily except when the Defence Minister was out of Delhi and was effective in ensuring better coordination amongst the Services and in speeding the build up of the forces. But the system underwent a change as the crisis mounted in August 1965. There have been various claims about the decisionmaking at that time. One claim is that a small group, with the Prime Minister at its head, took all decisions and the whole process functioned very smoothly. There are, on the other hand, complaints that there was unnecessary political interference, with the result that achievement fell short of what was feasible and desirable".

Mr PVR Rao also recalls:-

"The idea that there was no communication between the Chiefs and the Government is quite incorrect, because communications can be either oral or in writing. After Mr Chavan became the Defence Minister, there used to be a meeting every morning at 9.30 in the Defence Minister's room, attended by the three Chiefs of Staff and the Defence Secretary. The Cabinet Secretary used to come sometimes but he was not a regular visitor. Regular minutes of meetings were kept which were circulated to all concerned.

"As regards written Directives, the Navy, and particularly the Army, are very fond of saying that there were no written directives. I think it is a very ridiculous thing. In my view, decisions were not taken by the Cabinet. The decisions were always taken at the Defence Minister's morning meetings. If the decisions required further written authority, then only would they go to the PM and Defence Committee of the Cabinet. So, for operational purposes and that is what I am concerned with, all three Chiefs were in the picture every day of what was happening in the Government. It is not correct to say that the Service Chiefs were isolated or insulated and they wanted written orders that were transparent.

"Mr Shastri was staying at the relevant time at 4 Motilal Nehru Place and he had his office at the adjacent interconnected building at 10, Janapath. From about the 6th August 1965, I was asked to go to his office and I used to go there after office on my way home to report to him about the events of the day. As the situation in the valley vis a vis the infiltrators continued unabated and to drift, Shastri was clear that the troops should go across the Cease Fire line and wipe out the infiltrator's bases in POK. This became an issue for regular discussion at the morning meetings, one or two of which Shri Shastri also attended. It was Government's policy that if our action across the CFL brought out the Pak regular forces into the open, we would not confine ourselves to operations in Kashmir but be free to respond wherever we thought best on the West Pakistan Front. In this situation, General Chaudhuri demanded that if operations became necessary against West Pakistan, the whole might of the Indian Armed forces (all the three arms) should be thrown in and asked for a written directive from Government in this regard. This developed into a tussle of wills between General Chaudhuri on the one hand and the PM/DM on the other. As things continued to drift, I drafted, on Shri Shastri's instructions, a directive to the Chiefs of Staff accordingly. This was about the 10th or 11th August. There was, even then, never any question of extending the operations to the eastern sector. When I took the draft directive to 10 Janpath, Shastri took it from me and kept it, saying he would read through it. On the 11th, 12th and 13th, every evening, I asked for the paper back but he would just smile. The Indian Army crossed the Cease Fire Line on the 13th, destroyed the infiltrator's bases and in the process, captured Haji Pir by a brilliant operation. The operation was wholly Army; the IAF was not used. On the 14th or 16th August, Shastri returned to me my draft directive, saying that it was no longer necessary. No written directive (apart from the minutes of the morning meetings) were issued to any of the Chiefs of Staff. Incidentally, General Chaudhuri also did not further pursue the matter and he was in full agreement that the Navy had no role at that stage in the operations and that the operations should not be extended to the Eastern sector.

"The absence of a written directive and the see-saw that went on in this respect resulted in a curious incident. The Chief of Air Staff had apparently given standing instructions to his field commanders that if open hostilities broke out, they should spring into action without further orders. As news came out of the Pak attack on the Chamb front, the IAF on the night of 1/2 September, attacked Lalmanirhat and other targets in the East and the Pak Air Force, on its part, attacked Kalaikonda airbase near Kharagpur. Evidently, the Chief of Air Staff had not been able to countermand his earlier instructions to his field officers in the East in time. General Chaudhuri was very upset and protested to CAS/DM. The situation was rectified and the incident smoothed over.

"I have no knowledge of the happenings in the meetings between PM/DM and a Chief of Staff. Chiefs of Staff have direct access to the President, the PM and the DM. However, the P.M. and the D.M. were very punctilious and, if any action was required, the material would usually come down for suitable action. The DM would normally mention the point requiring action in the morning meeting; or, as in one or two cases, where personalities were involved, he mentioned the problem privately. That the Naval Chief remained uninformed at any stage about Government policy is just shibboleth.

"With regard to the 1965 war, it should be realised that the Government of India, that is the civil Government, wanted to keep the operations at as low a key as possible. Kashmir had to be defended and, to the extent that Pakistan was creating trouble there, it had to be faced. But it was the determined policy of Prime Minister Lal Bahadur Shastri and the Indian Government not to allow the operations to escalate.

"It is correct that the Navy was told not to approach Pakistan or threaten it. There is no question of going to Shastri or anything of the sort. But the Navy is quite correct in saying that they were asked not to escalate the fighting. They are absolutely correct. And India did not want to escalate the war. In point of fact, even in the east we did not take any action. In 1965, we wanted to limit the fighting as much as possible".

In the 1973 National Security Lecture of the United Service Institution of India, Air Chief Marshal Lal, who was the Vice Chief of Air Staff in 1965 (and subsequently Chief of Air Staff in 1971) stated:

"Early in 1965, Pakistan attacked us in Kutch, in Western India. The attack caught the armed forces unawares. The Army took the field without any prior planning or preparation. Its reaction was fast but there was no joint Army-Air Force plan, and all that the Air Force could do was to provide logistic support with light aircraft. The possibility of tactical support was considered after the fighting began. It was then realised that our bases were so far from the battle zone that our aircraft would have to operate at extreme range with reduced weapon loads while Pakistani aircraft could dominate the entire combat area from bases close by. Given time, we could also have improvised an airfield or two in or near Kutch, but the fighting ended before that. The incident was soon defused but, apparently, not before it had encouraged Pakistan in the belief that the time had come to settle the Kashmir dispute by force of arms. "Then in August and September 1965 came the second Kashmir War. It began with skirmishes in the valley by so-called freedom fighters, in reality agents of Pakistan. These were followed, towards the end of August, by an all-out attack by Pakistani armour in the Chamb area of Jammu province, with the obvious objective of cutting the Jammu-Srinagar highway. Our Army, working under the restrictions of the Cease Fire agreement, was lightly equipped in that sector and though it fought valiantly, its AMX tanks were no match for the more powerful Pakistani Pattons. While there was some hope of the Army holding the Pakistani attack on its own, there was no talk of bringing the Air Force into the conflict. But on 1st September, with the Pakistanis pressing forward from Jaurian, General Chaudhuri, the Army Chief, was compelled to ask for air support.

"There had been no prior joint planning for such an eventuality. Air Marshal Arjan Singh, the Air Chief, had on his own alerted the air bases in the Punjab. When the call came, a force of fighter bombers from Pathankot mounted a strike on the Pakistanis within minutes of being ordered to do so. It was a touch-and-go affair, because the demand for air support came late in the afternoon and the strike had to be mounted in an area with which our pilots were not familiar. With only a few minutes of daylight left, they could have missed the battle zone or attacked the wrong targets. Fortunately they did neither and so helped to bring the Pakistani force to a halt.

"At this point it is interesting to consider in somewhat greater detail why there was no prior planning of Army -Air operations even though, as General Chaudhuri said in his 1971 National Security lecture, he expected the Pakistanis to attack in Kashmir after the Kutch incident. Basically, I think, it was because he and his commanders were wedded to the idea that military operations were principally an Army affair and that the other services could only operate on the fringe, as it were, with an occasional bonus from the Air Force. This was compounded by a big-brother attitude towards the Air Force which led to its being treated with a certain amount of indulgence but prevented it being accepted as a vital and equal partner in war. Matters were further complicated by the belief that if the Indian Air Force took part in the fighting then the Pakistani Air Force would do likewise, thus increasing the likelihood of a general war between the two countries instead of a localised conflict in J & K. There was a good deal of truth in this, of course, but this was a possibility from which there was no escape. Indeed, this was a possibility that could not be ignored for Pakistan had already been warned that any attack on Jammu and Kashmir would be treated as an attack on India. With a political direction as clear as that on the record, it was incumbent on the Chiefs of Staff to have their plans ready for such a contingency. The fact that they did not is indicative of the thinking at the time.

"The events in the Chamb-Jaurian sector leading to the call for air support took matters out of the Army's hands. At that stage the Government had to decide whether to enlarge the area of conflict, and it did so without hesitation. That, indeed, appeared to be the only way to divert Pakistani forces from the vulnerable Jammu-Srinagar highway, the loss of which would have jeopardised the defence of the Valley. With the decision to fight Pakistan outside J & K, the Army had to move up forces from peace time stations, some from the Deccan and further south, and formulate an operational plan at short notice.

"During the five days that elapsed between the Government decision and the date set for implementing it, there was some discussion of how the Army and the Air Force should operate. On the Army side, the notion persisted that it would fight on its own, with the Air Force providing an occasional bonus;

and in the Air Force, where I was Vice-Chief, we thought of fighting mainly an air war against the PAF and what we considered to be strategic targets, assigning relatively low priority to support the Army. Separate plans were hastily drawn up by each Service with no joint consultation worth the name. And again, no tasks were envisaged for the Navy.

"Please note that in 1965 the higher defence organisation was functioning and the Chiefs of Staff Committee met regularly under the chairmanship of General Chaudhuri. Officers in positions of authority had read and studied and taught the procedures for inter-service co-operation. It was not realised, however, that even when the general drill is known, each particular task still requires a great deal of preparatory work, that the persons taking part need to be trained for it, that supporting facilities have to be arranged for in advance, and this has to be done for every contingency that can be envisaged. Flexibility in battle is gained only through long and arduous preparation.

"That we discovered when we entered Pakistan. Soon the Army found that it could not fight entirely on its own, for the PAF was constantly harassing it. The Army needed air defence and tactical support but no detailed arrangements had been made for either.

The Air Force was willing to help and it did all it could but in the absence of joint plans, large gaps remained in the air cover in the combat zone. Neither did the air operations through which we hoped to immobilize the PAF and reduce Pakistan's ability to make war achieve much, for we had no well thought out target system for the purpose. Having had some responsibility for all this, I must confess that the air war became a somewhat hit-and-miss affair, that depended heavily on finding targets of opportunity for its success. The aircrew performed magnificently, doing all that was expected of them and more; had there been a coherent joint war plan, we would have derived much fuller benefit from their courage and sacrifice.

"Our advance into Pakistan caught the Pakistani forces by surprise. I imagine they had not thought the Indian Government and Armed Forces capable of swift decisions and speedy action. The initial successes of our Army were soon checked by stiff resistance, a notable feature of which was the close co-operation between the Pakistani Army and Air Force. The two of them had obviously done their homework well, for our jawans reported that the PAF were quick to appear whenever the Pakistani ground forces were in difficulties, and gave them most effective support. This was the more remarkable because unlike our set-up, in which all three Service Chiefs and their Headquarters were based at Delhi, the Pakistani Air Chief was located at Peshawar, the Army Chief at Islamabad, near Rawalpindi, and the Naval Chief at Karachi.

The fact that their forces managed to work well together speaks well for their mutual understanding, which is more important than physical proximity. Furthermore, since Pakistan had been the one to start the fighting in J & K, it is to be presumed that its Service Chiefs had given some thought to the possibility of a more widespread conflict and prepared for it accordingly.

"Despite its preparations, however, Pakistan failed to make any inroads in J & K and just about held its own elsewhere. We advanced up to the Ichhogil canal, West Pakistan's first line of defence, and towards Sialkot. Pakistani forces came into Indian territory around Gadra Road in Rajasthan. Except for a single PAF attack on an Indian Air Force base near Calcutta, there was no fighting in the east.

Our Navy had no operational tasks but suffered a sea-borne attack at Dwarka in the west. The fighting was brought to a halt by 22nd September, the Army having been engaged in combat for nearly a month and a half and the Air Force for 22 days. At the turn of the year came the Tashkent agreement, negotiated by our then Prime Minister, the late Mr Lal Bahadur Shastri.

"In retrospect, it is clear that the 1965 war was successful as a defensive action, for it managed to preserve the status quo in Kashmir, but the operations in the Punjab and Rajasthan were inconclusive. We failed to make a real dent in Pakistan's forces, both on the ground and in the air. The Navy being far removed from Kashmir took no part in the fighting.

"With the benefit of hindsight, we can now see what part the higher defence organisation played in the 1965 war. Frankly, I do not think it made any significant contribution. I say this after careful thought, knowing that one of our distinguished Army Chiefs, General J N Chaudhuri, was then Chairman of the Chiefs of Staff Committee. Even at the risk of his displeasure, I must say that he failed to get the organisation working as it should have done. The General himself admits as much, without meaning to, in the published version of the National Security lectures that he delivered in this institution in 1971. He said in those lectures that he saw the Kutch incident as a prelude to an attack by Pakistan in Jammu and Kashmir, and he therefore began the Army's preparations well in advance. He omits to mention that the Air Force and the Navy were kept in the dark about this. He goes on to say that he often discussed the threat with the Defence Minister and the Prime Minister and that, once in a while, he took the Air Chief along with him. The impression conveyed is that he looked upon the impending conflict as an Army affair, in which the use of the Air Force would be incidental. To my mind, this reflects an attitude long prevalent in the Army, and only recently dissipated, to the effect that its larger size and greater age gave it a commanding superiority over the other services and invested it with the sole right to decide how wars should be fought. I may be reading too much into a single statement, but to me it is axiomatic that effective co-operation between the Services can grow only out of mutual trust and full understanding of each others capabilities and limitations. I think that was lacking in 1965.

"In any case, the Air Force and Navy, not having been alerted about the possibility of another war over Kashmir, no inter-service contingency plans were drawn up, nor was any course of action agreed upon with the Air Force in the event of its being called out to support the Army.

This mental block against consultation and joint planning continued right through the phase of guerrilla activity and was only partly removed when Pakistani armour threatened to cut the Jammu-Srinagar highway. It was at that critical stage, on 1st September 1965, that the Air Force was asked for air support, which it gave at short notice. Complaints from our forward troops about the limited extent of air cover in the war that followed were well-founded, for in the absence of precise plans the Air Force had simply maintained its normal forces at its bases in the Punjab and in Jammu and Kashmir. To do its job properly, some redeployment of squadrons and of logistic and communication facilities should have been effected before the commencement of hostilities. Had the joint planners been able to do their work in advance, I am certain more positive results would have been achieved in 1965. However, apart from preserving the status quo in Kashmir, the 1965 war was valuable for the many practical lessons it taught us in the conduct of operations from the highest level to combat in the field. In the years that followed these lessons were absorbed and applied."

The above excerpts indicate that until early August 1965 the Chief of the Naval Staff, Vice Admiral Soman, was unaware of two things - that information was available to the Chief of Army Staff that Pakistan may attempt to seize Kashmir later in the year and that the Chief of Army Staff had obtained the Government's approval in principle for the Army to counter attack Pakistan, if Pakistan attacked Kashmir.

THIRD INDO-PAK WAR WAS FOUGHT IN 1971

The peace, however, was short-lived. The third Indo-Pak war was fought in 1971 over the issue of former East-Pakistan and the creation of Bangladesh. The political division of Pakistan as East Pakistan became the sovereign and independent Bangladesh was another humiliating defeat that affected Indo-Pak relations as recalcitrance over Kashmir grew and became a prime contest for national pride and prestige. 1971 saw the signing of the Simla Treaty which cemented the border between PoK and Indian Kashmir as an international border that would be respected by both sides as any other international territorial confine (Varshney 1013). This border has come to be known as the Line of Contol (LoC) which frequently experiences border skirmishes and cross-fires.

In the midst of this growing Indo-Pak political animosity, there has also been a progressively intensifying discontent and disillusionment of the Kashmiri people against the Indian government. There has been an increasingly popular insurgency movement since December 1989 in Kashmir as various ideological groups claim the right to an independent state and oppose Indian rule in Kashmir (Ganguly, 1996, 76). These include the Jammu and Kashmir Liberation Front (JKLF), Hizb-ul-Mujahideen, and Lashkar-e-Toiba (LET) among others. During the rise and high points of the insurgency in the 1990s, Islamic insurgency groups were actively supported by Pakistan. "Almost every shop in the main bazaar of every town, large or small, in Pakistan had a Lashkar collection box to raise funds for the struggle in Kashmir" ("Profile…" 2006). If I may jump ahead in my historical analysis for a brief moment, it would be pertinent to point out that the 11th July 2006 co-ordinated attacks on the Mumbai metro system were carried out by LET ("Asia…" 2006). Many of these insurgent groups aim not only for the freedom of Kashmir from Indian rule but also to extend Islamic rule to India. They also benefit immensely from the chaotic political situation in Kashmir because it provides them with a huge bulk of a vulnerable population with enough grievances to recruit to fight for their ideologies.

The insurgency has only soured Indo-Pak relations further and in most cases delayed bilateral talks between the two countries. Further, since the September 11th attacks on the US and the global war on terror, Pakistan has been pressured to clamp down on these terrorist groups. President Musharraf has banned LET and three other terrorist groups although "after the ban [his] government did not try to break up Lashkar but it restricted the movements of its leaders and the group members were told to keep a low profile" ("Profile…").

Ganguly (1996) argues that there are two main reasons for the rise and steady presence of the insurgency in Kashmir which extends its violent nature into the rest of India. As the Indian government promoted development of its states through education, a new generation of young Kashmiris were made more cognizant of their rights and called for political mobilisation and the freedom of Kashmir (80). This was also accompanied by a "deinstitutionalisation of politics in the state, which drove the expression of political discontent into extra-institutional contexts" – mainly insurgent groups (80). The insurgency has undoubtedly embittered Indo-Pak relations and led to an intensification of the security threat that both feel. The insecurity of the region was heightened in 1998 when India announced its nuclear capability with Pakistan following soon after. Both have also not signed the Nuclear Non-Proliferation Treaty (NPT). Since then both countries have increased their defence budgets despite a number of sanctions in light of the nuclear tests (Ganguly & Biringer, 908).

With the Indian subcontinent now nuclear, the threat of the Kashmir conflict began to attract increasing international concern. Both India and Pakistan trudged along the path of uncompromised ideals. However, 1999 began with the Indian prime minister Atal Bihari Vajpayee taking an historic bus trip to Lahore on the invitation of then Pakistani premier Nawaz Sharif (Kapur, 195). There was much celebration as the Indian and Pakistani PMs exchanged garlands of flowers and the local people cheered. Hopes for a real peace building effort were rekindled. Countless Indians and Pakistanis forced to move at the time of partition dreamed of going back to their ancestral homes. Five decades after the conflict began, there seemed to be a real chance that the political process would move forward and there would a real attempt at a cessation of hostilities. However, deeply-rooted historical conflicts with identities, political interests, and national pride at stake are rarely forgotten with an unusual bus ride into enemy territory.

While political niceties between the Indian and Pakistani leaderships were going on, Parvez Musharraf, then chief of the Pakistani army, was planning an incursion into Indian territory by Pakistani troops and Kashmiri militants in an effort that was reminiscent of the 1965 war.

The LoC passes through extremely rugged territory among the craggy slopes of the Himalayan range with impassable weather for most of the year. There had been a tacit agreement between India and Pakistan that certain areas of the LoC would be unmanned during the peak of winter with the expectation that neither side would take advantage of this vulnerability and respect the international border ("War..."). The hope was that the Indian army would not detect the infiltrators until May which they didn't. This gave the Pakistani army and militants considerable time to occupy strategic positions along the LoC. The main Srinagar-Leh national highway was in clear range which gave them tactical advantage as it was the only route the army had to the higher reaches of the border between India and Pakistan. Had the incursion been successful, the LoC would have inevitably been redefined because India would not have been able to fight back with its only highway connecting them to the infiltrators being manned by the infiltrators themselves. The Indian offensive was launched on 26th May 1999 and called Operation Vijay (victory). Patriotism was flying high as India was deeply offended by the under-handed infiltration with a clear goal of redefining the international border and claiming Indian territory. The war ended with India successfully pushing back the infiltrators across the original LoC and Pakistan condemned by the international community for what was a clear act of unprovoked aggression and infiltration into Indian territory. Soon after, Musharraf led a military coup against Prime Minister Sharif and declared himself President. With mistrust high between the two countries and the demise of democracy in Pakistan, any diplomatic progress that had been made toward peace was stalled.

September 11th brought the Indo-Pak conflict over Kashmir back into the limelight as the US pressured Pakistan into banning terrorist organisations and providing refuge for the Taliban. The Indian and Pakistani people share a common history and a hard struggle against colonialism.

Yet they were separated along religion which can be a deeply contentious identity issue. I would argue that the Kashmir conflict between India and Pakistan is deeply rooted in identity and emotion. The pride of the Indian and Pakistani people relies on the future of Kashmir. The insurgency has shown that what the Kashmiris themselves want is independence and autonomy. Thus, you have the three main stakeholders in the conflict at cross-purposes, each fighting for a non-negotiable national identity. It is no wonder that this is a classically defined intractable conflict.

But to define the stakeholders as simply the Pakistanis, the Indians, and the Kashmiris would naturally be too simplistic and belie the complexity of the conflict. The promised plebiscite to the Kashmiris is long overdue; there isn't even a permanent provision for the state in the Indian constitution. However, the state of Jammu and Kashmir consists of three distinct territories with three diverse religious populations.

The Kashmir conflict makes them all important stakeholders especially as most of the people living there have lived their lives under constant threat of violence. The future of Kashmir will determine not only the future of the Kashmiris, but also the people of Ladakh, Jammu, and other parts of J&K. An important question that needs to be asked is what an independent Kashmir would mean for the rest of the state.

The Kashmir conflict has also inflamed religious animosity between Hindus and Muslims in India which threatens the secularity that the country proudly claims. The 1992 Mumbai and 2002 Gujarat Hindu-Muslim riots horrified not only the international community but also the Indian population. India was reminded of the deep cleavages in its population. The Hindu nationalist party (BJP) in government at the time was undoubtedly threatening to a significant size of the population.

Though the majority of Indians are Hindus, on account of sheer size of the population, India has a fair number of Muslims, Christians, and Buddhists among other religions. The Kashmir conflict threatens the delicate balance that the diversely secular Indian population lives in. Military insurgency groups such as the LET are increasingly attempting to ruin this balance in hopes for a resolution to Kashmir. The 2005 bombings in a public market in New Delhi during the festive celebrations of the Hindu festival of Diwali and the Muslim festival of Eid-ul-Fitr and the 2006 Mumbai metro bombings by the LET were strategically implemented to fracture religious communities and tolerance in India and weaken the Indian government.

INDIA'S FOREIGN POLICY SEVERELY MAULED BY PAKISTAN

Severely disconnected and in utter disregard of Indian public opinion, it has become the hall-mark of Prime Minister's tenure from 2004 onwards to stubbornly pursue an obsessive peace dialogue with Pakistan. This stubborn obsessiveness generates a "blind spot" in India's foreign policy planning on Pakistan. This "blind spot" induces in the Indian policy establishment a strategic obliviousness to the predominating structural reality of Pakistan, that Pakistan's policy postures are commanded and controlled by Pakistan Army. The latest utterances by Pakistan Army Chief, General Kayani should leave no doubts in any perceptive Indian's mind that Pakistan-India peace is strategically impossible.

India's peace policy approaches towards Pakistan primarily crafted by the Indian Prime Minister Singh and former Foreign Secretary now the Prime Minister's National Security Adviser Shankar Menon, from the ill-advised Havana Accord (2206) to the infamous. Sharm-al-Sheikh Declaration (2009) proved to be utter failures. Pakistan is still not strategically inclined towards "sustainable peace" with India despite India's appeasement policies towards Pakistan. The latest Indian policy initiative of resumption of peace dialogue with Pakistan, disregarding that it involves a total "U-Turn" from Prime Minister Singh's declaratory assertions following Mumbai 26/11 of no talks with Pakistan till it makes amends on Mumbai 26/11, also bears the imprint of Prime Minister Singh and the new NSA. As per Indian media reports the outgoing NSA, MK Narayanan had taken a hard line against resumption of dialogue with Pakistan until India's demands on Mumbai 26/11 were met. Within days of India's announcement of readiness to resume the peace dialogue with Pakistan, in typical Pakistani official responses, Pakistan's Foreign Minister Qureshi in an arrogant and vituperative public speech in Pakistan on February 10, 2010, covered live on TV for all the world to note, asserted that while Pakistan had stuck to its stands, it was India that had come crawling to Pakistan to seek resumption of peace dialogue.

India's political and strategic analysts have totally missed the point that this was not an isolated act of political demagogy of Pakistan's Foreign Minister. Attendant on this assertion were similar contextual assertions by Pakistan Prime Minister Gilani and Pakistan Army Chief, General Kayani.

Pakistan Prime Minister Gilani asserted that Pakistan will not give any guarantees that it can stop terrorism attacks against India, emanating from Pakistan's territories, a key demand made by India following Mumbai 26/11. The Pakistan Army Chief, who controls Pakistan's foreign policy towards India in a Press Conference last week, consistently harping on Pakistan's 'India-centric threat perceptions' gave the impression that peace with India was strategically impossible.

Pakistan's marked re-emergence of intransigence towards India arises from its born-again strategic confidence that in 2009-2010 Pakistan has reinvented its strategic utility to the United States and the West, as the outcome of the London Conference 2010 would indicate.

More importantly, Pakistan has become fully aware that by re-inventing its strategic utility to the United States and the West, Pakistan has been successful not only in severely mauling India's foreign policy towards Pakistan, but also India's foreign policy relationships with the United States and the West. Pakistan is not far wrong in this perception as the infirmities in India's foreign policies in the last few years, enabled Pakistan in one master-stroke to neutralize India's key strategic objectives that it attempted to achieve, banking on the strength of its perceptions that in the ultimate analysis.

Pakistan would count more in relation to India in the current regional security environment. The perceptional damage on India, regionally and globally by Pakistan's mauling of India's foreign policy objectives is extensive.

Pakistan could do so because the Indian Prime Minister and his former Foreign Secretary and now NSA, perceptional readings on Pakistan and Pakistan's linkages with the United States and the West have been faulty.

This Book intends to focus on the following aspects in this regard:

- India's Key Foreign Policy Objectives Mauled by Pakistan

- Pakistan Army Chief's India-Centric Demands Accepted by United States and NATO
- India's Timid Pakistan Policy Encourages Pakistan for Strategic Diminution of India in Regional and Global Terms
- India's Strategic Imperatives for Strong Policy Postures Against Pakistan.

INDIA'S KEY FOREIGN POLICY OBJECTIVES MAULED BY PAKISTAN

India's key foreign policy objectives in the period 2004-2009 particularly, and earlier too, can be listed in brief as follows: (1) Pakistan as the springboard of widespread terrorism attacks against India be neutralized by a policy of peace-engagement with Pakistan and persuasive diplomacy (2) India to establish a substantial presence in Afghanistan both to further her regional power aspirations and also as a strategic pressure point against Pakistan (3) Implicit in the US-India Strategic Partnership was the component hat the United States would facilitate attainment of India's policy objectives as indicated.

India's obsessive peace-engagement with Pakistan by diplomacy, Track II diplomacy, Special Envoys and other back-room channels have not delivered on India's objectives.

Pakistan Prime Minister's latest statement quoted above vividly indicates that Pakistan still views terrorism as an instrument of state policy. India's persuasiveness stands out-matched by Pakistan's continued intransigence.

On Afghanistan, the latest developments indicate (1) Pakistan has succeeded in side-lining India in Afghanistan (2) Pakistan outmatched India's utility in Afghanistan to US strategic interests (3) India'soft-power' approaches on Afghanistan have been a dismal failure (4) Pakistan has got ruled out India from any future role in Afghanistan as part of the US regional initiative.

In terms of India's key objectives in the US-India Strategic Partnership in relation to Pakistan and Afghanistan, no success has been forthcoming to India. Pakistan reigns supreme in US military strategy and the United States has given centrality to Pakistan's strategic interests in Afghanistan, over India.

In light of the central pillars of Indian Prime Minister's policy on Pakistan and Afghanistan being knocked down by Pakistan's success in prevailing over the United States, it can be argued that India's Pakistan policy of the existing political dispensation is a failure. It would take a long time for India to retrieve the damage inflicted on India's long term strategic interests by the current Indian weak-kneed policies towards Pakistan.

Centric Demands Accepted by United States

Pakistan Army which double-timed the United States for nearly 10 years on Afghanistan and till date has not handed over Osama bin laden and Mullah Omar to the Americans, and yet got away to emerge again as the central pillar in US strategic calculus in South Asia is a reality which the Indian Prime Minister can ill ignore. Pakistan Army Chief's demands made on USA and NATO in relation to Afghanistan, India and Pakistan strategic preferences stand accepted in full.

The list of Pak Army Chief's demands accepted by the United States could make any Indian incensed as to how such acceptance has mauled India's misperceived foreign policy. The list is as follows (1) Pakistan Army will not withdraw troops from the borders with India (2) Pakistan would be given a central role in Afghanistan (3) Pakistan Army will not accept any Indian role in training of Afghan National Army or Police (4) Pakistan will be part of any US discussions with the Taliban (5) Pakistan Army demands for US military weapons systems will be met (6) India will not be given any role in a regional solution initiative for Afghanistan. The Indian Government also seems to have forgotten that it was General Kayani on taking over as Pakistan Army Chief who ordered the breach in the four year old ceasefire in 2008 to be broken by firings and escalation of tension along the LOC and the international border. When it comes to impeding the Pakistan – India peace engagement it is the Pakistan Army which does so by firing from the shoulders of the Pakistani President, the Prime Minister and Pakistan Foreign Minister intransigent assertions against India and that too on the verge of resumption of a peace dialogue. The Indian foreign policy establishment needs to get their perceptive readings on Pakistan right.

PAKISTAN 2014: A REALITY CHECK FOR INDIA'S FOREIGN POLICY

Prime Minister Designate Narendra Modi's political reachout to SAARC nations to attend his swearing-in ceremony is a bold and imaginative foreign policy initiative especially in relation to Pakistan. Scheduled interaction between PM Modi is due to take place the day after the swearing-in ceremony. This would enable PM Modi and the SAARC heads to take a measure of each other. In the process of these interactions PM Modi would be able to dispel the negative images of him projected by India's Opposition parties during the 2014 Election Campaign.

It would be a pity therefore that the Pakistan Prime Minister is unable to attend especially when no other external engagements stand scheduled for him. PM Sharif is reputed to have friendly inclinations towards and keen to enhance economic and trade ties with India. If he is dissuaded in declining PM Modi's invitation when the new Indian Prime Minister is on the threshold of initiating foreign policy changes, Pakistan would have missed a significant opportunity towards moving Pakistani relations to a new footing.

PM Nawaz Sharif is now in office for a year now in what was the first democratic change of regimes in Pakistan. I had written last year and articulated on TV debates that PM Nawaz Sharif would require a year at least to bring about major changes as at that time Pakistani political dynamics were in a flux with impending changes of the Pakistan Army Chief and the Chief Justice of Pakistan. Indian establishment and media were advised not to be euphoric.

It needs to be noted that Pakistan's India and Afghanistan foreign policies are controlled by the Pakistan Army and the new Pakistan Army Chief seems disinclined to let go of this hold to sustain the institutional significance of the Pakistan Army in Pakistani domestic political dynamics and also as leverage with the United States and China. While all SAARC nations have accepted the invitation, Pakistan is dithering for the last two days indicating the serious institutional divide within Pakistan over its approaches to India.

A reality- check on Pakistan is therefore contextually relevant both for PM Designate Modi and the foreign policy establishment which would need to break-out of the earlier appeasement mode of the last ten years.

Pakistan's reality –check in mid-2014 would indicate the following:

- Pakistan Army continues to maintain a stranglehold on Pakistan's India policy and can never be accepted to change its hostile anti-India mind-sets.
- PM Nawaz Sharif despite all best intentions to move forward in relations with India would be unable to do so.
- Significance of Pakistan Army in United States strategic calculus will enhance as US is in the process of exiting Afghanistan.
- United States in view of above is unlikely to goad Pakistan Army to go along with any friendly approaches made by PM Modi.
- Pakistan Army's notorious ISI intelligence agency has been US cat's-paw in Afghanistan twice over in recent times. US may need it again and those in India who advocate that US assistance should be sought to tame it are being unrealistic of realities.
- China's strategic calculus imperatives also dictate an over-riding importance to the Pakistan Army and its ISI.

In view of the above strategic realities, what are the options available to the new Indian Prime Minister to reorder India's neighbourhood into a more stable and secure region? While PM Modi should continue to strive and persist in giving windows of opportunity to PM Nawaz Sharif to respond positively to Indian foreign policy initiatives, PM Modi can expectedly be hoped not to repeat the 'mantras' of the previous government in terms 'unending appeasement' and 'peace at any cost'

PM Modi's election slogan modified in the foreign policy context should read as "Friendship for All, Appeasement of None". Advocated in my earlier Papers on Pakistan that India should adopt the US's China strategy of 'CONGAGEMENT" towards Pakistan would be a worthwhile advocacy at this juncture.

In sum, it implies that Pakistan Army's military adventurist policies towards India in India-proper or in Afghanistan must be met with a strategy of diplomatic and military containment with political and economic engagement in tandem. In pursuance of India's engagement processes with Pakistan, India-at-large expects PM Modi that the Government under his political leadership would be "sensitive to "India's National Honour" and if India's power leverages have to be used as a last resort then India would display the "Will to Use Power" in a judicious and calibrated manner to ensure India's National Security interests are secured.

INDO-PAK RELATIONS: PRAGMATISM ON KASHMIR

Though its use in development of WMD is terrible, science has delivered uncountable comforts to mankind. No only that, it is a great social equalizer also. It has helped the humanity to break the millennia old chained social connections. No individual is superior now on the basis of race, religion and region. Whosoever excels in knowledge can enter into the world of his choice. It was not possible earlier because differentiation and its worst forms such as apartheid, caste system and slavery were being practiced puritanically. The science-induced civility has influenced the psyche of nations also. Hence, assimilation or annihilation of small nations is no more possible. Subjugation, however, still continues, and the poverty of knowledge is the only reason behind it. The victims instead of learning and improving their economies are engaged in confrontation from within and without. Who are to be blamed more, literate outsiders or indifferent insiders?

Chances to bring about change inside are always there, and chances to end external confrontation also appear quite often, but they are not availed due to the indecisiveness of leadership. Though the repeated indecisiveness of small nations usually makes them lose more, it does not spare the big nations either? After WW II, the Soviets should have gone for revision of their stagnant system; fifties was the proper time: they wanted to do it, but didn't, and when they did it, they were too late; and eventually the break-up of the Soviet Union was the only remedy left with them.

The situation in the Indian subcontinent is not so grim, so far. But, given the faulty perceptions and indecisiveness of its rulers, it is likely to become so. The concept that militancy in Kashmir is keeping the Kashmir issue alive, and it is bleeding the Indians, is simplistic, cruel, retaliatory, and self-destructive: In this age of enlightenment it is not possible to assimilate or annihilate small nations. So, until Kashmiris are satisfied, their peaceful struggle too will create an impact, which would not be negative as created by the militancy. It would be humane and reconciliatory, and hence positive. As far as Pakistan is concerned, it has become totally dependent economically, as its strategy of bleeding India has backfired. Accordingly India too has failed. Its militarism, even if in retaliation to militancy, has made it lose much; if not technically, on moral front certainly. What is needed is immediate end to confrontation and start of positive engagement. Both activities should start simultaneously. It is a difficult decision but it must be taken.

Leadership of Indian subcontinent took many bold and timely decisions in the past. It arrived at a consensus plan to divide India. Afterwards the Liaqat-Nehru Pact on the question of refugees saved Pakistan from unthinkable miseries. Similarly the most difficult of all the questions, the question of lifeline, the water dispute, was resolved through Indus Basin Treaty. But all the good that happened between India and Pakistan is neither discussed nor appreciated in both the countries. However not everything that happened between the two was good. There were grey areas as well, such as wars of 1948, 1965 and 1971, and warlike clashes in Khem Karn, Siachin and Kargil. Alongside these open examples of extreme confrontation, both countries subtly attempted to increase the intensity of each other's internal and external conflicts. Pakistan supported Sikh and Kashmiri struggles and India attempted to fuel the ethnic tension in Sindh.

Why did the good and bad strategies run side by side in Indo-Pak relationship is a very complicated question. However, if answer is to be summarized in one sentence then it can be said with clarity that the fears created problems, and commonness and commonsense led to solution of some of them and those, which remained unresolved remained so mostly due to indecisiveness of the leadership who had faulty perceptions about the ground realities. Any way the prevailing situation demands complete halt to the confrontation, militancy and militarism, because it has already done a lot of damage, and its continuity would inflict more, and that may eventually lead to irreversibility.

It is widely believed that the source that created tension and ills in the subcontinent is issue of Kashmir. Though it is not even the half-truth, let us take it as such. Again the key to solution of Kashmir issue lies with the leadership of India and Pakistan, and not with the Kashmiris. If India could surrender twenty percent of Kashmir to China in Aksi Chin, if Pakistan could settle Kashmir border issue with China—on Chinese terms, and if India and Pakistan could decide the fate of three rivers of Kashmir, then what does stop them from solving the issue in totality?

However, to find an achievable and acceptable solution is not that easy. The process would first require that the parties involved must turn to acceptance of existing realties and try to know how they were shaped. Kashmir was a part of undivided India, though with a status of princely state. Couple this sub-continental status with enormous confronting diversities that are located and locked in a complex and economically unviable geography of Kashmir, no one can and will take the Kashmiris as a separate nation in totality, no matter what they do, and how they fight; and the earlier this is understood, by the Kashmiris of valley, the better. Allow me to elaborate the argument. Kashmir cannot become independent – though in future it may get a special status under the joint Indo-Pak protection – because of its geography and small resources, and also due to the fact that there is a terrible division among the Kashmiris themselves that has basis in religion, ethnicity, geography and desires. The Gilgatis and Baltis do not count themselves as Kashmiris, and they will prefer that their area should become a province of Pakistan at the earliest. The people of Jammu and Ladakh will be happier if their areas are given separate status of states within the Indian Union. The Azad Kashmiris have socially and economically merged themselves with the Pakistanis and it won't make any difference to them if the status of Azad Kashmir is changed to a province of Pakistan.

Accordingly, whether India is in Kashmir due to inhuman Instrument of Accession (designed jointly by the Muslim League and the Congress; on the insistence of the former) and muscle power, or Pakistan has annexed a part of Kashmir through war and support of Kashmiris, the fact remains that both have attained some kind of legitimacy and fifty-six years of occupation has further entrenched their claims. But Indians' legitimacy is, surely, under constant question in the valley of Kashmir. Though it has roots in the concept that divided India, the politico-economic mismanagement by the Indians played a bigger part. And the rest was done by the Pakistan backed resistance, though at a colossal cost that has brought destruction to everything – to life, to soul, to spirit, to intellect and even to the environment. Probable reconciliation between India and Pakistan would save the Kashmiris of valley from further destruction and recover the paradise lost, we can only hope and pray for that. But what is almost certain is that both countries will again be on the right road that was jointly built by their leadership through Liaqat-Nehru Pact, Indus Basin Treaty, Tashkent Declaration, Shimla Accord and Lahore Declaration. Now, once they are on the road, they should remain on it.

Why is the right road left so often, it looks strange when seen through a broader angle of affinity? That no two nations have as much common between them as Pakistanis and Indians, and this relationship could have been used positively to resolve the remaining contradictions: Instead they are persistently on a warpath. If the reason for that lies within India and Pakistan, then its solution needs to be searched within India and Pakistan, and not in Kashmir. If conflict of Kashmir is the reason, then that certainly has a solution within the premises of Kashmir: Let me elaborate the point. Many analysts present an attractive parallel logic that Kashmir conflict would continue, because it is being used to cover or delay or solve the bigger and terrible conflicts of ethnicity and communalism that exist within Pakistani and Indian societies.

Whatever the reasons and their epicenter, the solution of Kashmir problem must be found. After all for how long innocent Kashmiris, Indian soldiers and Pakistani soldiers would bleed due to it. The solution, however, would not be searched unless we accept many more realities alongside the ones that were debated above. Kashmir of 1947 exists no more and neither Pakistan nor India would surrender a single inch of Kashmir under their control to each other or to create an independent area for Kashmiris. Pakistan cannot afford to do so due to strategic and life (water) related compulsions. India too has strategic compulsions vis-à-vis China: Not only that any unfavorable alteration in area under its control will either create or aggravate immensely societal imbalances between its various ethnic and religious diversities. That is one reality; the other is that neither Pakistan nor India nor the Kashmiri militants can alter the status of the universally recognized Line of Control through force.

These realities and their relationship with the volatile situation in valley, and also with the Indo-Pak societies form the fundamentals, to which leaders of the two countries would certainly pay attention, when they sit to discuss the Kashmir conflict. There are time-bound rational solutions, to be implemented in various phases, which India would like to propose. It could be conditional Independence or greater autonomy or self-rule for Indian Controlled Kashmir (ICK). But differences would surface on whether or not such solution should remain within the parameters of the Indian Constitution. India would insist on keeping its constitutional link and Pakistan would, likely, disagree.

So, if efforts to put the Kashmir issue on front-burner fail, they would fail only due to egoism. Does that mean to remain on the road and to move forward, the issue should be put on backburner? Not necessarily, the Kashmiris of valley can do what elders of India did: Those who are involved in militancy should turn to peaceful struggle. On their part, India and Pakistan should enter into an interdependent economic engagement as early as possible. It will not only help in finding an ultimate solution of Kashmir problem, but also help resolve the class, communal and ethnic contradictions of Indo-Pak societies. However, due to size and scope of its economy, the responsibility to evolve and nourish a mutually beneficial relationship mostly or perhaps totally lies with the Indians and the actual blueprint for that has to be prepared by them. How superbly it would work is not difficult to visualize. In this regard a simple example of gas pipelines from Iran and Central Asia to India, passing through Pakistan, would suffice. It would earn Pakistan 700 million dollars per annum and India would save billions of dollars through adoption of cheaper land route. Wouldn't it be an extraordinary achievement for both? Imagine how many doors Pakistan knocks at for assistance of a few hundred million dollars. Imagine also the after-affects of conditionalities attached to such assistance. Similarly look at the costly attempts and agreements that India is making or would make with various countries of the Gulf to secure its growing energy needs. Can't they adopt a wise route?

Besides gas pipelines, even oil lines are a possibility, and extending the interaction further would do magic for the economies of the two countries as the trade route, via land, from India to Europe would be opened. Here it must be understood that Pakistan would not act as an excise collecting state only. It would also gain in the fields where it is lagging far behind, and it is lagging in almost all the fields. Knowledge based manufacturing, which it couldn't attain through fifty years of its friendship with the others, China and America, would surely be achieved by acquiring this new relationship; and that is what the economic blueprint would also mean, and that would require India to invest a lot financially in gas lines and also in other areas.

The economic engagement would eventually lead to opening of Indo-Pak borders including that of Kashmir, and to defend them would also become a collective responsibility. Similarly with that magnitude of economic inter-activity the subjects of communication and the foreign policy would mostly become a mutual affair. Moreover the relationship in itself and social goodwill and the economic uplift connected to it would also help in solving the internal problems of ethnicity and communalism that have gripped the Indo-Pak societies. And a day would certainly come when Kashmir would be given a special status jointly by a prosperous Pakistan and a super power India, though that may happen after many decades.

The great nations have no ego problems. America withdrew from Vietnam and Russia from Afghanistan and it didn't reduce their honor and authority. West Germany recognized East Germany, and Egypt recognized Israel and that were the jobs no one would ever think of. And can there be a better example in entire history of mankind than the one that the Indian subcontinent provided. Division of a subcontinent was not a small thing. That it was attained peacefully through a consensus decision, taken by the Congress and the Muslim League, made the whole exercise unique and exemplary. If we were wiser fifty-five years ago, why cannot we act wisely now? And the time demands that the direction of wisdom should now be steered towards evolving a relationship on the pattern of European Union. Given the encouraging environment of today, and the political will of the present Indo-Pak leadership, it can be done. It must be done.

What if the newly appeared chance is not availed, which according to Prime Minister Vajpayee is the last attempt from his side? If cruelties continue, the Kashmiris would obviously continue to suffer. The Pakistanis would continue to live with the unaffordable conflicts, and that would certainly add to their poverty.

The Indians may not suffer as much immediately, but ultimately they too would repent. If the westward land route remains closed on them, they would lose a lot. Contained as they are now, they would remain so, for a long time to come; and that would surely stop them from becoming a major player in the world, and internally too their economic and social development would be curtailed drastically. Would Pakistan or India go for a war to change the status quo? No, they will not; at least not during the current decade.

Yet, the continuity of tension for a longer period would amount to the same, because the losses that a war brings in a short period would also be brought, though gradually, by the confrontation. But, whether it is slow or sudden, poisoning remains poisoning. The times ahead would see the developed world preparing itself for a journey to a planet outside our solar system. Meanwhile where would the nations carrying the unbearable load of conflicts go: may be back to the mud houses: may be into the black holes of history: Who knows?

POSSIBLE SOLUTIONS TO THE KASHMIR ISSUE

Many consider that the best way to end present violence in Kashmir is negotiations between various Kashmiri-separatists groups, Pakistan and India. Here are a few possible solutions to the Kashmir dispute-

The Status Quo Currently a Boundary: The Line of Control (LOC)- divides the region in two, with one part administered by India and one by Pakistan. India would like to formalize this status quo and make it the accepted international boundary. *Factors Opposing-Pakistan rejects the plan partially as it will get lesser control over the region and wants greater. Kashmiri political parties too would oppose the plan as it violates the UN resolution for a referendum*

Kashmir becomes a Part of India: Though New Delhi and much of the Hindu population of Jammu and Buddhists in Ladakh would have no objections to such a plan. *Factors Opposing– The Muslim majority population of Pakistan-administered Azad Kashmir, might object the outcome as would a majority of those in Kashmir valley in India*

The Status Quo for something else: Pakistan accepts the status quo in return for India giving away disputed Sir Creek

Kashmir becomes a part of Pakistan: Kashmir joining Pakistan. *Factors Opposing– The communities of Hindus of Jammu and the Buddhists of Ladakh would object the outcome. Hindu Kashmiri Pandits, who were forced out of Kashmir by militants are also a major topic to consider.*

Kashmir becomes an Independent Sovereign Republic: As an independent state, the region would most likely be economically viable with tourism probably being the largest source of income, however being a landlocked country, it would be heavily dependent on India and Pakistan. *Factors Opposing-The outcome is unlikely because it requires both India and Pakistan (and potentially China) to give up territory.*

A smaller Independent Kashmir: A smaller independent Kashmir formed out of the current strip of Kashmir (administered by Pakistan) and the Kashmir valley (controlled by India). This would leave the Northern areas with Pakistan while India retains Jammu and Ladakh. However this region should maintain good relations with both India and Pakistan as it is landlocked and is covered with snow in winter. This region can also have its defence and foreign relations jointly handled by India and Pakistan. *Factors Opposing-The outcome is unlikely because it requires both India and Pakistan to give up territory.*

Re-evaluation

The insurgents who initially started their movement as a pro-Kashmiri independence movement, have gone through a lot of change in their ideology. Most of the insurgents portray their struggle as a religious one. Indian analysts allege that by supporting these insurgents, Pakistan is trying to wage a proxy war against India while Pakistan claims that it regards most of these insurgent groups as "freedom fighters" rather than terrorists Internationally known to be the most deadly theatre of conflict, nearly 10 million people, including Muslims, Hindus, and Buddhists, have been fighting a daily battle for survival. The *cross-border firing* between India and Pakistan, and the terrorist attacks combined have taken its toll on the Kashmiris, who have suffered poor living standards and an erosion of human rights.

Kargil Crisis

Attempts to restart dialogue between the two nations were given a major boost by the February 1999 meeting of both Prime Ministers in Lahore and their signing of three agreements. These efforts have since been stalled by the intrusion of Pakistani forces into Indian territory near Kargil in Jammu and Kashmir in May 1999. This resulted in intense fighting between Indian and Pakistani forces, known as the Kargil conflict. Backed by the Indian Air Force, the Indian Army successfully regained Kargil. A subsequent military coup in Pakistan that overturned the democratically elected Nawaz Sharif government in October of the same year also proved a setback to relations.

In 2001, a summit was called in Agra; Pakistani President Pervez Musharraf turned up to meet Indian Prime Minister Atal Behari Vajpayee. The talks fell through. On June 20, 2004, with a new government in place in India, both countries agreed to extend a nuclear testing ban and to set up a hotline between their foreign secretaries aimed at preventing misunderstandings that might lead to a nuclear war. As of early 2005, both countries are committed to a process of dialogue to solve all outstanding issues. Baglihar Dam issue was a new issue raised by Pakistan in 2005.

Sporting Ties

Cricket and hockey matches between the two (as well as other sports to a lesser degree such as those of the SAARC games) have often been political in nature. During the Soviet invasion of Afghanistan Generah Zia-ul Haq travelled to India for a bout of "cricket diplomacy" to keep India from supporting the Soviets by opening another front. Pervez Musharaff also tried to do the same more than a decade later but to no avail.

Diasporic Relations

Indians and Pakistanis living in the Britain are said to have friendly relations with one another. There are various cities such as Birmingham, Blackburn and Manchester where both communities live alongside each other in peace and harmony. Both Indians and Pakistanis living in the UK fit under the category of British Asian. The UK is also home to the Pakistan & India friendship forum. The MEP Saj Karim is of Pakistani origin. He is a member of the European Parliament Friends of India Group, Karim was also responsible for opening up Europe to free trade with India. He has given his full support to the Indian government for a death sentence to be given to Ajmal Kasab, who was involved in the 2008 Mumbai attacks.

EGYPTIAN ISLAMIC JIHAD

The Egyptian Islamic Jihad, formerly called simply Islamic Jihad originally referred to as "al-Jihad," and then "the Jihad Group", or "the Jihad Organization", is an Egyptian Islamist group active since the late 1970s. It is under worldwide embargo by the United Nations as an affiliate of al-Qaeda. It is also banned by several individual governments including that of the Russian Federation. Since 1991 it has been led by Ayman al-Zawahiri. The organization's original primary goal was to overthrow the Egyptian Government and replace it with an Islamic state. Later it broadened its aims to include attacking the United States and Israel interests in Egypt and abroad. EIJ has suffered setbacks as a result of numerous arrests of operatives worldwide, most recently in Lebanon and Yemen. In June 2001, Al Qaeda and Egyptian Islamic Jihad, which had been associated with each other for many years, merged into "Qaeda al-Jihad."

History

Al-Jihad or "Tanzim al-Jihad" was formed in 1980 from the merger of two clusters of Islamist groups: a Cairo branch, under Muhammad abd-al-Salam Faraj, and a Saidi (Upper Egypt) branch under Karam Zuhdi. Faraj wrote the 1980 book *al-Faridah al-Ghaiba (The Neglected Obligation),* setting forth the standards for EIJ, of which 500 copies were printed.

After the assassination of Egyptian president Anwar Sadat, the Egyptian government succeeded in rounding up the membership of Tanzim al-Jihad, but "was rather lenient in the ensuing trial". In prison, the Cairenes and Saidis reverted into two factions, the Cairo militants later becoming the Egyptian Islamic Jihad, and the Saidis later forming the al-Gama'a al-Islamiyya, or the

Islamic Group. According to Zawahiri, the EIJ was "different from the Takfir wal Hijra group as we do not consider people infidels because of their sins. And we are different from the Muslim Brotherhood because sometimes they do not oppose the government". The leader of the Cairo militants was Abud Zumour, "a onetime army intelligence officer serving a life sentence for his part in the plot to kill Sadat." This faction, the Islamic Jihad, "was small and tightly disciplined".

Most of the middle-rank members were discharged from prison after only three years and fled to Pakistan and Afghanistan to help the mujahideen there and escape persecution at home.

Pakistan and Afghanistan

In the mid-1980s, in Peshawar Pakistan, the militants reconstituted themselves as the Egyptian Islamic Jihad, "with very loose ties to their nominal imprisoned leader, Abud al-Zumur." A physician by the name of Sayyed Imam Al-Sharif or "Dr. Fadl" was head of EIJ for some time, although eventually Ayman al-Zawahiri, "whose leadership style was autocratic," would take over. During this time EIJ became more extreme, with for example, Dr. Fadl emphasizing the importance of takfir and execution of apostates, which he argued should include those who registered to vote, since this was a violation of God's sovereignty over governance. It was also at this time that some saw "the Egyptians" of the EIJ begin to exert an influence on Osama bin Laden, who at the time was known as a wealthy and well-connected fundraiser for the Jihad in Afghanistan. Egyptian filmmaker Essam Deraz, "bin Laden's first biographer," met bin Laden in the "Lion's Den" training camp in Afghanistan and complained that the Egyptians "formed a barrier" around bin Laden and "whenever he tried to speak confidentially to bin Laden, the Egyptians would surround the Saudi and drag him into another room." One of those who complained of being elbowed aside was a former mentor of bin Laden Abdullah Azzam, the original exponent and organizer of global Jihad on behalf of the Afghan mujahideen.

In 1991, EIJ broke with al-Zumur and al-Zawahiri took control of the leadership. At this point, Marc Sageman (a former foreign service officer who was based in Islamabad from 1987 to 1989), says "the EIJ became a free-floating network without any real ties to its original society or to its surrounding society."

Sudan

Al-Jihad (EIJ) had a blind-cell structure, meaning members in one group did not know the identities or activities of those in another, so that if one member were captured they would not be able to endanger the whole organization. However, Egyptian authorities captured the membership director of EIJ, the one member who had all the other members names. The database in his computer listed every member's address, aliases, and potential hideouts. Al-Jihad leader al-Zawahiri bitterly lamented "the government newspapers" elation over "the arrest of 800 members of the al-Jihad group without a single shot being fired."

In August 1993 al-Jihad unsuccessfully attempted to kill the Egyptian Interior Minister, Hasan al-Alfi, who was leading a crackdown on Islamic militants. A bomb-laden motorcycle exploded next to the minister's car, fatally wounding Nazih Nushi Rashed and killing Tarek Abdel-Nabi (Dia al-Deen) instantly.

The attack marked the first time Sunni Islamists had made use of suicide in terrorism, a technique made famous by Shia Hezbollah in Lebanon. It is "likely that the notion of suicide bombing" was inspired by Hezbollah as al-Zawahiri had been to Iran to raise money, and had sent his underling Ali Mohamed, "among others, to Lebanon to train with Hezbollah".

A few months later in November Al-Jihad made another bombing attempt, this time to kill Egypt's prime minister, Atef Sidqi. The car bomb exploded close to a girls' school in Cairo as the minister was driven past. The minister, protected by his armored car, was unhurt, but the explosion injured 21 people and killed a young schoolgirl, Shayma Abdel-Halim. Unfortunately for al-Jihad this bombing was preceded by two years of terror by a larger terror group, al-Gama'a al-Islamiyya that had killed 240, and the patience of the Egyptian public had run short. "Little Shayma's death captured people's emotions as nothing else had" and "when her coffin was borne through the streets of Cairo, people cried, `Terrorism is the enemy of God!`" A harsh police crackdown followed and 280 EIJ members were arrested, with 6 eventually given a death sentence.

EIJ's longtime association with al-Qaeda became closer at this time when "most" of its members were reported to have gone "on the al-Qaeda payroll." EIJ leader hoped this would be a temporary measure but later confided to one of this chief assistants that joining with bin Laden had been `the only solution to keeping the Jihad organization abroad alive.`"

Mubarak Assassination Attempt

In June 1995 another failed assassination attempt caused yet a greater setback. Operating from its exile base in Sudan, EIJ joined forces with the Egyptian al-Gama'a al-Islamiyya and Sudanese intelligence in an attempt to kill Egyptian President Hosni Mubarak while he was in Ethiopia for a conference of the Organization of African Unity. The leader of the plot was "Mustafa Hamza, a senior Egyptian member of the Al-Qaeda and commander to the military branch of the Islamic Group." The plotters had been planning the attack for more than a year, and even married local women in Ethiopia. They received assistance from Sudanese intelligence services, which smuggled weapons into their embassy in Ethiopia. Their hope was to decapitate the Egyptian government thereby eliminating the "iron grip" of the state security services, and creating a power vacuum which Islamists could then fill. Unfortunately for this plan, the attack was foiled by a malfunctioning grenade launcher and Mubarak's bulletproof limousine.

Expulsion From Sudan

Back in Egypt, Mubarak launched a ruthless campaign to crush anyone involved in Islamist terrorism, but in Sudan the EIJ had even worse troubles. In 1994, Ahmad Salama Mabruk's 17-year old son Musab, as well as the 15-year old son Ahmed of Mohammed Sharaf, were captured by the Egyptian General Intelligence Directorate and sexually abused. They were blackmailed with videotape of the sodomy, until they agreed to act as informants against their fathers' group. Musab went through his father's files and photocopied them for the Egyptians, but the Sudanese intelligence service saw the covert meetings and alerted al-Jihad, recommending that they treat the boys leniently if they confessed. al-Zawahiri convened a Sharia court, where Musab confessed he had been given explosives by the Egyptians which he was told to detonate at the next Shura council meeting. They were each found guilty of "sodomy, treason, and attempted murder", and sentenced to death by firing squad. The trial, and the execution, were filmed and copies of the film were distributed by al-Jihad. When the Sudanese found out about the executions in its jurisdiction, al-Zawahiri and the rest of EIJ were ordered to leave the Sudan. It was a devastating blow to the group. "In Zawahiri's hands, al-Jihad had splintered into angry and homeless gangs."

Bin Laden was also weakened by this failed operation. The core of his al-Qaeda group was made up of members of Islamic Jihad. Because of Sudan's collaboration in the plot, the United Nations voted to impose sanction on the country. To rehabilitate itself in the international community, the Sudanese government pressured bin Laden to leave the country. Bin Laden and many EIJ returned to war torn Afghanistan having lost many members and almost all of bin Laden's assets. On November 19, 1995 EIJ bombed the Egyptian embassy in Islamabad killing 16 and wounding 60. The attack served as a prototype for future attacks by its sister organization al-Qaeda, such as the 1998 bombings of American embassies in Africa.

Albania

According to journalist Lawrence Wright, based on testimony given at the trial of the Albanian cell members in the late 1990s or early 00's, EIJ membership had dwindled to 40 members outside Egypt, and none at all inside the country where "the movement had been eradicated". In 1998, three al-Jihad members were arrested in Albania, and the United States intervened to ensure they were extradited to Egypt to face charges.

In Afghanistan Zawahiri wrote the 1998 fatwa for the "International Islamic Front for Jihad Against Jews and Crusaders," calling for the killing of Americans and their allies, both civilian and military, which was signed by representatives of several jihadi organizations, including EIJ. In August 1998, Issam Abdel-Tawab was extradited to Egypt from Bulgaria.

Dissent among EIJ members to this change of direction and abandonment of the taking over Egypt as the group's primary goal, was so strong that "in the end, Zawahiri pledged to resign if the members failed to endorse his actions.

The organization was in such disarray because of arrests and defections, and so close to bankruptcy, that the only choice was to follow Zawahiri or abandon al-Jihad." One of those who did abandon al-Jihad was Zawahiri's own brother Muhammed, the military commander of EIJ.

Merger with al-Qaeda

In June 2001, Al Qaeda and Egyptian Islamic Jihad merged into an entity formally called jamaa'at Qa'idat al-Jihad, with leadership of EIJ "comprises the majority" – six of nine seats – "of al Qaeda's ruling council (shura)."

Consequently it often considered synonymous with Al-Qaeda, (for example by the U.S. Treasury Department), although some refer to it as a separate organization with al-Zawahiri as its leader and global Jihad's main ideologist.

Activities

The organization specializes in armed attacks against high-level Egyptian Government personnel, including cabinet ministers, and car-bombings against official US and Egyptian facilities. The original Jihad was responsible for the attempted assassinations of Interior Minister Hassan al-Alfi in August 1993 and Prime Minister Atef Sedky in November 1993. Egyptian Jihad and rival armed group launched a wave of violence against Egypt's secular government in 1992, a campaign they only abandoned at the end of the decade. Nearly 1300 people died in the unrest, including policemen and government officials. It is responsible for the Egyptian Embassy bombing in Islamabad, Pakistan in 1995. In 1998 a planned attack against the US Embassy in Albania was thwarted by a roundup of suspects who are now called the Returnees from Albania.

Leadership

Al-Sharif passed the Jihad leadership to Ayman al-Zawahri amid dissent within the movement in the mid 1980's. The al-Zawahri faction subsequently formed an alliance with Al-Qaeda leading over time to the effective merger of the two groups operations inside Afghanistan.

Although al-Zawahri is frequently referred to as a 'lieutenant' or 'second in command' of Al Qaeda this description is misleading as it implies a hierarchical relationship.

The modern Al Qaeda organization is the combination of Bin Laden's financial resources with al-Zawahri's ideological and operational leadership. Despite the effective merger of al-Zawahri and Bin Laden's groups in the *Afghanistan* area of operations there is evidence that suggests that at least part of the Islamic Jihad group continuing to operate in Egypt remains independent of Bin Laden's organization and reports to al-Zawahri personally.

External Aid

The extent of its aid from outside of Egypt is not known. The Egyptian Government claims that both Iran and Osama bin Laden support the Islamic Jihad. It also may obtain some funding through various Islamic non-governmental organizations, cover businesses, and criminal acts. Unlike other militant counterparts, EIJ was noted for condemning only the government as *apostate,* and seeking to recruit soldiers, reporters and government workers who were untainted by jahiliyya. Iraq March 1993 agreed to renew relations with the Islamic Jihad Organization in Egypt.

LASHKAR-E-TAIBA

Lashkar-e-Taiba literally *Army of the Good,* translated as *Army of the Righteous,* or *Army of the Pure*) — also transliterated as Lashkar-i-Tayyaba, Lashkar-e-Tayyaba, Lashkar-e-Tayyiba, Lashkar-i-Taiba, Lashkar Taiba or LeT — is one of the largest and most active militant Islamist terrorist-designated organizations in South Asia, operating mainly from Pakistan.

It was founded by Hafiz Muhammad Saeed and Zafar Iqbal in Afghanistan. With its headquarters based in Muridke, near Lahore in Punjab province of Pakistan, the group operates several training camps in Pakistan-administered Kashmir. Lashkar-e-Taiba members have carried out major attacks against India and its objective is to introduce an Islamic state in South Asia and to "liberate" Muslims residing in Indian Kashmir. The organization is banned as a terrorist organization by India, Pakistan, the United States, the United Kingdom, the European Union, Russia and Australia. As of December 2008 U.S. intelligence officials believed that Pakistan's main intelligence agency, the Inter-Services Intelligence (ISI), continued to give LeT intelligence help and protection.

Objective

The group was recently taken out in a covert operation undertaken by the Indian cabinet. Most praise is given to the Minister of Power for constructing several dams around the region and cutting all communication. While the primary area of operations of the their terrorist activities is the Kashmir valley, the outfit is also active in the Jammu region besides having undertaken repeated and confirmed terrorist attacks in other parts of India and on Indian humanitarian mission in Afghanistan. Their professed goal is not limited to challenging India's sovereignty over Jammu and Kashmir. Their aims include establishing an Islamic state in South Asia and uniting all Muslim-majority regions in countries that surround Pakistan to raise Jihad against all non-Muslim communities.

LeT sees the issue of Kashmir as part of a wider global struggle. The group has repeatedly claimed through its journals and websites that its main aim is to destroy the Indian republic and to annihilate Hinduism and Judaism. LeT has declared Hindus and Jews to be the "enemies of Islam", as well as India and Israel to be the "enemies of Pakistan". In a pamphlet entitled "Why Are We Waging Jihad?" the group defined its agenda as the restoration of Islamic rule over all parts of India and declared India, Israel and the United States as existential enemies of Islam.

In the wake of the November 2008 Mumbai attacks, investigations of computer and email accounts revealed a list of 320 locations worldwide deemed as possible targets for attack. Only 20 of the targets were locations within India. Analysts believed that the list was a statement of intent rather than a list of locations where LeT cells had been established and were ready to strike. In January 2009 the LeT publicly declared that it would pursue a peaceful resolution in the Kashmir issue and that it did not have global jihadist aims.

Formation

LeT gained prominence in the early 1990s as a military offshoot of Markaz-ud Dawa-wal-Irshad. In May 1990, as hostilities between India and Pakistan over the Kashmir issue and the Siachen conflict had increased considerably to be on the verge of war, Lashkar-e-Taiba was formed in Afghanistan's Kunar province, with the sole aim of providing volunteers for the Pakistani Army aided militancy in Indian Kashmir. The logistical and intelligence support was provided by ISI.

It was at a time when militancy in Kashmir was at its peak (which had started in 1987), but most Kashmiri militants were secular nationalists who advocated an independent Kashmir as opposed to "secession to Pakistan" which the religiously-motivated militant groups advocated. Lashkar-e-Taiba was at that time the only militant organization whose aim was to forcefully secede Kashmir to Pakistan. It was formed in 1990 with the blessings and design of the then Army chief General Mirza Aslam Baig and the Prime Minister Nawaz Sharif. The newly formed organization was assured supply of arms and veterans left over from the anti-Soviet Afghan War of the 1980s, as well as access to the training camps which were used to train the Afghan Mujahideen in the 1980s.

Most of these training camps were located in North-West Frontier Province (NWFP) and many were shifted to Azad Kashmir for the sole purpose of training volunteers for the Kashmir Jihad. From 1991 onwards, militancy surged in Indian Kashmir, as many Lashkar-e-Taiba volunteers were infiltrated into Indian Kashmir from Azad Kashmir with the help of the Pakistan Army and ISI. As of 2010, the degree of control that Pakistani intelligence retains over LeT's operations is not known.

PAKISTANIS AND INDIANS WANT IMPROVED RELATIONS

Even though tensions between Pakistan and India loom large, publics in both countries are supportive of greater diplomatic and economic ties across the border. Large majorities of Pakistanis (70%) and Indians (74%) say it is important that relations between the two countries improve. Both publics also want more bilateral trade – nearly seven-in-ten (69%) Pakistanis see increasing trade with India as a good thing, while 67% of Indians also support this idea. In addition to trade ties, majorities in both countries are supportive of further diplomatic talks between the two nations.

At the crux of tensions between India and Pakistan lies the Kashmir dispute.

Nearly three-fourths (73%) of Pakistanis consider the Kashmir dispute a very big problem. Majorities in both countries think it is important to find a resolution to the Kashmir issue, but Pakistanis are more likely than Indians to give this issue high salience (80% vs. 66% very important). Majorities of Pakistanis across age, education and ethnic groups agree that resolving this issue is very important.

Many Say U.S. Tilts Toward India

Pakistanis are considerably less likely than Indians to see American policies in the region as fair toward both countries. Only 9% of Pakistanis see the U.S. approach in the sub-continent as fair, while more than half (52%) say U.S. policies favour India. Only 6% believe that U.S. policies favour Pakistan. Solid majorities of Punjab residents (63%) and PML-N supporters (69%) believe that American policies are biased in favour of India.

Indians are more divided on this issue. Nearly three-in-ten (27%) say that U.S. policies in the region are balanced, while a similar proportion (29%) believes that the U.S. favors India. Only 13% say that Pakistan garners greater favour.

Many in both countries think the India-U.S. relationship has grown stronger in recent years. A plurality of Indians (46%) says relations between their country and the U.S. have improved. An equal number (46%) of Pakistanis agree that India-U.S. relations have improved, up from 37% last year.

2011 India–Pakistan border shooting

The 2011 India–Pakistan border shooting incident took place between 30 August (Tuesday) and 1 September 2011 (Thursday) across the Line of Control in Kupwara District/Neelam Valley resulting in one Indian soldier and three Pakistani soldiers being killed. Both countries gave different accounts of the incident, each accusing the other of initiating the hostilities.

Incident

Pakistani sources claimed that the fighting started when Indian border security forces opened fire on a Pakistani checkpoint based on the Line of Control in the Neelam Valley of Azad Kashmir, Pakistan. The Inter Services Public Relationsspokesman Major General Athar Abbas confirmed the incident had taken place while talking to BBC Urdu. Abbas dubbed the attack as unprovoked and said the attack had been protested with India during a border meeting. He claimed that three soldiers were moving from one post to another when they got lost during bad weather and after a 24-hour search, their bodies were recovered. Lieutenant-Colonel J.S. Brar, spokesman for the Indian Army, claimed that the incident started when Pakistan made an infiltration bid in the Keran Sector of Kupwara District,Jammu and Kashmir on Tuesday (30 August 2011) which was foiled by Indian security forces. He claimed that on Wednesday (31 August 2011) night, at around 20:00 hours, an Indian border post was fired on by Pakistani troops. Following the first shots, both sides engaged in a firefight, with the Indians claiming that heavy mortars and machine guns were used, and that the shooting lasted for about 50 minutes. Accusing Pakistan of two ceasefire violations in the space of fifteen hours, India claimed that the exchange of fire continued at 1100 hours the following day after a brief lull.

Casualties

India confirmed the death of one soldier during the incident. He was identified as *Naib Subedar* Gurdayal Singh. Pakistan announced that three soldiers of the irregular Mujahid Battalion were also killed.

Diplomatic damage from latest India-Pakistan border clashes

On 6 August 2013, five Indian soldiers were shot dead in an ambush in Indian-controlled Kashmir, near the India-Pakistan Line of Control (LoC). While it is unclear who was responsible for the attack, blame has been attributed to either militants backed by the Pakistan Army, or the Pakistani Special Forces themselves. Although Pakistan has denied any involvement and its Prime Minister, Nawaz Sharif, has sent his condolences over the killings, tensions have markedly increased. Intermittent exchanges of small arms fire across the LoC have occurred throughout the week, wounding several soldiers and civilians. The most recent incident occurred on 11 August, with both sides using machine guns.

Comment

While the incident on 6 August and the following border skirmishes are unlikely to escalate into more serious military actions, they are likely to damage the efforts of the Indian and Pakistani governments to improve relations between their countries. Both governments are showing restraint and a willingness to co-operate at the moment, but political pressure over a similar incident in January 2013, forced the Indian Prime Minister, Manmohan Singh, to suspend the official dialogue with Pakistan.

Talks between Indian and Pakistani bureaucrats over their territorial disputes were scheduled to restart this month, but that is now doubtful; many in India's opposition are stridently opposed to them taking place. The main Indian opposition party recently demanded that Singh's government cancel a planned meeting with Sharif in New York next month and even scale down relations with Pakistan by recalling the Indian High Commissioner to Islamabad. With elections in India due next May, Singh's government is particularly susceptible to agitation from the Indian opposition and the notoriously jingoistic media, which could force it to take a harder stance against Pakistan. Although the current administration favours dialogue to reach a consensus with Pakistan, the public mood in India will make this politically difficult.

Singh's government is frequently painted as being weak on border protection, owing to the incursions by Chinese and Pakistani forces at various times through the past year. Since the Indian Government is already contending with domestic anger over the rising cost of living, it is likely that it will heed calls to take some action to shore up its support, rather than just wait out the media storm before quietly restarting talks. While India's reaction is unlikely to be as extreme as the opposition and sections of the media are calling for, the government will almost certainly suspend the talks and make a diplomatic protest.

Perhaps a greater concern not just for relations in the sub-continent but for the region and beyond, is that this event highlights the Pakistani government's lack of control over at least some elements of its military forces and the militants aligned with Pakistan. The government of Prime Minister Sharif has been seeking to re-engage in dialogue with India for some time now, making it highly unlikely that it would have authorised such an attack. Consequently, although the efforts by Sharif to ease tensions and rebuild trust are widely seen as sincere, questions will again begin to rise about his government's ability to deliver on its peace agreements.

When India, or indeed any country, enters into security-based talks with Pakistan, the issue of how Pakistan can control its rogue elements and prevent them from tarnishing any deal, will need to be factored into the discussions. Given that Pakistan's democracy is newly established, it is unlikely to be able to give any reliable guarantees in this area. That alone may provide the Indian Government with a reasonable excuse for suspending the talks with Pakistan, now that it is politically expedient for them to do so.

Indo-Pakistan Border

India shares 3323 km long and complicated boundary with Pakistan. The India-Pakistan boundary is categorised under three different heads. The first is the international boundary also known as the 'Radcliff line'. It is 2308 km long and stretches from Gujarat to parts of Jammu district in Jammu and Kashmir. The second is the line of control (LoC), or the Cease Fire Line, which came into existence after the 1948 and 1971 wars between India and Pakistan. This line is 776 km long, and runs along the districts of Jammu (some parts), Rajouri, Poonch, Baramula, Kupwara, Kargil and some portions of Leh. And the third is the actual ground position line (AGPL), which is 110 km long and extends from NJ 9842 to Indira Col in the North. The LoC and the AGPL has been a scene of constant tensions with border skirmishes and firing between the armies and border guarding forces of both countries. The LoC has been vulnerable to constant infiltration by foreign terrorists, Kashmiri separatists and Pakistani army regulars for long.

Like the Bangladesh boundary, the India-Pakistan boundary also does not follow any geographical barrier. It runs through diverse terrain like deserts, marshes, plains, snow clad mountains, and winds its way through villages, houses and agricultural lands making it extremely porous. Porosity of this border has facilitated various illegal activities such as smuggling, drugs and arms trafficking, and infiltration. Heroin and fake Indian currency are the two predominant items of smuggling along this border. Other items include saffron, textile, mercury, which are smuggled from Pakistan. The villagers adjacent to the border are alleged to be involved in smuggling in a big way. Money laundering is also quite rampant along the border. A large scale hawala network is flourishing in Punjab, especially in Ludhiana. In addition, the border population has also been subjected to hostile propaganda by Pakistan designed to mislead and sway their loyalties. The Sir Creek area, due to its peculiar terrain, makes the movement of border guarding forces very difficult and thus, provides scope for illegal fishing in the creeks.

Future Options for Declaration of the Dispute

Over the past fifty years, besides the UN resolutions, observers and intellectuals have proposed various other options for resolving the Kashmir dispute time and again at the UN fora and at the bilateral India-Pakistan levels.

UN Resolutions: The Plebiscite Option

The UN Security Council resolutions of August 13, 1948 and January 5, 1949, proposed the plebiscite option for resolving the Kashmir dispute. However, it is important to note that the Government of India itself accepted *plebiscite* or *referendum* as a right of the Kashmiri people, when it filed the initial complaint against Pakistan before the United Nations on January 1, 1948, as pointed out in Part I of this paper. Beginning with Governor General Mountbatten, Indian leaders like Prime Minister Nehru also repeatedly made the commitment to 'the will of the Kashmiri people'.

After India filed its initial complaint, the UN Security Council passed the two important resolutions of August 13, 1948 and January 5, 1949. These resolutions laid down the principles and procedures for a free and impartial plebiscite under UN auspices. Broadly, the resolution of January 5, 1949, stated: '(a) the question of the accession of the State of Jammu and Kashmir to India and Pakistan, would be decided through the democratic method of a free and impartial plebiscite after the cease-fire and truce agreement provided for in the Resolution of August 13 had been carried out; (b) the Secretary General of the UN would nominate a Plebiscite Administrator, who would be appointed by the government of Jammu and Kashmir and given powers which he considers necessary for holding a free and impartial plebiscite; (c) on implementation of the ceasefire and the truce agreement, the Commission and the Plebiscite Administrator would determine, in consultation with the Government of India, the final disposal of Indian and State Armed Forces, as well as the Forces in Azad Kashmir (in consultation with the local authorities); (d) persons who had entered the State since August 15, 1947 would be required to leave the State, and citizens of the State who had left the State on account of disturbances would be allowed to return.' Both India and Pakistan accepted the above UN Resolutions. However, later, differences arose over the interpretation of various clauses of the resolutions, especially on the issues of demilitarisation and disbandment/disarming of the 'Azad Kashmir' forces.

India gave its own interpretation to the agreement and suggested that the Azad Kashmir forces be disbanded and the defence and administrative responsibility of the region be given to India and Indian Kashmiri authorities. Pakistan, on the other hand, was in favour of a complete and simultaneous withdrawal of armed forces personnel by both the countries.

On this issue, the President of the Security Council, General McNaughton, in his proposal of December 22, 1949, in para 2, clarified that the Resolutions of 1948 and 1949 called for demilitarisation of the whole State of Jammu and Kashmir and not merely Azad Kashmir: that 'demilitarisation should include the withdrawal from the State of Jammu and Kashmir of the regular forces of Pakistan; and the withdrawal of the regular forces of India not required for purposes of security or for the maintenance of local law and order.'

The UN Security Council passed Resolution 80 on March 14, 1950, which called upon the Governments of India and Pakistan 'to prepare and execute within a period of five months from the date of this resolution a programme of demilitarisation on the basis of the principles of paragraph 2 of General McNaughton's proposal, or of such modifications of those principles as may be mutually agreed.' Pakistan accepted that Resolution as well, but India maintained its position as regards the demilitarisation issue.

The UN Security Council passed Resolution 98, in December 1952. The UNSC Resolution, regarding demilitarisation issue clarified that: (Article 4) 'the Governments of India and Pakistan to enter into immediate negotiations under the auspices of the United Nations representative for India and Pakistan in order to reach agreement on the specific number of forces to remain on each side of the cease-fire line at the end of the period of demilitarisation, this number to be between 3,000 and 6,000 armed forces remaining on the Pakistan side of the cease-fire line and between 12,000 and 18,000 armed forces remaining on the India side of the cease-fire line.'

Though during the discussions Pakistan's representative to the UN, Mr. Zafrulla Khan, pointed out that the number of forces proposed was not fair, yet he said that Pakistan 'is prepared to go forward on the basis of this resolution.' The Indian representative, Mrs. Pandit, in her speech, however, categorically said, 'I should like to repeat that we reject the proposal in it and we are not prepared to enter into any talks on the basis suggested.'

Regarding the question of plebiscite, Pakistan was in favour of giving complete authority to the UN for holding, organising and supervising the plebiscite. India, on the other hand, only wanted the non-binding advice of the UN. Various UN mediators were appointed to resolve this issue, but no one was successful in convincing India on a compromise. Sir Owen Dixon, the UN mediator, in his report submitted in 1950, wrote: 'In the end I became convinced that India's agreement would never be obtained to demilitarisation in any such form, or to provisions governing the period of plebiscite of any such character, as would in my opinion, permit of the plebiscite being conducted in conditions sufficiently guarding against intimidation and other forms of influence and abuse by which the freedom and fairness of the plebiscite might be imperilled.'

Dr. Frank P. Graham, appointed UN representative for India and Pakistan in 1951, submitted five reports, up to March 1953, but his efforts at mediation also proved to be unsuccessful as India would not agree on the size of the forces to be left on either side of the cease-fire line after demilitarisation. India, therefore, consistently refused to take recourse to all proposals of various statesmen and UN representatives for the holding of a plebiscite in Jammu and Kashmir. On the other hand, it is on record that Pakistan supported all such international mediation and UN efforts. Defending the Indian position on plebiscite, Sisir Gupta, an Indian scholar, wrote: 'it became obvious even at the early stages of the Kashmir dispute that a plebiscite -an "ideal" solution according to some – because of the complexities in Kashmir was difficult to accomplish. Even as a democratic solution, it had loopholes. Kashmir, clearly, is not composed of one people: in religion, it has three major groups; in language, four. If there is a section which wants to secede from India, there are others who do not.' However, the fact of the matter is that, right from the beginning, India feared that if a plebiscite was held it would lose what it had already occupied. According to a Kashmiri activist, Prof. Mrs. Shamim Shawl, 'plebiscite is the most plausible solution of the problem. This has been accepted in the Resolutions of August 48 and January 1949. It is these resolutions, which confirm the disputed character of the problem and negate the Indian position that says Kashmir is an irrevocable part of India. India is in fact challenging the rightful and legal authenticity of the United Nations by delaying the implementation of UN resolutions.' Keeping in view the basic genesis and nature of the dispute, the option incorporated in the then UN resolutions is still valid. The UN resolutions are not time-barred, as observed in 1956, by the UN Secretary General, Dag Hammarskjold, who clarified the important principle that 'the UN decision is valid until it has been invalidated by the organ which took it.'

The UN Trusteeship Option

Generally, this option proposes that Kashmir should be placed under UN Trusteeship and then plebiscite may be held for the final resolution of the dispute. It is argued that this will provide a face-saving for India, and will also give Kashmiris, on both sides of the Line of Control, enough time to come up with a joint option. The JKLF Chairman, Ammanullah Khan in December 1993, proposed: (1) complete, simultaneous withdrawal of Indian and Pakistani troops and civil administration, non-Kashmiri personnel from Jammu and Kashmir; (2) the reunification of Indian and Pakistani-controlled parts of Kashmir; (3) placement of the State under UN control for five to ten years; and (4) holding of a plebiscite. Well-known Pakistani economist, the late Dr. Mahbubul Haq, in an interview he gave to an Urdu Weekly *Hurmat,* in 1994, proposed that only the Kashmir Valley be placed under UN Trusteeship for ten years and then plebiscite be held in the Kashmir Valley.

As India regards Occupied Kashmir as its integral part, it is obvious that it will never voluntarily agree to the placing of the State, or the Kashmir Valley under UN trusteeship. *Secondly,* both the above trusteeship options support the plebiscite option under the UN auspices, an option that has been rejected by India even though in the early years of the dispute India committed itself to holding of the plebiscite.

As regards Pakistan and the Kashmiris, since the above proposals support a UN role and the option of plebiscite, in view of the already existing UN resolutions which provide the plebiscite option under UN auspices, the above proposal would mean unnecessarily prolonging the solution beyond five or ten years. Moreover, according to Article 76 of Chapter XII of the UN Charter one of the basic objectives of the trusteeship system is 'to promote the political, economic, social, and educational advancement of the inhabitants of the trust territories, and their progressive development towards self-government or independence, as may be appropriate to the particular circumstances of each territory and its peoples…' The case of Jammu and Kashmir does not require placement under UN trusteeship as the Kashmiris have, over the years, demonstrated their political will by waging an indigenous movement in Occupied Kashmir for their right of self-determination, underscoring the fact that their preferred option is self-determination.

The Partition Option

Regarding the option of the partition of Jammu and Kashmir, this has largely been an academic debate and various scholars have suggested different proposals. The *first* is a division-related option for Jammu and Kashmir, based on the holding of regional plebiscites.

This proposal was first given by UN Representative, Sir Owen Dixon, in his report of 1950-51. Called the 'Dixon Report', it proposed the idea of holding regional plebiscites, instead of a general plebiscite as proposed in the UN resolutions. The Owen Dixon Plan proposed the division of the State of Jammu and Kashmir into four main regions: Jammu, Ladakh, the Vale of Kashmir including Muzaffarabad, and Gilgit-Baltistan. According to his plan the district of Poonch was to remain with Pakistan. He proposed that of the four regions, Jammu and Ladakh should go uncontested to India and the Northern Areas to Pakistan. He concluded that in the Valley a plebiscite might be held to decide about its future. Pakistan, did not outrightly reject the proposal, but was in favour of a general plebiscite in the whole of Jammu and Kashmir. India on the other hand regarded Jammu and Kashmir as a unit of the Indian Federation and thus was not in favour of any regional plebiscite.

The second partition proposal is an option based on a 'Trieste-type' solution. The Trieste issue, between Italy and Yugoslavia, arose as a result of the two World Wars. After World War I, Trieste and the adjoining areas, including the whole valley of the Adige river and Istria, went to Italy, but in 1945 it was claimed by Yugoslavia on the grounds that Italy was guilty of aggression against Yugoslavia. However, Trieste and its environs and the Gorzia region to the northwest (Zone A) remained under Anglo-American control and the southern portion (Zone B) was under the control of the Yugoslav troops. Finally, in 1954, Italy and Yugoslavia agreed to a partition and Zone A (including Trieste) was given to Italy and Zone B to Yugoslavia. Italy agreed to maintain a free port at Trieste. Later, the agreement was given a *de jure* status by the 1975 Treaty of Osimo between Italy and Yugoslavia.

The 'Trieste'-type option for Jammu and Kashmir proposes that the Valley along with some adjoining parts of Jammu and the Pakistani side of Kashmir (Azad Kashmir), be made an autonomous units, under India and Pakistan, respectively. The LoC would be a soft border between the two autonomous units. The remaining areas on both sides of the LoC may be merged with India and Pakistan, respectively. India and Pakistan would be required to withdraw their forces under UN supervision. Again, this proposal lacks viability, as it does not address either the genesis of the dispute, nor the complexities that have accumulated since then to date. The struggle in Jammu and Kashmir is not for autonomy of any one region but for the right of self-determination to be expressed by the Kashmiris, as granted to them under UN resolutions. Also, India and Pakistan being parties to the dispute will continue to have a clash of interests in the proposed autonomous regions; therefore, this would certainly not result in any stability in the region. Moreover, the option implies that the existing Line of Control (LoC) may serve as the line of division. The LoC remains the UN-recognised ceasefire line (CFL) and was not drawn with any basis for serving as a permanent border, but with the intention of bringing about cessation of military hostilities.

The third partition proposal considers the conversion of the Line of Control (LoC) into an international border. This means maintenance of the prevailing *status quo*. This option is in principle supported by India. If it were accepted, India would take additional advantage by then propagating that it had conceded Indian territory to Pakistan and would try to emerge as a peacemaker in the region. As assessed by Robert Wirsing, 'by asserting the primacy of actual military *control* over punitive legal *entitlement*, it tacitly acknowledges India's dominant political standing in the region. By requiring Pakistan to relinquish its claim of the coveted Valley of Kashmir and the Kashmiri separatists their claim of independence, while at the same time entailing little or no detachment from India of territories now in its possession, it leaves existing political and economic arrangements essentially undisturbed. Thus, of the several conceivable forms of partition, it is clearly among the most generous to India.' However, the 'the LoC as a border' option has to take into account the fact that the LoC is merely a ceasefire line, as well as take stock of the struggle for the right of self-determination that is going on in the Indian-held Kashmir. Moreover, Kashmiris do not recognise the LoC. Prof. Mrs. Shamim Shawl, a Kashmiri scholar from Srinagar, has argued that 'the proposal of division is in contravention of the basic principle that Jammu and Kashmir is an indivisible entity. It also violates the fundamental fact that the Kashmir problem is basically the problem of the people of Jammu and Kashmir. It is not a bilateral problem between India and Pakistan. Nor is it a territorial dispute.' Secondly, the present LoC is an altered ceasefire line, whereby India acquired territory through military aggression in 1971. Therefore, accepting LoC would mean legitimising Indian military aggression. Thirdly, the LoC as accepted by both Pakistan and India at Simla in 1972 does not exist anymore. Indian incursion into Siachen in 1984 has destroyed the sanctity of the ceasefire line.

Fourthly, some Western scholars have proposed the partition of Kashmir along ethnic/cultural, religious, and linguistic lines. For example the *Kashmir Study Group*, a US-based group comprising academics and diplomats from various countries as members, has made various proposals along these lines in its report entitled, *Kashmir: A Way Forward* (September 1999). The proposals suggested are as follows:

Two hypothetical sovereign entities, self-governing in all aspects, established on both sides of the Line of Control on cultural and linguistic grounds. According to the study, 'On the Indian side of the LOC every tahsil in Kashmir proper and in Doda district in Jammu, and Gool Gulab Ghar tahsil in Udhampur district in Jammu would seek incorporation in the proposed state. All these areas are imbued with "Kashmiriyat" or interact with Kashmiri speaking people. On the Pakistani side it is conceivable that the whole of Azad Kashmir would opt to have a sovereign status. This is predominantly Punjabi-speaking, wholly Muslim area';

A new sovereign state on the Indian side of LoC with no territorial exchange between India and Pakistan. The state would include 'within its maximum potential area the whole of Kashmir proper as well as adjoining areas in which Kashmiri is either the majority language or that of a plurality of the population';

Desirable territorial changes along and beyond the Line of Control in Jammu and Kashmir. Viewing that 'LoC is dysfunctional and has been violated innumerable times', it proposes that a new state be created with territorial exchanges between India and Pakistan. However, it proposes that Pakistan gives almost twice as much area (7,366 sq. km) to India, than India ceding territory (4,501 sq. km) to Pakistan. The rationale given for such an exchange is ' overall, the territorial adjustments should not be excessively disruptive of the established order and yet should appear significant and be of such a nature as to allow all parties to claim a victory.'

The above proposals are again not viable solutions, as they tend to complicate the situation in Jammu and Kashmir and result in a further division of the region, rather than leading to a stable solution. Moreover, the 'Kashmir Study Group's' proposals make no provision for the right of self-determination of the people of Kashmir to which presently a military struggle is underway by the Kashmiris in Indian-occupied Kashmir.

The Independence Option

An option gradually evolved as a result of the impasse on the Kashmir issue is that of independence, generally known as the 'Third Option'. Under this option, the pre-Partition status of the Jammu and Kashmir State is to be restored and an independent state established.

The proposal is mainly advocated by the JKLF. Its Chairman, Amanullah Khan, in one of his articles says, 'the future independent Kashmir is to be neutral, like Switzerland, with friendly and trade relations with all its neighbours.'

According to Amanullah Khan's proposal, 'Independent Kashmir is to consist of five federating units: Kashmir Valley, Jammu province, Ladakh, Azad Kashmir and Gilgit-Baltistan, each enjoying considerable internal autonomy, having its own elected provincial government. At the centre there will be a bicameral parliament.' He further says, 'the re-unification and independence of the state can be brought about without making any drastic changes in the existing socio-economic, political and administrative structures of any of the present three units i.e. Indian occupied areas, Azad Kashmir and Gilgit-Baltistan.'

According to Indian scholars 'independence, either for part or all of J&K, is equally unrealistic.

They maintain that although an artificial product of war, the Line of Control does follow a rough and ready ethno-cultural divide in some measure.

Further, "self-determination" within the two parts of J&K could result in the Balkanisation of a mosaic put together by history, with every new 'self-determined' minority being assailed for a newly-created majoritarianism, which lesser minorities refuse to accept. Such an unravelling would be a recipe for strife, insecurity, and destabilisation of the region.' The option for an independent Jammu and Kashmir state does not seem to be a viable solution, as the State would be land-locked and, therefore, permanently dependent on its neighbours. For India the proposition would be unacceptable because it could lead to a similar unravelling in other areas where separatist movements are going on in India.

As regards Pakistan, the 'third option' can be advantageous. An independent Jammu and Kashmir state would have a preference for good relations with a neighbour that has consistently extended its support to the principles of self-determination. Pakistan's position on the 'third option' has been that it should not confound the existent problems further, and, therefore, it stresses the need to address the issue in the light of the Security Council Resolutions, as a first step in the resolution of the dispute.

The Irish Model

Recently, various scholars have suggested the Irish model, based on the 'Good Friday Agreement' signed in April 1998 between the Governments of the United Kingdom of Great Britain and Northern Ireland and the Government of Ireland, as a possible option for resolving the Kashmir dispute between India and Pakistan.

The main features of the 'Good Friday Agreement' are: (a) it recognises the consent principle: that change in the status of Northern Ireland can only come about with the consent of the majority of its people. It acknowledges that while a substantial minority in the North and a majority on the island want a united Ireland, the majority in the North currently wishes to maintain the Union. However, it says that if that situation changes, there is a binding obligation on both governments to give effect to whatever wish the people of the North express; (b) it recognises 'the birthright of all the people of Northern Ireland' to identify themselves and be accepted as Irish, British or both; (c) it proposes concrete legislative and constitutional changes; such as, the Government of Ireland Act, claiming British jurisdiction over all of Ireland is to be replaced, future polls in the North on its status are to be held on the order of the Secretary of State for Northern Ireland. Such polls must be at least seven years apart; (d) it proposes a 108-member Assembly elected by proportional representation; (e) it establishes a North-South Ministerial Council under legislation at Westminister and the Oireachtas, to bring together ministers from the North and the Republic; (f) it establishes a British-Irish Council consisting of representatives of the British and Irish Governments, devolved in situations in Northern Ireland, Scotland and Wales, the Isle of Man and the Channel Islands; (g) it establishes a new British-Irish Conference; (h) reaffirms commitment to the total disarmament of all paramilitary organisations, and confirms intention to work constructively with the Independent Commission on Decommissioning; and, (i) establishes an independent commission to make recommendations for future policing arrangements in the North.

Based on the Irish model, some Indian scholars have made suggestions supporting autonomy for various regions of Jammu and Kashmir. For example, Amit A. Pandya, an Indian scholar, has proposed the following steps: (1) An India-Pakistan commission to discuss boundary issues in Jammu and Kashmir, and to engage in joint monitoring of the LOC; (2) Phased demilitarisation at the LOC, contingent first on substantial cessation of 'cross-border' terrorism; (3) Three-way (Indian, Pakistani, Kashmiri) commission on internal law and order. Kashmiris to be chosen from Pakistan-occupied Azad Kashmir and all Indian-occupied segments—Valley, Jammu and Ladakh. (4) Indian and Pakistani commitments to proceed with a scheme of local government reform and strengthening of local institutions and local autonomy in respective areas of Kashmir. (5) Issue-specific consultative bodies (water, power, tourism, finance) comprising such local units, and Indian Jammu & Kashmir State and Azad Kashmir governments. (6) Regularly scheduled and publicity-free consultative mechanism for Indian government's talks with all parties, and with non-party civil society institutions, within Indian Kashmir on political issues. (7) Corresponding mechanism for Azad Kashmir. (8) Consultative mechanism for talks among all parties on ethnic and religious minority protections. (9) Consultative mechanism for dialogue between these processes on the Indian and Pakistani side of the LOC. (10) Indian commitment to allow free access, consistent with security requirements, to independent and credible Indian human rights monitoring organizations, and to Indian, and Pakistani press. Corresponding commitment by Pakistan for Azad Kashmir.

Another Indian scholar, Professor Sumantra Bose, basing his suggestions on the Irish model proposes three dimensions. *Dimension one: the New Delhi-Islamabad axis,* involving the 'establishment of a permanent India-Pakistan Intergovernmental Conference to promote the harmonious and mutually beneficial development of the totality of relationships between the two countries.' As suggested by Professor Bose, this body is to be chaired by the respective prime ministers, and its twice-yearly meetings to be rotated between Indian and Pakistani cities. *Dimension two: the New Delhi-Srinagar and Islamabad-Muzaffarabad axis,* here the 'objective in Kashmir would be the gradual, incremental normalisation of politics within Kashmir in both Indian-and Pakistani-controlled zones, and the devising and implementation of political frameworks which can foster a working degree of internal accommodation and cooperation between the representatives of communities holding radically different basic political allegiances.' *Dimension three: the Srinagar-Muzaffarabad axis,* proposes 'along with the progressive normalisation of the overall framework of India-Pakistan relations and the gradual normalisation of life and politics in both sides of the Kashmir border', that there is greater need to make the border porous. He further suggests 'the establishment of a cross-border Jammu and Kashmir Council for Cooperation, with representatives from inclusive, elected and autonomous governments from both sides of the line of control.'

These Indian proposals, selectively use the Irish model, but basically support autonomy for the regions of Jammu and Kashmir under the supervision of India and Pakistan. The central aspects focusing on self-determination and total disarmament after implementation of the agreement are ignored. The Indian proposals are similar to the idea of a condominium with dominant Indian influence. Also, the LoC has been proposed as the dividing line and a soft border. This is against the genesis of the Kashmir dispute, which is not for greater autonomy or 'self-government', as proposed, but for the right of self-determination to be expressed by the Kashmiris. However, as Dr. Mazari has suggested, it is the central aspects of the Irish model, which are relevant in case of the Kashmir dispute and could be used as guiding principles for a resolution of the conflict. For instance the underlying principle is *recognition of the right of the people as of Northern Ireland* to choose their political future through a referendum. Also, the principle of deweaponisation is linked to it, as following the implementation of the Agreement.

NEW FACETS IN INDIA-PAKISTAN RELATIONS

The terrorist attacks of September 11, 2001 in New York and Washington have had profound implications on developments in India-Pakistan relations. The American led offensive against the Taliban resulted in an end to Taliban rule and the installation of a democratically elected Government headed by President Hamid Karzai in Afghanistan.

But, the Taliban, the Al Qaeda and their allies affiliated to the "International Islamic Front" formed by Osama bin Laden in February 1998, retreated into safe havens across the Afghanistan-Pakistan border. They set up base in Baluchistan and the tribal areas (North and South Waziristan) of Pakistan's Northwest Frontier Province. While Pakistan assisted the US and its western allies in tracking down some Al Qaeda leaders, the Taliban leadership was not touched.

It has now regrouped and commenced attacking American led NATO forces in Afghanistan's Southern and Eastern Provinces, adjacent to Afghanistan's borders with Pakistan. One major impact of the removal of the Taliban from power and the passage of UN Security Council Resolution 1363 was the decision by western powers to ban all those organizations affiliated with Osama bin Laden's "International Islamic Front".

The organizations that were thus banned included four extremist Islamist groups backed by Pakistan's Inter Services Intelligence (ISI) that were playing a leading role in terrorist violence in Jammu and Kashmir (J&K) The terrorist organizations banned internationally included the *Lashkar e taiba*, the *Harkat ul Mujahidee* n, the *Harkat ul Jihad ul Islami* and the *Jaish e Mohammed*. While these organizations continue to operate under new names, the Pakistan Government came to realize that mere resort to terrorist violence in an attempt to force India out of J&K was proving counterproductive and that political initiatives had to be undertaken, if the international community was to be persuaded of Pakistan's commitment to ending terrorist violence and normalizing relations with India.

These developments have resulted in a sustained dialogue between India and Pakistan over the past three years, to enhance cooperation and promote confidence. An agreement has been signed on prior notification of missile tests and measures to avoid incidents at sea between the two navies are being finalized.

New border routes have been opened for travel between the two countries and travel between the two sides of Jammu and Kashmir between Srinagar and Muzzafarabad has resumed after lapse of nearly half a century. It has been agreed for the first time to promote trade across the LOC in J&K. Similar travel arrangements are envisaged between Poonch in the Jammu Region and Rawalkot across the LOC. India has proposed further easing of restrictions for travel between the two sides of Jammu and Kashmir by opening bus routes between Kargil and Skardu in the isolated "Northern Areas" of the State. Most importantly, a cease fire across the Line of Control has been observed by both sides since November 2003.

It was in this background that President Musharraf stated that progress could be made in resolving the issue of J&K only if both sides explore mutually acceptable proposals. He has proposed that J&K should be divided into seven different regions, followed by the "demilitarization" of identified regions. He has specifically demanded that Indian forces should be withdrawn from the urban centres of Baramulla, Kupwara and Srinagar. President Musharraf has also advocated "self governance" in J&K without clarifying whether such "self governance" would be equally applicable to areas under Pakistan's control. Finally, he has proposed that there should be a system of "Joint Management" of Jammu and Kashmir by India and Pakistan. While welcoming "new ideas" from President Musharraf, India's Prime Minister Dr. Manmohan Singh has proposed that while borders cannot be changed they can be made "irrelevant" or just "mere lines on a map".

He has said that people of both sides of the Line of Control (LOC) in J&K should be allowed to move and trade freely across the LOC. Responding to General Musharraf's proposal of "Joint Management", Dr. Manmohan Singh has suggested that India and Pakistan should devise "cooperative and consultative mechanisms" to promote cooperation across Jammu and Kashmir. Discussions between India and Pakistan on these proposals have been taking place in recent months. Measures to resolve the issue of J&K figured prominently for the first time when the Foreign Secretaries of India and Pakistan met in New Delhi in November 2006. New Delhi appears to be ready to discuss General Musharraf's proposal for "selfgovernance" and would be quite prepared to discuss greater devolution of powers and autonomy in a manner under which there is harmonization in the nature and extent of self-governance and devolution of powers on both sides of the LOC in J&K. At the present moment, the State of J&K under Indian Administration enjoys far greater autonomy than the regions of "Azad Kashmir" and the "Northern Areas" under Pakistan's control. Both "Azad Kashmir" and the "Northern Areas" are directly administered by governing "Councils" presided over by the Prime Minister of Pakistan who wields his authority through the Federal Ministry of Kashmir Affairs. Local representatives of these areas have virtually no powers, even in the appointment of Government functionaries.

Given Pakistan's continuing assistance to armed terrorist groups functioning out of Muzzafarabad in "Azad Kashmir" under the banner of a "United Jihad Council" India cannot obviously agree to any proposal for the "demilitarization" of areas it presently governs in J&K. Moreover, J&K lies on the vital lines of communications to India's western borders with China. Free movement and deployment of India's forces in J&K is, therefore, essential for the security of its frontiers with China. But, should Pakistan effectively ban and disarm groups waging *"Jihad"* in Jammu and Kashmir from territory under its control, India could consider redeployment and reduction of its forces in J&K, provided Pakistan takes corresponding measures on its side of the LOC, both in "Azad Kashmir" and the "Northern Areas'.

These are issues that appear to have figured in both formal and informal discussions between India and Pakistan in recent months. While these "new ideas" for resolving Jammu and Kashmir have figured prominently in discussions and have been the focus of extensive media attention, one has to inject a sense of caution and realism on the path ahead.

President Karzai has made no secret of his conviction that the Musharraf Government is actively aiding, arming, training and providing safe haven for the Taliban on Pakistani territory. There are, similarly, strong sentiments in India that the Pakistan Government continues to use terrorism as an instrument of State policy to promote its interests and territorial ambitions. The revival of the Taliban has encouraged Pakistan based terrorist groups like the *Lashkar e Taiba* that the climate is ripe to promote *Jihad* not merely in Jammu and Kashmir, but in other parts of India also.

Further, if borders are indeed to be made "irrelevant" as proposed by Dr. Manmohan Singh then Pakistan will have to remove existing trade and economic restrictions on relations with India and join with other South Asian countries in SAARC to make South Asia and Economic Community for the free movement of goods, services and investment within the next fifteen years. Pakistan appears to be totally averse to moving in this direction. There is thus a climate of continuing uncertainty about the directions Pakistan's policies will take in coming months. Much will depend on political developments within Pakistan in coming months. Both India and Afghanistan will have to wait and see whether the post-election political scenario in 2007 in Pakistan results in moderate elements opposed to religious extremism taking over the reins of Government, or whether the Islamist elements in the army and in the political set up will retain their hold over the conduct of Pakistan's policies.

PAKISTAN'S POLICY IN THE CHANGING SCENARIO

The events of 9/11, the attack on the Indian parliament, and the following war-like situation between India and Pakistan not only greatly impacted the Kashmiri resistance movement but also compelled Islamabad to change its track on Kashmir. Moreover, the unfriendly international environment and Pakistan's deep involvement in Afghanistan forced Islamabad to rethink its relations with India and its Kashmir policy. The decision of General Pervez Musharraf to join the US-led War on Terror was also a factor in changing Islamabad's strategic position on Kashmir, particularly in terms of its ideological foundation. The economic condition of the country, unrest in the tribal areas, and — allegedly externally sponsored — violence in some parts of Balochistan, and the growing engagement along the Afghan border also played an instrumental role in bringing about a paradigm shift in Islamabad's thinking towards India. It is also said that Pakistan's trusted friends, like China and

Saudi Arabia, advised it to seek an unconventional way out for a lasting deal with India over the Kashmir issue and bilateral relations; besides, constant persuasion from the United States also continued.

Pakistan's capacity to protract the low cost conflict in Kashmir is beyond any doubt. Although the likely spillover effects of this on Pakistan's polity are obvious, they will be, to a great degree, manageable. On the other hand, despite its conventional military superiority and strong diplomatic backing from the world, India could not subdue the resolve of Pakistan to support Kashmir's right to self-determination and its demand for sovereign equality with India. Pakistan's ties with the United States, and its role as an ally of the West, are considered advantageous for seeking a settlement of the Kashmir issue. As the country's former Foreign Secretary Shamshad Ahmad observed:

> We cannot deny the post-9/11 reality that our "friends," the Americans, now have deeper than ever stakes in India-Pakistan rapprochement as a factor of stability for regional and global peace.

The 'covert' US engagement with Islamabad, Delhi and Kashmiris is no longer a secret. Washington has expressed its desire at a number of times to help settle the Kashmir issue within the existing territorial parameters but with minor realignment. It views India as a potential rival to China, not only in the region but also in global affairs. Siddharth Srivastava, a New Delhi-based journalist, observes:

> The US is striving to build India as a strategic counterweight to China, along with Japan and Australia.

Termed as naïve by critics, Pakistan's calculations of the ground realities are optimistic, being based on the belief that India will never be able to bring normalcy into Kashmir because Kashmiris are highly skeptical towards it, and that India will need Pakistan's support and will ultimately make tangible transformations in its current stance over Kashmir. The majority of Kashmiris do not trust the Indian government and, ever since the eruption of the resistance, their aspiration for the right of self-determination has multiplied manifold and now cuts across even the hardcore pro-India circles in the Kashmir Valley. India's carrot and stick tactics and the brutalities of its forces have alienated the local population and invoked armed resistance, which may not die down easily. It is this assessment of the situation that emboldened Islamabad to make tangible concessions on Kashmir and bring India to the table for talks. Some also believe that the personal ambition of the President Musharraf — his wish to be regarded in history as a statesman who settled one of the world's most complicated disputes — is a driving factor that has brought essential changes in Islamabad's policies.

Besides various other factors that caused India and Pakistan to change their policies on the Kashmir issue, back channel diplomacy led by the US played a major role in alleviating the crisis and creating a viable atmosphere for initiatives towards a comprehensive normalization process.

Change in India's Approach

For a long time, India's approach for dealing with Pakistan had revolved mainly around zero tolerance in any concerns related to India's security or political ideology. However, its inability to 'punish' Pakistan and to break its back economically (by creating a war-like environment in the region) had a sobering impact on the Indian mindset and led New Delhi to conclude that its conventional policies vis-à-vis Pakistan and Kashmir were getting nowhere. In the past, New Delhi had publicly pronounced several times that it would take punitive action and destroy what it alleged were militant training camps inside Azad Jammu and Kashmir (AJK) by air strikes. However, its hostile attitude did not yield the desired results and Islamabad did not succumb to its pressure.

At the same time, economic tycoons and multinational companies were pressuring the Indian government to normalize relations with Islamabad as hostile relations between the two neighbors and the constant fear of war had a negative impact on business activity and international investment. New Delhi needed peace in the region and internal stability to continue its current annual growth rate of 8-10 percent and obtain further foreign investment. As one researcher on the peace process put it:

Improved relations would lead to improved trade: there was money to be made, and this had become a strategic objective for both Islamabad and New Delhi.

India realized that its successful economic journey would cease if it did not settle disputes with Pakistan. It had to think about the immense potential in bilateral trade and in trade with landlocked Afghanistan and Central Asia via Pakistan. Besides, India aspires for a permanent seat in the UN Security Council for which it had to ensure friendly relations with neighbors and settle the Kashmir issue in the context of which India is regarded among those countries that did not comply with the UNSC resolutions. Moreover, the Kashmir resistance poses a huge financial burden on the Indian treasury. It is also acknowledged that the Indian security forces do not have the capacity to fix the problem; rather, they invite anger by frequently committing severe human rights violations that aggravate the already complex situation.

After the withdrawal of Indian forces from the Pakistani borders, Pakistan made a chain of unilateral concessions pronounced by President General Musharraf himself. It began with a unilateral ceasefire on LoC announced by Prime Minister Zaffarullah Khan Jamali in November 2003. In the following month, speaking to *Reuters*, General Musharraf said he had "left aside" the 55-year-old demand for a UN mandated plebiscite on Kashmir and wished to meet India "halfway" in a bid for peace in the subcontinent.

These multiple pulls created a sense of obligation among the Indian ruling elite to at least take some measures to show that they were serious about settling the problems. Eventually, the Indian Prime Minister Atal Behari Vajpayee went to Kupwara in the south of the Kashmir Valley and offered a hand of friendship to Pakistan in April 2004. This was regarded a departure from the conventional Indian thinking on Kashmir and Pakistan, and paved the way for further initiatives on Kashmir. It also created a palatable environment for Vajpayee to visit Islamabad to attend the South Asian Association for Regional Cooperation (SAARC) summit.

Musharraf's 'Out of the Box' Thinking

Islamabad has consistently said that it supports the resistance in IHK diplomatically and politically, and has nothing to do with the armed struggle. It has also invariably linked talks with India with progress on the Kashmir settlement. But it relinquished both of these stands in the quest to find a compromised solution. Pakistan accepted the responsibility to rein in militants operating from areas under its control. It also pledged to stop all kinds of cross-border activities from Azad Kashmir. Pakistan had never acknowledged the armed resistance in IHK as terrorism, but astonishingly, it ceded even this stance and conceded to the Indian interpretation of the movement. As a retired former Ambassador aptly commented: This amounted to an admission of its guilt and was unprecedented in that Pakistan unilaterally took on a responsibility that was not only almost impossible to honor, but even more importantly, it was given without any reciprocal obligation by the other side. To further the shift in policy, the Pakistani President articulated his ideas on Kashmir for the first time while speaking to journalists during an *iftar*dinner held in Islamabad in October 2004. Although he said these were "off the cuff" ideas, the nature of the proposals on the Kashmir settlement that he forwarded suggests that he had in mind a well-conceived and thought-out plan, on which he was gauging feedback. The crux of the proposals is outlined below:

- Identify seven regions, demilitarize them, and change their status before looking for possible options to resolve the dispute.

- The status quo in Kashmir is unacceptable and the LoC cannot be a solution to the lingering dispute.
- As a starting point for a step-by-step approach on the option of demilitarization, the regions on both sides of the LoC need to be analyzed for local culture and demographic composition. After identifying these regions, there could be gradual demilitarization, following which the two sides could discuss who should control these areas.
- Pakistan and India could also have joint control of these areas or the United Nations could be asked to play a role.

Later, Musharraf dilated upon his ideas with the *CNBC* anchorperson, Karan Thapar, on January 8, 2006. He suggested the concept of self-governance and joint management of the entire Kashmir area. In his words, "self-governance is more than autonomy but less than independence. In other words, both India and Pakistan will keep the parts of Kashmir they control but under their joint management. Self-governance is devolved to the Kashmiris, independence being firmly ruled out."

The interviewer, Karan Thapar, afterwards elaborated this concept in his article, saying, "...The self-governance would apply to the full state of Jammu and Kashmir as it existed in 1947. This means it would be implemented in Northern Areas (Gilgit Baltistan). Additionally, the border within old Kashmir state would be open and thus irrelevant."

Subsequently, Musharraf had a comprehensive discussion on his proposals with the noted Indian lawyer and journalist, A. G. Noorani, who published it in the Indian magazine *Frontline* on August 12-25, 2006. Later on, President Musharraf also spoke to *NDTV* on similar ideas, going further to clearly articulate his position as follows:

- Kashmir will have the same borders but people will be allowed to move freely back and forth in the region;
- The region will have self-governance or autonomy, but not independence;
- Troops will be withdrawn from the region in a phased manner
- A joint supervision mechanism will be set up with India, Pakistan and Kashmir represented in it.

The proposals offered by Musharraf sent clear signals that: a) Islamabad was ready to compromise its traditional stance that the people of Kashmir will decide their destiny through free and fair plebiscite; b) Indian and Pakistani sovereignty would remain as it currently was at the end of the day; c) The

LoC would be irrelevant, except as a line on a map to demarcate both parts of the state; d) Self-governance or self rule would be granted to both parts of Kashmir and joint management established.

Pakistan's proposals paved the way to move forward on a slightly faster track as India did not view them as being against its strategic or political interests. Previously, Pakistan had banked on the UNSC resolutions that guaranteed the right of self-determination to the Kashmiris, besides recognizing Pakistan as a principal party to the dispute. Musharraf relinquished these positions unilaterally without seeking any quid pro quo. In other words, he came close to almost acknowledging the Indian claim that Kashmir could not be receded from the Union. India also tactfully rephrased its traditional stance that "J&K is its integral part" in more acceptable language, now asserting that "Borders cannot be redrawn but any kind of solution could be acceptable to India." Musharraf agreed to this proposition while rejecting the status quo and showed willingness to embrace some kind of joint management of the state.

Moreover, Pakistan accepted the pro-Indian Kashmiri leadership's role in the future dispensation and changed its position that only the All Parties Hurriyat Conference (APHC) should be the representative of Kashmiri people in the negotiation process. President Musharraf said that the President of the National Conference, Omer Abdullah, and Mahbooba Mufti had a role to play in the Kashmir political landscape. This gesture comforted the Indian establishment as Pakistan's demands were in line with their own views and interests.

These major departures from the traditional stance made Musharraf a good bet for India to deal with Pakistan on Kashmir and settle other issues broadly allied to Pak-India trade and access to markets in Central Asia and Afghanistan.

A Review of the Composite Dialogue

The dialogue process between Islamabad and New Delhi is slowly progressing despite several ups and downs. It is often said that the continuation of the process is in itself a success because, in the past, the two countries have been unable to remain engaged in a sustainable dialogue. However, the substance of the process and prospects of its success need to be analyzed.

Until February 1994, India and Pakistan were engaged in sporadic dialogues that always ended with zero progress. This is why both countries formally suspended dialogue in 1994. Islamabad's approach was to settle the Kashmir issue first, after which the other problems would get settled almost automatically, whereas India was interested in dilating first on other issues, such as trade and travel. Eventually, to bridge the gap between the two positions, both governments agreed to address all political and territorial issues simultaneously, including Jammu and Kashmir. Consequently, the foreign secretaries of the two countries met in Islamabad and resumed the stalled dialogue process in June 1997. They institutionalized the process by identifying eight areas to deliberate upon and established working groups to make progress on each issue separately but simultaneously.

This entire process was called off when the Kargil confrontation occurred. As discussed earlier, post-9/11 events also contributed in the stalemate between the two countries. Later, in 2004, India and Pakistan launched a renewed peace process aimed at resolving all their longstanding disputes. However, the Kashmir dispute still dominates over other issues. Even after voicing his new approaches, President Musharraf said that if progress on Kashmir could not make headway, the entire process would be back to square one. Recently, Prime Minister Shaukat Aziz has underscored the settlement of Kashmir as a precondition for further progress on other related disputes as well as for offering trade and business opportunities to India.

Since January 2004, both neighbors have been engaged on two different levels. The first is the official level, at which concerned officials from both sides meet periodically and report their progress to foreign secretaries, who meet to review the outcome and discuss the Kashmir, peace and security issues, before, finally, the foreign ministers meet to take stock of developments and set the rules for further dialogue. The second level of engagement is back-channel diplomacy. Pakistan's National Security Secretary, Tariq Aziz, who is known to be a close aide of President Musharraf, and India's S. K. Lamba, former High Commissioner to Pakistan, are engaged in a serious dialogue. However, it has been said that only five people in Pakistan are truly in the loop on the actual state of bilateral negotiations. Therefore, no one can really assess the behind-the-curtains activities or predict the contours of solutions.

So far, at the official level, both countries have completed four rounds of a composite dialogue. This process received a dent when the Mumbai train blasts on July 11, 2006 caused a postponement in the foreign secretary-level talks. India blamed elements from Pakistan for their involvement in the blasts but no evidence was provided by the Indian government to Pakistan.

This decision was in violation of the joint statement, issued on April 18, 2005, by the leaders of Pakistan and India, which states that, "Terrorist acts would not be allowed to derail the peace process." Eventually, sanity prevailed and the stalled process was resumed in November 2006. Likewise, in February, the Lahore-bound Samjhauta Express became a target of bomb blasts that killed 68 passengers, most of whom were Pakistani.

Islamabad reacted with caution and did not allow the peace process to derail, despite the immense loss of its citizens' lives. The question does arise how New Delhi would have reacted had Indian citizens been the victims.

The fourth round of composite dialogue was held in Islamabad on March 13-14, 2007, with a focus on the Jammu and Kashmir dispute and peace and security. In the context of peace and security, the two sides discussed a wide range of issues relating to their conventional and nuclear military capabilities and reviewed the entire process. The Pakistani team sought India's response to President Musharraf's "ideas" on the resolution of the Kashmir issue and emphasized the need for forward movement on Jammu and Kashmir, saying it was time to move from confidence-building measures to dispute resolution.

Among related issues, Pakistan pushed for early finalization of the agreements on speedy return of inadvertent line crossers; quarterly flag meetings of the sector commanders at the LoC; and liberalization of the visa regime. Pakistan also proposed some new cross-LoC confidence building measures, including allowing sports activities and launch of helicopter and postal services between Srinagar and Muzaffarabad.

In addition, Pakistan tabled a new proposal on anti-ballistic missiles. Siachen, Sir Creek and economic cooperation were among the other issues discussed.

Following are the significant consensus points of the fourth round of foreign secretary-level talks:

- After years of reluctance, Pakistan agreed to the Indian proposal of launching a bus service between Kargil and Skardu in the Northern Areas.
- It was agreed that a truck service between Srinagar and Muzaffarabad would be launched in a few months;
- It was agreed that the Joint Committee of Retired Judges, set up to look into the prisoners issue, would begin its work soon and suggest ways to ensure the humane treatment of Indian prisoners in Pakistani jails and Pakistani prisoners in Indian jails;
- The two countries agreed to conclude an agreement on "No Development of New Posts and Defense Works" along the LoC and proposed drafts for new border control guidelines along the International Border;
- The two sides agreed to work on finalizing a liberalized visa regime, including a proposal for group tourism.

Although the meeting could not settle the problem of demilitarizing Siachen, it was able to narrow down differences on some elements. The political leadership of both countries appears optimistic about resolving this issue in the days ahead.

Likewise, the formation of a Joint Counter-Terrorism Mechanism is also a significant development. India has long blamed Pakistan for any terrorist activities occurring on its territory. The Mechanism offers an opportunity for thorough investigation of incidents prior to the pronouncements of conclusions. However, it was reported in sections of the Pakistani and Indian press that Islamabad seeks to keep the armed resistance in J&K out of the ambit of the Joint Anti-Terrorism Mechanism. At a joint press conference with the Indian Foreign Secretary Shivshankar Menon, his Pakistani counterpart, Riaz Mohammad Khan, said that Jammu and Kashmir was "disputed" and should not be "mixed" with the initiatives that are between India and Pakistan only. The visible achievement of the four rounds of foreign sectaries' level dialogue is the initiation of a Srinagar-Muzaffarabad bus service and, of late, the opening of entry points along the LoC for civilian crossing. Although the 42-month dialogue process has not yielded the desired results, both the governments seem to be closer to agreements on a number of issues.

Besides, the two countries have also exchanged some proposals through the back channel on the settlement of the Jammu and Kashmir dispute. However, very few people of the two governments are fully aware of what is going on behind the scene. Concerned citizens and the general public on both sides know virtually nothing. This makes the back channel process vulnerable: nobody knows how stakeholders and the public will react when the solution is finally made public.

India's Mixed Response

Initially, the Indian leadership was quick to turn down President Musharraf's proposals on Kashmir, making it clear that sharing the sovereignty of Jammu and Kashmir with Pakistan was out of the question. However, due to the host of factors outlined above, it eventfully realized that it had to reciprocate and take the proposals into serious consideration.

The Indian Prime Minister made some reconciliatory remarks that encouraged pro-settlement forces in Kashmir and Pakistan. India resumed the negotiation process with APHC's Mirwaiz faction and also held meeting with Sajjad Ghani Lone, Chairman of the People's Conference and to the leader of Jammu & Kashmir Liberation Front (JKLF), Yasin Malk. The Indian Prime Minster held three Kashmir-related roundtables with the pro-India leadership of IHK and formed five working groups to seek recommendations on various issues.

The pro-independence leadership was also invited but it did not participate, demanding that a separate meeting be held with it instead of a joint sitting with pro-India politicians. Notably, President Musharraf personally encouraged the pro-independence APHC leadership to join talks with India and Pakistan separately, as this would be a step in the direction of trilateral talks. There is a feeling in a large section of the Indian establishment and public opinion that Pakistan has narrowed down its position and come closer to that of India's, despite its use of different jargon and nuances.

It is interesting to note that, in the last two years, Indian Prime Minister Manmohan Singh has spoken on his vision of how to settle the Kashmir issue several times. On March 24, 2006, in Amritsar, he argued for a step-by-step approach and commencement of dialogue with the people "in their areas of control" to improve the quality of governance. Regarding the future status of the LoC, he said that it might eventually become a mere line on a map, and that people might be able to visit and trade freely. He made a departure from his government's earlier stated position by acknowledging that the "the two parts of Jammu and Kashmir can, with the active encouragement of the governments of India and Pakistan, work out cooperative consultative mechanisms so as to maximize the gains of cooperation." He also offered a treaty of friendship between India and Pakistan.

Subsequently, at the Second Round Table Conference held in Srinagar in May 2006, the Indian Prime Minister indicated that he might take some institutional arrangements to bring people from both sides of the LoC closer to each other. While meeting with a APHC Conference delegation in New Delhi, he said India might create an environment in which a person could live in Srinagar or Muzaffarabad without any legal restriction. He reiterated that India was willing to move beyond its stated position, and expressed his openness to any ideas that might contribute to the ongoing thought process.

Finally, speaking to a meeting of Indian businessmen in New Delhi, Prime Minister Manmohan Singh repeated his hope for a treaty of peace and friendship with Pakistan and emphasized the need for linkage among South Asian states for economic development. This was the second time he had spoken of such a treaty in the period of about a month.

Just one month earlier, he had initiated his idea of a treaty of peace and friendship at a public rally in Amritsar. Echoing the same line a few days earlier, the Indian External Affairs Minster Paranab Mukarjee had said that

India had to be prepared for some give and take in the border talks with China and Pakistan and should be prepared to shun rigid claims of national sovereignty if the talks were to be meaningful.

These pronouncements indicate that the Indian leadership is willing to have a phased-out formula for the resolution of the Kashmir issues. Nevertheless, it is neither relinquishing Indian sovereignty over Jammu and Kashmir, nor ready to trade off territory. At the end of the day, the people of Jammu and Kashmir may have de facto reunification of the state, which will give them psychological satisfaction. Apart from Monmohan Singh's reconciliatory remarks, a number of other key political stakeholders, such as Mufti Muhammad Sayyed's People's Democratic Party (PDP), National Conference, and APHC's Mirwaiz faction all support the Islamabad approach on Kashmir with slightly varied interpretations.

In this context, the Indian government has adopted a policy of engaging both Kashmiris and Pakistan in the dialogue process, separately but simultaneously. It suggests that New Delhi has attached huge expectations to an internal agreement with the people of Kashmir, giving relatively less importance to the external factor. However, it recognises the significance of people-to-people contacts across the LoC and, therefore, agreed to initiate the Srinagar-Muzaffarabad bus service and allowed Kashmiri leaders to travel on it to Muzaffarabad in July 2005. It has also given relatively better political space to the Mirwaiz faction of APHC and frequently facilitated its travel outside the country.

On the other hand, a number of Indian officials and commentators are restlessly following the beaten track of bitterness, continuing to hurl accusations at Pakistan with no regard for the emerging environment. Officials in India's top echelons quite frequently use isolated events to accuse Pakistan of terrorism without offering any substantial evidence. At times, Islamabad's sincerity is questioned. For instance, according to Satish Chandra, former Deputy National Security Advisor to the Indian government:

Is the military in Pakistan sincere in wanting good relations with India? Pakistan's engagement in the current dialogue process is due to compulsion of external pressures and military exigencies which have tied up substantial Pakistani forces on the West.

In April 2005, when Musharraf visited New Delhi, both the gov-ernments made announcements that the peace process was irreversible and no incident would be permitted to derail it. But immediately after the Mumbai bomb blasts, New Delhi called off the dialogue process and stalled the foreign secretary-level talks for almost three months. Indeed, New Delhi left no stone unturned to prove that Pakistan was a haven for terrorists and was involved in promoting terrorist networks inside India, particularly in the occupied Jammu and Kashmir. Satish Chandra observed:

Pakistan's involvement in terrorism is well-known. It is not limited to Jammu and Kashmir, but extends to several parts of India, including the northeast. One of my major concerns was that in many parts of India, including New Delhi, we are a hair's breadth away from a major terrorist attack.

In view of such contradictions, it may be assumed that either opinion within the Indian establishment is divided on the future course of action, or New Delhi has a well-defined, official double-edged policy of conducting talks with Islamabad and, at the same time, continuing its blame game to keep the latter under pressure. It is possible that New Delhi wishes to maintain tactical ambiguity to keep both pro- and anti-peace process forces confused with mixed signals. Such an approach also allows the Indian government to drag its feet on the peace process whenever it desires. It appears that India does not care if its stance sends negative signals to the people of Pakistan, or if it reinforces the argument before them that Delhi is not responding to Musharraf's flexibility, even in diluted form. On the other hand, Musharraf has consistently applauded Vajpayee and Manmohan Singh, calling them statesmen, but the Indian leadership has never reciprocated the gesture. Musharraf has earned a lot of appreciation across the world for his efforts to solve the Kashmir problem but this too has made little impression on the Indian establishment.

Some leading Indian opinion makers believe that Pakistan had no option but to comply with Indian demands. This view has been echoed by former Indian Prime Minister Inder Kumar Gujral in the following words:

What options does he [Musharraf] have? His country faces innumerable problems. He also finds India growing taller and taller. His friends, the Americans, have told him not to rock the boat.

Thus, the process of reconciliation and the blame game are continuing simultaneously, indicating that the Indian establishment has yet to enter true reconciliation mode. Naturally, several questions arise about this complex Indian attitude. The answer primarily lies in the changed ground realities; for instance, back and forth movement across LoC has admittedly gone down, while militants are no longer a major threat to the security forces. Moreover, with the tacit approval of Islamabad, the fencing of the LoC has been completed without any real hassle. The unfaltering commitment on the part of Pakistan to respect the ceasefire along the LoC is a further encouraging factor. Inside Kashmir, the APHC stands divided into two factions and one of them, headed by Mirwaiz Omer Farooq, is in touch with Indian interlocutors, seeking a compromised settlement of the issue within the Indian Union.

New Stakeholders

Recently, Kashmiri domestic politics took a dramatic turn when the President of the pro-India National Conference, Omar Abdullah, made a striking demand. He said that no solution for Kashmir was possible without the involvement of Hizbul Mujahideen (HM) in the dialogue process. He urged India and Pakistan to hold talks with the United Jihad Council and HM's chief, Syed Salauddin.

Besides Omer Abdullah, the PDP chief Mehbooba Mufti has also consistently advised New Delhi to bring HM on board. JKLF leader Yasin Malik, known as the pioneer of militancy, also sets dialogue with HM as a precondition to a peaceful resolution of the Kashmir dispute. Moreover, a number of intra-Kashmir dialogue conferences organized by the Centre for Dialogue and Reconciliation, Delhi, have persistently been arguing for a seat for militants in the ongoing process.

HM has welcomed the suggestion for the first time in its 17-year armed resistance. Its inclusion in the dialogue has become a bipartisan demand of the Kashmiri stakeholders, cutting across the political divide. However, several questions arise regarding HM's future course of action. It is a fact that HM has played an instrumental role in highlighting the Kashmir issue by rendering huge sacrifices. It commands immense respect and credibility among the masses. Its chief, Syed Salauddin, is a household name in Kashmir and is regarded as one of the most trusted leaders of the state.

CBMs: A Blank Cheque for HR Violations

Despite a number of Confidence Building Measures (CBMs), the articulation of positive statements in the top echelons of the two countries, and several rounds of high level tête-à-tête between Indian and Pakistani officials, there has not been even a slight decline in the level of human rights violation in Indian-held Kashmir. Fake encounters and disappearances are still staged. The violations are so high that even the pro-Indian mainstream, along with the "separatist parties" — as India calls them — are up in arms against the government and security forces on this issue.

In the context of the ongoing peace process, it was not a misplaced expectation that, at least to improve its democratic image, the Indian government would take special measures to ensure respect for human rights and stop indiscriminate killings of civilians in the state. It was also necessary to get public support for the ongoing dialogue process. But events show that human rights abuses have actually doubled and random killings continue as a routine matter in IHK. It is quite surprising that the world community does not let a single opportunity slip to condemn human rights violations by resistance outfits but is silent on the acts of barbarism committed by the forces.

The Indian brutalities fuel feelings of vengeance among Kashmiris and invite more violence, which helps in providing fresh blood to the dissidents. It should be borne in mind that, in the initial years, the character of the resistance movement was not violent or communalized as it later became. However, even peaceful protests were dispersed with gunfire. The Indian forces imprisoned all renowned political figures and ceased all avenues for the peaceful and non-violent components of the struggle. Eventually, not only the youth but also professionals and the political leadership were dragged into armed struggle. These views were echoed in the editorial comments of the Jammu-based *Kashmir Times* on January 5, 2005:

> The poor track record of Indian forces on human rights front, which includes not just physical torture but also the mental trauma and agony of being looked upon with suspicion and subjected to every day humiliation in one's own home by a man in uniform who is for all practical purposes an outsider, thus becomes a major source of spread of militancy in its fanatic form, as is evident today.

Given, Kashmiri leaders often say that the current Indian strategy is aimed at crushing the Kashmiri struggle for self-determination under the disguise of parlays with Pakistan. This is why Indian forces are vigorously pursuing their military operations in the state. Secondly, as long as the two sides remain engaged in talks, the international community and human rights organizations will not voice any concerns lest it derail the dialogue process and spoil the atmosphere. Besides, Pakistan is consciously avoiding making human rights a point in the talks, fearing that it might annoy India to the extent that it backs out of the negotiations. India is taking undue advantage of this deliberate silence. On the other hand, it has practically given India a soft opportunity to suppress all the significant voices in the state.

It is also a known fact that the Indian armed forces have developed stakes in the J&K conflict. Over a period of time, they have developed a huge infrastructure and extract immense benefits from the festering wounds of Kashmir. They are entrusted with several draconian powers and prerogatives to conduct arbitrary operations and commit custodial killings. It is a proven fact that the security forces take money from local people through intimidation and threats. Therefore, the huge military set-up in J&K has itself become a bottleneck in the peace process. Several Kashmir watchers believe that it was the military and intelligence establishment that compelled the Congress-led government to not budge from the Indian stated position on the issue. The ruling class in Delhi today also believes that Islamabad is on the receiving end and its game plan has been exhausted. So, eventually, the Indian writ on Kashmir shall be fully reestablished.

Dissident voices

Syed Ali Gilani, Chairman of his own faction of APHC, has emerged as a leading critic of the current peace process. He believes that the process is going to bury the Kashmir issue rather than settling it according to the people's wishes. His views have a strong following of politically aware lawyers, intellectuals, youth and women inside Kashmir.

Apart from his political and religious ideology, he commands respect from all segments of Kashmiri society because of his firm stand on resolution of Kashmir according to the wishes of its people. Militant outfits, too, regard him as a source of aspiration.

Hizbul Mujahideen, the largest indigenous militant outfit, has been especially under his influence since its inception. Armed groups, such as Lashkar and Jaish, have also expressed great respect for him. Because of his position within these outfits, he has emerged as one of the key influential leaders of the Valley. It is often said that he holds the key to the peaceful settlement of Kashmir.

On January 17, 2007 a strike was observed in the Valley to mark a protest against the visit of Mirwaiz Omer Farooq and his colleagues to Islamabad. Interestingly, however, public response to his recent strike call had been overwhelming, with the calling it a near to complete strike. This signifies the failure of the moderate APHC factions to take people into confidence. Mirwaiz visited Islamabad in January 19-27, 2007. He had meetings with President Pervez Musharraf twice and other government functionaries, besides sitting with a large number of political entities and Kashmiri parties. However, he could not get in touch with Syed Salahudin, the Hizbul Mujahideen commander-in-chief, as he declined to meet him. Likewise, in Azad Kashmir, apart from the ruling Muslim Conference, no other political party or civil society group supported the current formulation of the Kashmir settlement. Evidently, within Kashmiri opinion, the current moves do not enjoy reasonable support, which makes the entire process vulnerable and weak.

7

India-Sri Lanka Relation

India's national interests demand maintaining the unity and sovereignty of the Sri Lanka nation state. India's domestic Tamil politics should not become the touch stone of India's policies towards Sri Lanka. India needs to react forcefully to ensure that Sri Lanka remains a unified state with a set up that would meet the just aspirations of a majority of Tamils.

The above proposition entails once again the forging of mutual national interests convergence of India and the United States Sri Lanka is an important component of United States India Ocean strategy and it is felt that United States-India convergences exist already. Joint USA-India strategies and foreign policies towards Sri Lanka would be helpful in counter-acting Chinese and Pakistani overtures to wean away Sri Lanka from India's influence.

DEVELOPMENT OF BILATERAL RELATIONS

India and Sri Lanka established diplomatic relations when the latter gained its independence in 1948. Both nations proceeded to establish extensive cultural, commercial, strategic and defence ties to establish a common sphere of influence in the region, adopting nonalignment to control Western and Soviet influence. The close relationship between the then-Indian Prime Minister Indira Gandhi and then-Sri Lankan Prime Minister Sirimavo Bandaranaike led to the development of strong bilateral relations. In 1971, Indian armed forces helped squash a Communist rebellion against the Sri Lankan government.

Indian Intervention in the Sri Lankan Civil War

In the 1980s, private entities and elements in the state government of Tamil Nadu were believed to be encouraging the funding and training for the Liberation Tigers of Tamil Eelam, a separatist insurgent force..In 1987, faced with growing anger amongst its own Tamils, and a flood of refugees, India intervened directly in the conflict for the first time after the Sri Lankan government attempted to regain control of the northern Jaffna region by means of an economic blockade and military assaults, India supplied food and medicine by air and sea. After subsequent negotiations, India and Sri Lanka entered into an agreement. The peace accord assigned a certain degree of regional autonomy in the Tamil areas with Eelam People's Revolutionary Liberation Front (EPRLF) controlling the regional council and called for the Tamil militant groups to lay down their arms. Further India was to send a peacekeeping force, named the IPKF to Sri Lanka to enforce the disarmament and to watch over the regional council.

Even though the accord was signed between the governments of Sri Lanka and India, with the Tamil Tigers and other Tamil militant groups not having a role in the signing of the accord, most Tamil militant groups accepted this agreement, the LTTE rejected the accord because they opposed the candidate, who belonged to another militant group named Eelam Peoples Revolutionary Liberation Front (EPRLF), for chief administrative officer of the merged Northern and Eastern provinces. Instead the LTTE named three other candidates for the position. The candidates proposed by the LTTE were rejected by India. The LTTE subsequently refused to hand over their weapons to the IPKF.

The result was that the LTTE now found itself engaged in military conflict with the Indian Army, and launched their first attack on an Indian army rations truck on October 8, killing five Indian para-commandos who were on board by strapping burning tires around their necks. The government of India then decided that the IPKF should disarm the LTTE by force, and the Indian Army launched number of assaults on the LTTE, including a month-long campaign dubbed *Operation Pawan* to win control of the Jaffna peninsula from the LTTE. When the IPKF engaged the LTTE, the then president of Sri Lanka, Ranasinghe Premadasa, began supporting LTTE and funded LTTE with arms. During the warfare with the ltte IPKF was also alleged for human rights violation against the civilians. Notably, IPKF was alleged to have perpetrated Jaffna teaching hospital massacre which was the killing of over 70 civilians including patients, doctors and nurses. The ruthlessness of this campaign, and the Indian army's subsequent anti-LTTE operations made it extremely unpopular amongst many Tamils in Sri Lanka. The conflict between the LTTE and the Indian Army left over 1,000 Indian soldiers dead.

The Indo-Sri Lankan Accord, which had been unpopular amongst Sri Lankans for giving India a major influence, now became a source of nationalist anger and resentment as the IPKF was drawn fully into the conflict. Sri Lankans protested the presence of the IPKF, and the newly-elected Sri Lankan president Ranasinghe Premadasa demanded its withdrawal, which was completed by March 1990. On May 21, 1992, Rajiv Gandhi was assassinated and the LTTE was alleged to be the perpetrator. As a result India declared the LTTE to be a terrorist outfit in 1992. Bilateral relations improved in the 1990s and India supported the peace process but has resisted calls to get involved again. India has also been wary of and criticised the extensive military involvement of Pakistan in the conflict, accusing the latter of supplying lethal weaponry and encouraging Sri Lanka to pursue military action rather than peaceful negotiations to end the civil war.

Commercial Ties

India and Sri Lanka are member nations of several regional and multilateral organisations such as the South Asian Association for Regional Cooperation (SAARC), South Asia Co-operative Environment Programme, South Asian Economic Union and BIMSTEC, working to enhance cultural and commercial ties. Since a bilateral free trade agreement was signed and came into effect in 2000, Indo-Sri Lankan trade rose 128% by 2004 and quadrupled by 2006, reaching USD 2.6 billion. Between 2000 and 2004, India's exports to Sri Lanka in the last four years increased by 113%, from USD 618 million to $1,319 million while Sri Lankan exports to India increased by 342%, from $44 million to USD $194 million. Indian exports account for 14% of Sri Lanka's global imports. India is also the fifth largest export destination for Sri Lankan goods, accounting for 3.6% of its exports. Both nations are also signatories of the South Asia Free Trade Agreement (SAFTA). Negotiations are also underway to expand the free trade agreement to forge stronger commercial relations and increase corporate investment and ventures in various industries.

India's National Thermal Power Corp (NTPC) is also scheduled to build a 500 MW thermal power plant in Sampoor (Sampur). The NTPC claims that the this plan will take the Indo-Srilankan relationship to new level.

Fishermen Issue

There have been several incidents of firing on Indian fishermen fishing in Palk Bay.Indian Government has always taken up the issue of safety of Indian fishermen on a priority basis with the Government of Sri Lanka. Presently there is no bona fide Indian fisherman in the Sri Lankan custody. A Joint Working Group (JWG) has been constituted to deal with the issues related to Indian fishermen straying in Sri Lankan territorial waters, work out modalities for prevention of use of force against them and the early release of confiscated boats and explore possibilities of working towards bilateral arrangements for licensed fishing. The JWG last met in Jan 2006.

Development Cooperation

India is active in a number of areas of development activity in Sri Lanka. About one-sixth of the total development credit granted by GOI is made available to Sri Lanka.

Lines of credit: In the recent past three lines of credit were extended to Sri Lanka: US$ 100 million for capital goods, consumer durables, consultancy services and food items, US$ 31 million for supply of 300,000 MT of wheat and US$ 150 million for purchase of petroleum products. All of these lines of credit have been fully utilized. Another line of credit of US$ 100 million is now being made available for rehabilitation of the Colombo-Matara railway. A number of development projects are implemented under 'Aid to Sri Lanka' funds. In 2006-07, the budget for 'Aid to Sri Lanka' was Rs 28.2 Crs.

Small Development Projects: A MoU on Cooperation in Small Development Projects has been signed. Projects for providing fishing equipments to the fishermen in the East of Sri Lanka and solar energy aided computer education in 25 rural schools in Eastern Sri Lanka are under consideration.

Health Projects: We have supplied medical equipments to hospitals at Hambantota and Point Pedro, supplied 4 state of the art ambulances to the Central Province, implemented a cataract eye surgery programme for 1500 people in the Central Province and implemented a project of renovation of OT at Dickoya hospital and supplying equipment to it. The projects under consideration are: Construction of a 150-bed hospital at Dickoya, upgradation of the hospital at Trincomalee and a US$ 7.5 million grant for setting up a Cancer Hospital in Colombo.

Education Projects: Upgradation of the educational infrastructure of the schools in the Central province including teachers' training, setting up of 10 computer labs, setting up of 20 e-libraries (Nenasalas), Mahatma Gandhi scholarship scheme for +2 students and setting up of a vocational training centre in Puttalam. India also contributes to the Ceylon Workers Education Trust that gives scholarships to the children of estate workers.

Training: A training programme for 465 Sri Lankan Police officers has been commenced in Dec 2005. Another 400 Sri Lankan Police personnel are being trained for the course of 'Maintenance of Public Order'.

Concluding Observations: India's emergence as a regional power and a key global player depends largely on her image and standing in the South Asian neighbourhood. If India cannot effectively generate and ensure her key status in South Asia, how can the world be convinced that it can carve influence farther afield. India's nuclear weapons, space programmes, missiles development and her overwhelming superiority in military strength are of no use, if the South Asian neighbourhood takes India for granted and merrily tramples on India's national interests and her image. India needs to introduce an element of 'unilateralism' in her state-craft in South Asia.

Fortunately for India, with the exception of Pakistan, joint convergences of national interests exist between United States and India. This could greatly facilitate India's forceful assertion in South Asian affairs for greater regional good. Once this is achieved, a marginalised Pakistan in South Asia, may see the dawn of South Asia's strategic realities.

INDO-SRI LANKA ACCORD

The Indo-Sri Lanka Peace Accord was an accord signed in Colombo on 29 July, 1987, between Indian Prime Minister Rajiv Gandhi and Sri Lankan President J. R. Jayewardene. The accord was expected to resolve the Sri Lankan civil war. Under the terms of the agreement, Colombo agreed to a devolution of power to the provinces, the Sri Lankan troops were to be withdrawn to their barracks in the north and the Tamil rebels were to surrender their arms.

Importantly however, the Tamil groups, notably the The Liberation Tigers of Tamil Eelam (LTTE) (which at the time was one of the strongest Tamil forces) had not been made party to the talks and initially agreed to surrender their arms to the Indian Peace-Keeping Force (IPKF) only reluctantly. Within a few months however, this flared into an active confrontation. The LTTE declared their intent to continue the armed struggle for an independent Tamil Eelam and refused to disarm. The IPKF found itself engaged in a bloody police action against the LTTE. Further complicating the return to peace was a burgeoning Sinhalese insurgency in the south.

Background

Sri Lanka, from the early part of the 1980s, was facing an increasingly violent ethnic strife. The origins of this conflict can be traced to the independence of the island from Britain in 1948. At the time, a Sinhala majority government was instituted which passed legislation that were deemed discriminatory against the substantial Tamil minority population. In the 1970s, two major Tamil parties united to form the Tamil United Liberation Front (TULF) that started agitation for a separate state of Tamil Eelam within the system in a federal structure in the north and eastern Sri Lanka that would grant the Tamils greater autonomy. However, enactment of the sixth amendment of the Sri Lankan Constitution in August 1983 classified all separatist movements as unconstitutional, effectively rendering the TULF ineffective. Outside the TULF, however, factions advocating more radical and militant courses of action soon emerged, and the ethnic divisions started flaring into a violent civil war.

Indian Involvement

India had, initially under Indira Gandhi and later under Rajiv Gandhi, provided support to Tamil interests from the very conception of the secessionist movement. This included providing sanctuary to the separatists, as well as support the operations training camps for Tamilguerrillas in Tamil Nadu of which the LTTE emerged as the strongest force. This was both as a result of a large Tamil community in South India, as well as India's regional security and interests which attempted to reduce the scope of foreign intervention, especially those linked to the United States, Pakistan, and China. To this end, the Indira Gandhi Government sought to make it clear to the Sri Lankan President, Jayewardene that armed intervention in support of the Tamil movement was an option India would consider if any diplomatic solutions should fail. Following the anti-Tamil riots, the Tamil rebel movement grew progressively strong and increasingly violent. However,after Indira Gandhi's assassination, the Indian support for the militant movement decreased. However, the succeeding Rajiv Gandhigovernment attempted to re-establish friendly relations with its neighbours. It still however maintained diplomatic efforts to find a solution to the conflict as well as maintaining covert aid to the Tamil rebels.

From 1985 however, the Sri-Lankan Government started rearming itself extensively for its anti-insurgent role with support from Pakistan, Israel, Singapore and South Africa. In 1986, the campaign against the insurgency was stepped up and in 1987, retaliating an increasingly bloody insurgent movement, Operation Liberation was launched against LTTE strongholds in Jaffna Peninsula, involving nearly four thousand troops, supported by helicopter gunships as well as Ground attack aircraft. In June 1987, the Sri Lankan Army laid siege on the town of Jaffna. As civilian casualties grew, calls grew within India to intervene in what was increasingly seen in the Indian (and Tamil) media as a developing humanitarian crisis, especially with reports use of aerial support against rebel positions in civilian areas. India, which had a substantial Tamil population in South India faced the prospect of a Tamil backlash at home, called on the Sri Lankan government to halt the offensive in an attempt to negotiate a political settlement.

However, the Indian efforts were futile. Added to this, in the growing involvement of Pakistani and Israeli advisors, it was necessary for Indian interest to mount a show of force. Failing to negotiate an end to the crisis with Sri Lanka, India announced on 2 June 1987 that it would send a convoy of unarmed ships to northern Sri Lanka to provide humanitarian assistance but this was intercepted by the Sri Lankan Navy and turned back.

Following the failure of the naval mission, the decision was made by the Indian government to mount an airdrop of relief supplies in support of rebel forces over the besieged city of Jaffna. On 4 June 1987, in a blatant show of force, the Indian Air Force mounted Operation Poomalai in broad daylight. Five An-32s of the Indian Air Force under cover of heavily armed Indian fighter jets flew over Jaffna to airdrop 25 tons of supplies, all the time keeping well within the range of Sri Lankan radar coverage. At the same time the Sri Lankan Ambassador to New Delhi was summoned to the Foreign Office to be informed by the Minister External Affairs, K. Natwar Singh, of the ongoing operation. It was also indicated to the Ambassador that if the operation was in any way hindered by Sri Lanka, India would launch a full-force military retaliation against Sri Lanka. The ultimate aim of the operation was both to demonstrate the credibility of the Indian option of active intervention to the Sri Lankan Government, as a symbolic act of support for the Tamil Rebels, as well to preserve Rajiv Gandhi's credibility.

Faced with the possibility of an active Indian intervention and facing an increasingly war-weary population at home, the Sri Lankan President, J. R. Jayewardene, offered to hold talks with the Rajiv Gandhi government on future moves. The siege of Jaffna was soon lifted, followed by a round of negotiations that led to the signing of the Indo-Sri-Lankan accord on July 29, 1987 that brought a temporary truce. The terms of the truce specified that the Sri Lankan troops withdraw from the north and the Tamil rebels disarm, and saw the induction of the IPKF as a peace keeping force in Sri Lanka.

Peace Accord

Among the salient points of the agreement, the Sri Lankan Government made a number of concessions to Tamil demands, which included Colombo devolution of power to the provinces, merger (subject to later referendum) of the northern and eastern provinces, and official status for the Tamil language. More immediately, Operation Liberation — the successful, ongoing anti-insurgent operation by Sri Lankan forces in the Northern peninsula — was ended. Sri Lankan troops were to withdraw to their barracks in the north, the Tamil rebels were to disarm. India agreed to end support for the Tamil separatist movement and recognise the unity of Sri Lanka. The Indo-Sri Lanka Accord also underlined the commitment of Indian military assistance on which the Indian Peace Keeping Force came to be inducted into Sri Lanka.

In 1990, India withdrew the last of its forces from Sri Lanka, and fighting between the LTTE and the government resumed. The Liberation Tigers of Tamil Eelam committed serious human rights violations.

In January 1995, the Sri Lankan Government and the Liberation Tigers of Tamil Eelam agreed to a cease fire as a preliminary step in a government-initiated plan for peace negotiations. After 3 months, however, the Liberation Tigers of Tamil Eelam unilaterally resumed hostilities.

The government of Sri Lanka then adopted a policy of military engagement with the Tigers, with government forces liberating Jaffna from LTTE control by mid-1996 and moving against LTTE positions in the northern part of the country called the Vanni. An LTTE counteroffensive, begun in October 1999, reversed most government gains; and by May 2000, threatened government forces in Jaffna. Heavy fighting continued into 2001.

Reaction

On the eve of the signing of the Indo-Sri Lanka Accord, Rajiv Gandhi was assaulted by Leading Rate Vijitha Rohana at the Guard of Honour held for Gandhi in what seemed an attempted assassination. Four years later, in 1991, Rajiv Gandhi was assassinated by a LTTE suicide bomber. This radically reduced support for the LTTE within India. In 2009, 19 years after his assassination, the Sri Lankan army mounted a major military offensive in the north and eradicated the LTTE. The operation was not opposed by India and received Indian diplomatic and military support, despite condemnations from state of Tamil Nadu and Western nations for alleged human rights violations. Rajiv Gandhi's widow, Sonia Gandhi was the chairperson of India's ruling coalition at the time.

OPERATION POOMALAI

Operation Poomalai , also known asEagle Mission 4, was the codename assigned to a mission undertaken by the Indian Air Force to air-drop supplies over the besieged town of Jaffna in Sri Lanka on 4 June 1987 in support of Tamil Tigers during the Sri Lankan Civil War.

Jaffna was at the time under blockade by Sri Lankan troops as a part of Colombo's offensive against the Tamil separatist movement. Concerned over alleged violations of interests of the Tamils, who had broader support among the Tamil population of South India as well as the government, India attempted to negotiate a political settlement but the Indian offers had been rebuffed by Colombo. As civilian casualties grew, calls grew within India to intervene in what was increasingly seen in the Indian (and Tamil) media as a developing humanitarian crisis, especially with reports of aerial bombardment against rebel positions in civilian areas. The Indian Government under Rajiv Gandhi decided to attempt to deliver aid to the northern area of Sri Lanka as a symbolic act of support to the rebels. The first of these efforts, a small naval flotilla, was thwarted by the Sri Lankan Navy. Two days later, in a show of force, India mounted the airdrop over Jaffna.

Background

The ethnic conflict in Sri Lanka can be traced to the independence of the island in 1948 from Britain. At the time a Sinhala majority government was instituted that passed legislation deemed discriminatory by the substantial Tamil minority population. In the 1970s two major Tamil parties united to form the Tamil United Liberation Front (TULF) that started agitating for a separate state of Tamil Eelamwithin the system in a federal structure in northern and eastern Sri Lanka that would grant the Tamils greater autonomy. Outside the TULF, however, factions advocating more radical and militant courses of action soon emerged, and the divisions started flaring into a violent civil war.

The first round of violence flared in 1983 when the killing of 13 Sri Lankan soldiers sparked anti-Tamil riots in which nearly 400 Tamils died. The riots only aided in the deterioration of the already worsening ethnic strife. The militant factions, notably the LTTE, at this time recruited in large numbers and continued building on popular Tamil dissent and stepped up the guerrilla activities. By May 1985 the guerrillas were strong enough to launch an attack on Anuradhapura, attacking the Bodhi Tree shrine – a sacred site for Buddhist Sinhalese – followed by a rampage through the town. At least 150 civilians died in the hour-long attack.

The government stepped up its campaign against the insurgency, and the Sri Lankan army in 1987 laid siege to the town of Jaffna, an LTTE stronghold, as part of its campaign against the Tamil bases. This resulted in large-scale civilian casualties and created a condition ofhumanitarian crisis. India, which had a substantial Tamil population in the southern part of the country, had been aiding the Tamil factions and particularly the LTTE and called on the Sri Lankan government to halt the offensive in an attempt to negotiate a political settlement. However, the Indian efforts were futile. Failing to negotiate an end to the crisis with Sri Lanka, India announced on 2 June 1987 that it wound send a convoy of unarmed ships to northern Sri Lanka to provide humanitarian assistance but this was intercepted by the Sri Lankan Navy and turned back.

Following the failure of the naval mission, the decision was made—both as a show of force to the Sri Lankan government of symbolic support for the Tamil rebels as well as an act to preserve the credibility of Indian prime minister Rajiv Gandhi among the country's Tamil population—by the Indian Government to carry out an airdrop of the humanitarian supplies, designated Operation Poomalai or Eagle Mission 4.

Operation Poomalai

Mounted on the evening of 4 June 1987, the operation involved five An-32s of the Paratroop Training School in Agra, escorted by five Mirage 2000s of the No. 7 Squadron. On the morning of 3 June No. 7 Squadron was directed to send a five-ship detachment to Bangalore Airport, where they were re-directed to Yelahanka airbase north of the city. At the same time, under the supervision of the (then) Vice-Chief of Air Staff Air Marshal S. Raghavendran, five An-32s were loaded with the relief supplies and took off for Bangalore at 0800 hours. These were to fly out—led by Gp. Capt. B.K. Sunder, CO of Paratroop Training School—after dawn and carry out the supply drop under the cover of the Mirages, which were led by Wg. Cdr. Ajit Bhavnani, CO of No. 7 Squadron. A group of 35 national and international journalists also joined the flight. The Mirages were armed with two Matra Magic II AAMs as a measure against any opposition by the Sri Lankan Air Force, and also carried three drop tanks.

The Sri Lankan Ambassador to New Delhi was summoned to the Ministry of External Affairs at 1500 hours, where the message was conveyed by Minister of External Affairs Natwar Singh that the Indian Air Force would be flying a mission at 1600 hours to drop supplies over Jaffna. The ambassador was told that the aircraft were expected to complete their mission unhindered and any opposition by the Sri Lankan Air Force "would be met by force" by the escorting Mirage 2000s.

The first of the flights left Bangalore at 15:55 hours and flew towards the Coramandel coast, where they were met by four Mirage escorts. One Mirage stayed back acting as radio relay, along with two additional An-32s over Tamil Nadu, which acted as radio relay to Bangalore.

The flight leader attempted radio contact with Colombo ATC over the civilian air traffic radio channel at 1647 hours, but was unable to establish contact. The mission approached Jaffna peninsula at about 1650 hours and sighted Jaffna Town itself at 1700 hours. The aircraft descended from 12000 feet to about 1500 feet and carried out the drop at the drop zone about 7 km from the town of Jaffna. The aircraft then turned in a western direction, flying over Palay airbase before turning north, heading for the Indian coast. Unopposed by Sri Lankan forces, the mission arrived back over Bangalore at 1813 hours, where they were greeted with much jubilation.

Aftermath

In the wake of Operation Poomalai, Sri Lanka accused India of violating its sovereignty. However, India defended its actions as a mercy mission in aid of what were termed as the deteriorating conditions of the civilian population, refusing at the time to rule out further missions. Within India, the actions were endorsed across the political diaspora In India, it was seen at the time as an act of support against the beleaguered and besieged Tamil population of the north – an opinion that was destined to undergo a drastic reversal after the assassination of Rajiv Gandhi by the LTTE in 1991. At that time, Colombo deemed it as a blatant show of support for the Tamil Tigers. The total supply air dropped by India during the operation amounted to little over 25 tons, and this was clearly not sufficient to sustain a besieged city.

Faced with the possibility of an active Indian intervention, Sri Lankan President J. R. Jayewardene offered to hold talks with the Rajiv Gandhigovernment on future moves. The siege of Jaffna was soon lifted, followed by a round of negotiations that led to the signing of the Indo-Sri-Lankan accord on July 29, 1987 that brought a temporary truce. The terms of the truce specified that the Sri Lankan troops withdraw from the north and the Tamil rebels disarm, and saw the induction of the IPKF as a peace keeping force in Sri Lanka.

SRI LANKA'S PIVOT TO INDIA BREAKS CHINA'S DREAMS

Following elections earlier this year, a major shift in the geopolitical and perhaps military balance of power is taking place on this island that hangs like a jewel from the ear of India. Many Americans may have trouble finding Sri Lanka on the map, but sitting as it does in the Indian Ocean, so close to the sea lanes over which nearly half the world's trade travels, including nearly 70 percent of petroleum to energy-hungry China and Japan, Sri Lanka has a strategic importance beyond its small size.

The new regime is rebalancing its relationship with India and China which may affect China's maritime ambitions in the region. This will please both Washington and New Delhi which have been watching China's rising power with some trepidation.

During the 10-year rule of President Mahinda Rajapaksa, from November 2005 to January 2015, Sri Lanka threw its lot in with China. The Indian Ocean isle borrowed huge sums from China, asked the Asian superpower to build massive infrastructure, and allowed Chinese submarines to dock in its ports — all to the chagrin of India, Sri Lanka's closest neighbor and fierce China rival.

China's building spree, including a new, 500-acre Colombo Port City project in the capital, a new international airport, and another port in Rajapaksa's home district, was seen by many as a link in China's so-called string of pearls that is extending China's influence and naval potential all around the Indian Ocean littoral. China is building or planning new port facilities in Burma, Bangladesh, and Pakistan. Few are as controversial as the Colombo Port City project, which has been attacked on environmental grounds and for the fact that Rajapaksa had allowed China to own part of the port in perpetuity and another part on a 99-year lease — similar to what the British once had in Hong Kong.

China is Sri Lanka's top investor and biggest government lender and a major trading partner. Its building projects here have been described by author Robert Kaplan as "emblematic of China's budding yet exquisitely elusive empire built on soft power."

In January, however, in a surprising electoral upset, Rajapaksa lost power to his former ally, Maithripala Sirisena. Already, President Sirisena is pushing back on China's influence and has temporarily halted construction of the Colombo project while he assesses the situation, much to the alarm of China and delight of India. And although Sirisena visited China last week, his first state visit outside the country was to India. Earlier this month Prime Minister Narendra Modi returned the compliment with a state visit to Sri Lanka, the first Indian prime minister to do so in 29 years.

Sirisena is attempting a delicate balance of tacking back towards India without losing China's friendship. Such a move would please Washington, which is improving relations with India while carefully watching China's newly competitive maritime and naval expansion in the Indian Ocean. It may also offer Sri Lanka its first shot at true reconciliation after decades of civil war.

FOREIGN POWERS have long seen the strategic importance of Sri Lanka, lying so close to the shipping lanes over which travels nearly half of the world's seaborne trade, including oil from the Middle East to the great energy consuming nations of Japan and China. The island is bountiful and blessed by nature; Arab traders called it this island Serendip, from which Horace Walpole coined the word serendipity. Greek and Roman traders reached these shores in ancient times, and Sri Lankan traders were to be seen in imperial Rome. Then the prize was spices, gemstones, and the export of elephants. "A golden trade route between east and west," as author Michelle de Krestser put it, Sri Lanka was a "useful bauble fingered and then pocketed by the Portuguese, the Dutch, and British in turn" for a period of 443 years. The British gave the island, which they called Ceylon, its independence in 1948.

India, which got its independence a few months earlier, is so near and so big that Sri Lankans have long feared that they could be squashed when India rolls over in bed. The relationship was further complicated by the 26-year-long civil war between Sri Lanka's mostly Hindu Tamil minority and its majority Buddhist Sinhalese, which ended with a Tamil defeat in 2009. There is an even smaller Muslim minority — made up mostly of Malays from what are now the nations of Malaysia and Indonesia — who have been discriminated against by both Tamils and Buddhist extremist. A smaller minority are Christian, mostly Roman Catholics — a holdover from Portuguese dominion. The Sinhalese originally come from northern India while the Tamils come from southern India. Both communities feel they are an endangered minority. For although the Sinhalese are the majority of the 20 million people in Sri Lanka, the keepers of the Buddhist faith that has all but disappeared in India with a language that is spoken nowhere else, they fear the weight of the more than 70 million Tamils in the nearby southern Indian state of Tamil Nadu, with whom Sri Lankan Tamils share a common language and the Hindu religion.

Tamil and Sinhalese empires have risen and fallen on this island for thousands of years, but it was independence that severely damaged the relationship between the two communities. After independence, the secular traditions of the British were soon abandoned in favor of a Sinhalese-Buddhist nationalism that made Sinhala the official language of the country, discriminating against the Tamils, who could no longer read official government documents or even job applications.

The Sinhalese majority felt that the British had tended to favor Tamils in the days of the British Raj. Sri Lanka fell victim to the kind of majoritarian politics that has led to the detriment of linguistic, ethnic, and religious minorities in so many countries in the post-colonial world.

When Tamils began to feel their rights were being trampled by the Sinhalese majority, discontent grew and in due course Tamils began to agitate for their own independent country in the north and east where most of them lived. This soon deteriorated into rebellion and civil war with massacres between Sinhalese and Tamils reminiscent of the sectarian bloodlettings in India before the 1947 partition of the subcontinent.

The Tamil Tigers, under the leadership of the megalomaniacal Velupillai Prabhakaran, became one of the most vicious and powerful guerilla-cum-terrorist groups in the world. They killed off rival Tamil groups that threatened the Tigers' ascendancy, and moderate Tamils who sought compromise. Then they took on the mostly Sinahlese army, committing acts of terrorism that were the forerunner of what we have become so used to today. The Tamil Tigers pioneered the suicide vests that killed many Sri Lankan politicians as well as the prime minister of India, Rajiv Gandhi. The army, at times, responded with brutal suppression.

It was India's Indira Gandhi who began to seriously meddle in the affairs of her small neighbor to the south. Being pro-Soviet, she didn't like the way Sri Lanka had courted the West. She also wanted to appease her Tamil Nadu subjects, who generally supported the Sri Lankan Tamil cause. She began to train and equip Sri Lankan Tamil rebels, and nearby Tamil Nadu became a safe haven for Tamil rebels who had only to hop on a boat to cross the narrow body of water that separates Sri Lanka from the Indian state to find a safe haven.

It may have been Indira Gandhi's intention to eventually take the Tamil territories in Sri Lanka, including the great natural harbor of Trincomalee, for India. After all, Indira Gandhi took Goa from Portugal and ended the semi-independence of Sikkim. It was Indira Gandhi that severed Bangladesh from Pakistan. Or it may have been her intention just to have an independent Tamil nation in Sri Lanka as a friend and ally on her southern flank.

Her successor and son, Rajiv Gandhi, tried to bring an end to the Sri Lankan civil war and got both sides to agree to an Indian peace keeping force. But Prabhakaran and his Tamil Tigers soon revolted against what he saw was an Indian occupation, and after a two-and-a-half-year fight, he forced India to withdraw from the island and had Rajiv Gandhi assassinated. Even the government in Colombo got tired of the Indian peacekeeping force and asked it to leave. Indo-Sri Lankan relations were at their nadir.

RAJAPAKSA FINALLY managed to wipe out the Tamil Tigers and bring peace to the divided island six years ago, but, despite promises otherwise, he kept his foot on the neck of the Tamils and also strengthened his bond with China.

Perhaps, but under the new regime China is not going to play the dominant role it has under Rajapaksa. It was not so much the former regime's attachment to China that cost Rajapaksa the election, however. It was his extraordinary corruption and abuse of power, by which he and his brothers ran Sri Lanka as if they were the kings of old. President Sirisena has gone out of his way to present himself as more a man of the people.

Earlier this month I watched Sirisena's motorcade pass by in the northern and former rebel city of Jaffna with a minimum of security while a Sri Lankan told me that if it had been Rajapaksa the entire street would have been closed off and emptied of traffic. Even the potted flowers on the wall of the prime minister's official residence here in Colombo were taken away because they seemed an unnecessary government expense.

President Sirisena has begun a 100-day campaign to make political reforms, and although it has not been announced as such, a realignment with India was made possible by promising to give the Tamils a measure of autonomy that had previously been promised but never delivered. Sirisena fired an unpopular governor of the Tamil regions and has promised to give land seized by the army back to the Tamils as well. Sirisena seems to be pursuing a real policy of national reconciliation.

This has bought him respite from relentless Western and United Nations demands for an investigation of alleged war crimes committed during the last days of the civil war – which Rajapaksa refused to do. He has until the fall to look into the matter before the United Nations reacts.

The state visit of Narendra Modi symbolized a new relationship between India and its southern neighbor that, if continued, will mean that China's "elusive empire" will not extend as far into the Indian Ocean as China might have wished.

As for Mahinda Rajapaksa, he has a chance to return to power as prime minister if Sirisena carries out his intentions to limit the constitutional power of the presidency and put power in the hands of elected prime ministers. Never a good loser, Rajapaksa has accused the secret services of India, Britain, and America of conspiring against him in the last election, and has even said that after his defeat at the polls he no longer believes in astrology.

But whatever the outcome, the stars are aligned so that Sri Lanka is back in the middle of great power rivalry the way it was when Portuguese, Dutch, and British fought over it half a millennium ago.

KNITTING THE INDIA-SRI LANKA RELATIONSHIP CLOSER

On his three-nation Indian ocean tour, Prime Minister Narendra Modi has made it clear he envisions a new maritime security architecture for India island neighbours, which will draw them into a closer 'security net', making the Indian ocean, "India's ocean". Amongst the countries of the IOR, Sri Lanka is the most significant in this, and in his departure statement, Mr. Modi said he looks forward to "forging a new partnership" with "one of our most important neighbours", with major agreements and several development projects due to be inaugurated during the first bilateral visit by an Indian Prime Minister in 28 years.

However, three separate interviews by Sri Lankan leaders, including one by Prime Minister Ranil Wickremasinghe in the run-up to the Prime Minister's visit must give Indian foreign policy planners cause for worry, if not a re-look at how India is being seen by the country. Particularly, the question that arises is whether Mr. Modi's "muscular policy" with India's smaller neighbours is producing a pushback.

With Sri Lanka, the government has been clear about what it wants. On the Tamil issue, the PM met with TNA leaders in June, promising he would push for devolution and the implementation of the 13th amendment for them. Mr. Modi's planned visit to Jaffna and Talaimannar, the first Indian PM to go there is an affirmation of India's special concern for the Tamil-majority areas. Secondly, the government has been open about countering China's influence, over construction of major projects, as well as the docking of China's submarines in Colombo harbor, with NSA Ajit Doval issuing warnings to the Sri Lankan naval chief and former defence secretary over it.

Thirdly, despite the Prime Minister's "good luck" wishes to former President Mahinda Rajapaksa during the SAARC summit in Kathmandu, Indian officials have been clear that his electoral defeat was to India's advantage, and the four high level exchanges between Sri Lankan and Indian leaders — President Maithripala Sirisena, Foreign Minister Mangala Samaraweera in Delhi, Mr. Modi and External Affairs Minister Sushma Swaraj in Colombo — within 90 days of the government's formation are evidence of just how much India welcomes Mr. Rajapaksa's successors.

Statements by the new government, however, seem to indicate that the new government isn't necessarily viewing India's welcome the same way. In the first interview, which has now been debated in parliament, Mr. Wickremsinghe's comments on Sri Lanka's "right to shoot" Tamil Nadu fishermen like intruders, also accusing India of double standards on the

Italian marines issue, have been widely commented on. But Mr. Wickremsinghe said more. He accused Indian politicians of "amnesia" over helping former President Mr. Rajapaksa defeat the LTTE in 2009, and claimed that any "international genocide inquiry" as has been demanded by the Northern Provinces, must also inquire into killings by the Indian Peacekeeping Forces in the 1980s. Mr. Wickremsinghe, and the Indian opposition parties have been ably answered by Ms. Swaraj in parliament, who was herself in Colombo when the interview was broadcast, but Mr. Wickremsinghe's wasn't the only discordant voice out of the Sri Lankan capital this week.

The second interview came from Power and Energy Minister Patali Champika Ranawaka, who told *The Hindu* that India "must stop seeing Sri Lanka through the Tamil prism", and instead see it "as a whole", a startling statement. Given India's interests in energy cooperation, and building power plants in Sri Lanka, the power minister's statement that "India cannot tell Sri Lanka what its China policy should be", is also significant. Mr. Ranawaka then complained about Indian commitments on project costs and deadlines not being kept.

The view was echoed by Finance Minister Ravi Karunanayake in an interview to the South China Morning post this week (the third interview of concern). "The Tatas come in and say they will put in $250 million, but they put in $20 million, use our land, and sell it back to us for a higher price. How does that work?" Mr. Karunanayake said, indicating that like Chinese projects okayed by the Rajapaksa regime, Indian projects too would be reviewed by his government.

It would be easy to dismiss all three interviews as symptoms of "political compulsions" of the UNP government, even as the country heads into parliamentary elections sometime this year. Analyst Dr. P. Saravanamuttu of the Centre for Policy Alternatives, told a gathering in New Delhi this week that given accusations from the opposition of the government being "too India-friendly", it is necessary for the Sri Lankan government to make these statements. It would also be possible to speculate if the statements have less to do with India than with underlying tensions between the UNP led by Mr. Wickremsinghe and Mr. Sirisena's SLFP (Also Mr. Rajapaksa's party).

However, India would be dismissive of the comments at its own peril, as the history of India-Sri Lanka ties is replete with examples of minor strains in the understanding between their leaders quickly mushrooming into something much more serious.

Given that, Mr. Modi would do well to step lightly, as he criss-crosses the island during his two-day visit. His visits to Anuradhapura, Talaimannar and Jaffna are all novel ideas, but he may find a certain reservation over plans to distribute "India's largesse" including handing over 20,000 homes to formerly displaced residents in the North. A similar plan to distribute 3,000 bicycles in Nepal along with a public rally in Janakpur had been dropped in November last year, after the opposition and members of the ruling party had protested.

Secondly, while India is correct in wanting to counter China's strategic influence in its "backyard", as it is integral to India's own security, it would be unfair to deprive a smaller neighbour of China's economic prowess. As a result, while Indian officials have noted with some satisfaction at the suspension of the $1.34 billion Colombo port project, they must remember that India had declined the offer for that project earlier, and is unlikely to be able to supplant China financially on that and other projects under review. Even so, Mr. Modi's visit will hopefully make some announcements of investment, and also push along stalled negotiations over the CEPA (Comprehensive Economic Partnership Agreement), which President Sirisena recently said would not be signed until it addressed concerns of Sri Lankan businesses.

On the Tamil question, Mr. Modi has already hit the right note, expressing India's commitment to a full reconciliation process, while counseling TNA leaders who met with him in June last year to focus on their future "within Sri Lanka", as opposed to the interests of Tamilians outside the country. The truth is, the India-Sri Lanka relationship historically comprises five different dialogues: between New Delhi and Colombo, but also Delhi-Jaffna, Delhi-Chennai, Colombo-Jaffna and Colombo-Chennai. The only way forward, from the vexed problem of fishing rights to the larger question of India's strategic goals in the region is promote each of those dialogues and knit them together for a stronger comprehensive relationship.

Finally, with geography as well as its age-old cultural and ethnic ties to Sri Lanka, India cannot but be "first amongst equals" in terms of influence over its island neighbour. For that primacy to be kept, India must be seen as bipartisan, as a true friend of the people of Sri Lanka, rather than any one regime.

REBUILDING THE INDIA-SRI LANKA RELATIONSHIP

Briefing statements often veer between the effusive and the inane. The one issued by Prime Minister Narendra Modi on Monday, during the visit of Sri Lanka's president Maithripala Sirisena achieved this balance with aplomb. In the 27 paragraph-statement, the word Tamil was not mentioned even once. The only reference, and that too as a politically neutral expression—Internally Displaced Persons—occurs in the context of India helping build 27,000 houses in Sri Lanka. Forget contentious subjects such as the 13th Amendment to Sri Lanka's Constitution (that devolves greater power to Tamil-dominated Northern and Eastern regions), the statement was extraordinarily deferential to Colombo's sensitivities.

To be fair to the prime minister, the official spokesperson of the ministry of external affairs had clearly stated last week that return of Tamil refugees to Sri Lanka was work in progress. He also said that subjects such as the 13th Amendment would feature in the discussions between the two leaders.

The two countries did agree to four, rather low-key agreements on agriculture, nuclear cooperation (for medical and scientific purposes) and other subjects (cultural cooperation and enabling Sri Lanka to participate in the Nalanda University Project).

What is the reason for India's deference to Colombo? For starters, India does not want to queer the pitch for Sirisena by insisting on a solution to a tough problem. Sri Lanka's politics was polarized during the long fight with the Liberation Tigers of Tamil Eelam, which was further accentuated during the decade-long rule of Mahinda Rajapaksa who cynically used it to bolster his appeal and pulverize the opposition—or whatever remained of it—into submission. Sirisena has barely begun the process of return to normalcy. It is best not to make demands of him that will create problems for him. A complicating factor is his dependence on the same hardline Sinhala electorate that once supported Rajapaksa.

While the Tamil issue has an emotional resonance in India, it should not be allowed to distort India's interests in Sri Lanka. Foremost among these interests is to keep its southern flank free from any external political and military influence. Bringing back Colombo to a state of acceptable neutrality (code for reduced Chinese influence) should be India's primary goal at the moment. Rajapaksa had gone to an extreme that went against India's interests: if Chinese submarines begin calling on Sri Lankan ports for goodwill missions, then that is too much of goodwill for India.

Restoring balance in our relations with Colombo is important for another reason. In the second term of the United Progressive Alliance (UPA) government, the conduct of foreign policy had become hostage to interests of regional parties.

The refusal of prime minister Manmohan Singh to attend the Commonwealth Heads of Government Meeting in Colombo in 2013 hurt the Sri Lankans. India's abstention from voting at the United Nations Human Rights Council, during an NGO lobby-promoted resolution on human rights, was another irritant. These actions reduced the room for manoeuvre of the Union government in making informed foreign policy choices. If Modi does what is necessary to further India's interests in Sri Lanka without fear of domestic repercussions, he will restore insulation in foreign policymaking.

SRI LANKAN PRESIDENTIAL ELECTIONS: INDIA'S STANCE

Sri Lanka's presidential elections are to be held on January 8, 2015. President Mahinda Rajapakse will be up against his former Health Minister, Maitripala Sirisena, who defected from the ruling Sri Lanka Freedom Party (SLFP). Chandrika Kumaratunga, earlier the country's President from the SLFP, has stepped in to support Sirisena. For his part, Sirisena has arrived at a working arrangement with the SLFP's arch rival, the United National Party (UNP), to entrust the premiership to the UNP leader, Ranil Wikremasinghe, in the event of his victory. Along with Sirisena, a number of Members of Parliament have also defected from the SLFP and the United People's Freedom Alliance of which the SLFP is a constituent.

From the Indian perspective, there is no clear cut posture as yet that Sirisena has outlined on which New Delhi can work out its future policy options. Therefore, a neutral posture on India's part vis-à-vis the Rajapakse-Sirisena contest may be prudent. However, the Government of India may not be oblivious of the support extended to Sirisena by another defecting member of the Rajapakse Government, Rajitha Senaratne, Fisheries & Aquatic Resources Minister, who had advocated devolution of power to the provinces.

As for the electoral prospects of Rajapakse, the hard reality is that he still has the support of a large segment of the economically lower strata of the Sinhala middle class, particularly in the deep south and central parts of the country. This is so notwithstanding some erosion of support over the past two years as evident from the SLFP's narrow win in the provincial elections in Uva Province in September 2014. An apparent lack of cohesion among the political forces opposed to Rajapakse at the level of middle-level leaders and grass-root workers is likely to militate against an effective anti-Rajapakse campaign.

However, some leading figures in the Sinhala Buddhist clergy (Venerable Maduluwawe Sobitha thero) seem to have already positioned themselves against Rajapakse. The hard core Buddhist Party, Jathika Hela Urumaya, and the Peoples' Liberation Front (erstwhile Janatha Vimukti Peramuna) are already lined up against Rajapakse. A more active involvement of Chandrika Kumaratunga in the campaign may be a game changer. Active association of the minorities – Sri Lankan Muslims and the Tamil National Alliance (TNA) – with Sirisena, or even a moderately favourable posture on their part towards him may, however, divide the Buddhist clergy and eventually dissuade a majority in their ranks from working against Rajapakse.

In this backdrop, it may be in India's interest to adopt a neutral posture vis-à-vis the political contestants in these Presidential elections. While President Rajapakse has not moved forward in regard to political and administrative devolution of power to the Northern province, he has also allowed the C. Wigneswaran-led TNA Northern Provincial Government to function, though under substantial administrative constraints. These include, for instance, inadequate control on land-use matters, not appointing functionaries having the confidence of the provincial political executive, police and the armed forces functioning disharmoniously with the TNA Government, among others.

Sri Lanka's relationship with China has come under increasing scrutiny in recent times. Rajapakse has continued to build up a multifaceted relationship with Beijing with an underlying strategic content that involves procurement of weapon systems as well as provision of docking and refuelling facilities for Chinese submarines with extended operational capabilities. Sri Lanka has also continued to engage India in a cooperative relationship involving exchanges between the defence forces in training matters, anti-piracy operations, and working in a cooperative mode in the Palk Straits and the high seas around.

While India-Sri Lanka relations with Sirisena in power may not undergo much of a change, in the initial phase it is only in the domestic sphere that the nature of Sri Lankan polity may be a little different. It is pertinent to note that the SLFP of today is quite different from the SLFP of the Sirimavo-Chandrika period. Rajapakse has transformed the party into a political establishment run by a coterie. A Sirisena victory in the presidential elections may lead to a transformation of the SLFP, with consensual views having more impact in inner party decision making. Sirisena has not yet enunciated a clear policy on devolution. However, it is possible that his government may be more flexible on this issue and may devolve more powers to the provinces in general, with the Northern Province becoming a consequential beneficiary. A reappraisal of central and provincial government relations may ensue without, however, any alteration in the basic unitary structure of the state.

In such a scenario, India may not have much to lose as compared to its position today though some positive fallout may be expected eventually as a result of further devolution or re-distribution of powers from the centre to the provinces in general. Kumaratunga may also influence a favourable slant in Sri Lanka's relations with India, considering the past political profile of the Bandaranaikes towards India.

Given the above dynamics, in the run-up to the presidential polls, India has to be extremely cautious in its posture. The slightest tilt in favour of any of the contestants, or even a benign hint, is likely to be misconstrued. This is borne out by the adverse reaction in some quarters in Nepal to Prime Minister Narendra Modi's advice to Nepalese political parties for an early finalisation of their Constitution through consensus methodology. India perforce should be sensitive and tread cautiously in its approach to her smaller South Asian neighbours. Adopting an equidistant posture between Rajapakse and his opponent in the presidential elections would therefore be most prudent. Post-elections, India should intimately work with whoever is in power with a view to obtaining the best outcome in terms of devolution of powers to the Northern Province in the inherent interest of the original inhabitants of that province. It should also seek to foster the development of economic and cultural ties with Sri Lanka without external involvement in that country which militates against India's strategic interests.

8

India-Afghanistan Relation

Bilateral relations between India and Afghanistan have been traditionally strong and friendly. While India was the only South Asian country to recognize the Soviet-backed Democratic Republic of Afghanistan in the 1980s, its relations were diminished during the Afghan civil wars and the rule of the Islamist Taliban in the 1990s. India aided the overthrow of the Taliban and became the largest regional provider of humanitarian and reconstruction aid.

The new democratically-elected Afghan government strengthened its ties with India in wake of persisting tensions and problems with Pakistan, which was suspected of continuing to shelter and support the Taliban. India pursues a policy of close cooperation to bolster its standing as a regional power and contain its rival Pakistan, which it maintains is supporting Islamic militants in Kashmir and other parts of India. India is the largest regional investor in Afghanistan, having committed more than US$2.2 billion for reconstruction purposes.

INDIA AND AFGHANISTAN RELATIONSHIP

India has traditionally enjoyed friendly relations with Afghanistan. President Hamid Karzai graduated from a university in India. Despite that, India supported the Soviet invasion and occupation of Afghanistan. Relations deteriorated after the Taliban took power in 1996. India "unofficially" supported the Northern Alliance minority groups against the Pakistani-backed Taliban. During the course of the hijack of Indian Airlines Flight 814 in 1999, the Taliban requested recognition by India in exchange for help in negotiations. The request was not acted upon by the Indian government. After the fall of the Taliban in late 2001, India strengthened ties with the Islamic republic of Afghanistan by establishing consulates in most major Afghan cities. The Embassy of India is located in Kabul.

India has participated in multiple socio-economic reconstruction efforts, including power, roads, agricultural and educational projects. Some of these include building dozens of dams and reservoirs, a number of hospitals or clinics, schools and government institutions. The long road from Bandar-Abbas in southern Iran to highway 1 in southern Afghanistan is carried out by state-owned Border Roads Organization (BRO), the mission statement of which states that the BRO is India's "most reputed, multifaceted, transnational, modern construction organization committed to meeting the strategic needs of the armed forces." The killing of a BRO employee by the neo-Taliban in 2005 prompted the Indian authorities to dispatch approximately 200 Indo-Tibetan Border Police commandos to in 2006 to provide security for Indians working in various construction projects in Afghanistan.

Political contacts between India and Afghanistan have increased in 2011, especially after the death of Osama bin Laden in Pakistan. During Indian Prime Minister Manmohan Singh's May 2011 visit to Kabul, it was announced that India's total aid to Afghanistan reached $2 billion after a package of $500 million was added. There are also military ties between Afghanistan and India, which is expected to increase after the October 2011 strategic pact that was signed by President Karzai and Manmohan Singh. India's the largest regional provider of humanitarian and reconstruction aid to Afghanistan.

History

Relations between the people of Afghanistan and India traces to the Indus Valley Civilisation. Following Alexander the Great's brief occupation, the successor state of the Seleucid Empire controlled the region known today as Afghanistan. In 305 BCE, they ceded much of it to the Indian Maurya Empire as part of an alliance treaty.

Alexander took these away from the *Persians* and established settlements of his own, but *Seleucus Nicator* gave them to *Sandrocottus* (*Chandragupta*), upon terms of intermarriage and of receiving in exchange 500 elephants. —Strabo, *64 BCE – 24 CE*

The Mauryans brought Buddhism from India and controlled the area south of theHindu Kush. Their decline began 60 years after Ashoka's rule ended, leading to theHellenistic reconquest of the region by the Greco-Bactrians. Much of it soon broke away from the Greco-Bactrians and became part of the Indo-Greek Kingdom. The Indo-Greeks had been defeated and expelled by the Indo-Scythians in the late 2nd century BCE. Much of Afghanistan has been influenced by Buddhist, Hinduand Zoroastrian cultures until the arrival of Islam in the 7th century. But despite many Afghans accepting the message of Islam, the Muslims and Hindus lived side by side. "Kábul has a *castle* celebrated for its strength, accessible only by one road. In it there are *Musulmáns,* and it has a town, in which are *infidels* from *Hind.*" — Istahkrí, *921 CE*

Between the 10th century to the mid 18th century, northern India has been invaded by a number of invaders based in what today is Afghanistan. Amongst them were the Ghaznavids, Ghurids, Khiljis, Suris, and Durranis. During these eras, especially during the Mughal period (1526–1858), many Afghans began immigrating to India due to political unrest in their regions.

Khan Abdul Ghaffar Khan and Khan Sahib were prominent leaders of the Indian independence movement and active supporters of the Indian National Congress. Although the NWFP became part of the Muslim state of Pakistan in 1947, active Pashtun support for the Indian freedom struggle led to great sympathy in India for the cause of Pashtun autonomy and freedom. The Indian government continued to support Pashtun leader Khan Abdul Ghaffar Khan in lobbying for greater Pashtun freedom in the NWFP. Indians are working in various construction projects, as part of India's rebuilding efforts in Afghanistan, although the Indian intelligence agency RAW is accused by countries such as Pakistan of working to malign Pakistan and train & support insurgents. These workers are estimated to be anywhere between 3,000 and 4,000. Indian nationals stationed in Afghanistan have often faced continuous security threats in the country, with kidnappings and many attacks (such as the February 2010 Kabul attack) deliberately carried out on them.

Soviet invasion to Taliban takeover

The Republic of India was the only South Asian nation to recognise the Soviet-backed Democratic Republic of Afghanistan and the Soviet Union's military presence in Afghan territories, and provided humanitarian aid to President Najibullah'sGovernment in Afghanistan. Following the withdrawal of the Soviet armed forces from Afghanistan in 1989, India continued to support Najibullah's government with humanitarian aid. After its fall, India together with the international community supported the coalition government that took control, but relations and contacts ended with the outbreak of another civil war, which brought to power the Taliban, an Islamist militia supported by Pakistan. The Taliban regime was recognised only byPakistan, Saudi Arabia, and the United Arab Emirates (UAE). The destruction of the Bamiyan Buddha monuments by the Taliban led to outrage and angry protests by India, the birthplace of Buddhism. In 1999, the hijacked Indian Airlines Flight 814 landed and stayed in Kandahar in Afghanistan and the

Taliban were suspected of supporting them. India became one of the key supporters of the anti-Taliban Northern Alliance.

Post 9/11

During the U.S.-led invasion of Afghanistan in 2001, India offered intelligence and other forms of support for the Coalition forces. After the overthrow of the Taliban, India established diplomatic relations with the newly established democratic government, provided aid and participated in the reconstruction efforts. India has provided US$650–750 million in humanitarian and economic aid, making it the largest regional provider of aid for Afghanistan. India's support and collaboration extends to rebuilding of air links, power plants and investing in health and education sectors as well as helping to train Afghan civil servants, diplomats and police. India also seeks the development of supply lines of electricity, oil and natural gas. Also to give Afghan Students scholarships. The Indian Army's Border Roads Organisation constructed a major road in 2009 in the remote Afghan province of Nimroz, connecting Delaram to Zaranj. This has proved a viable alternative route for the duty-free movement of goods through theChabahar port in Iran to Afghanistan. Key to India's strategy in Afghanistan is to build up transportation links that bypass Pakistan, helping reduce the Afghan economy's dependence on Pakistan.

In 2005, India proposed Afghanistan's membership in the South Asian Association for Regional Cooperation (SAARC). Both nations also developed strategic and military cooperation against Islamic militants. Owing to the killing of an Indian national by Taliban militants in November 2005, India deployed 200 soldiers of the Indo-Tibetan Border Police (ITBP) to provide security for Indian nationals and the projects supported by India. Afghanistan strengthened its ties with India in wake of persisting tensions and problems with Pakistan, which was suspected of continuing to shelter and support the Taliban. India pursues a policy of close collaboration with countries such as Afghanistan, Bhutan, and Iran in order to bolster its standing as a regional power and contain its rival Pakistan, which stands accused of aiding and abetting Islamic militants in Kashmir and other states of India.

Three memorandums of understanding (MOUs) for strengthening cooperation in the fields of rural development, education and standardisation between the Bureau of Indian Standards (BIS) and Afghan National Standardisation Authority were signed between Afghanistan and India during Hamid Karzai's visit to India in April 2006. An agreement providing $50 million to promote bilateral businesses between Afghanistan and India was signed during the visit of the Afghan Foreign Minister Dr. Spanta between 29 June – 1 July 2006. During the same year, India raised its aid package to Afghanistan by $150 million, to $750 million. In 2007, Afghanistan finally became the eighth member of SAARC.

In July 2008 the Indian embassy in Kabul was attacked by a suicide car bomb – the deadliest attack in Kabul since the fall of the Taliban in 2001. The bombing killed 58 people and wounded 141. Senior Indian Army officer Brigadier Ravi Datt Mehta was entering the embassy gates in a car along with V. Venkateswara Rao when the attack took place. Both were killed in the blast. The Afghan government's official position implies that Pakistan's ISI was involved in the attack. This position has found support in recent leaks of classified information by Wikileaks.

During the 15th SAARC summit in Colombo, India pledged another USD $450 million alongside a further US$750 million already pledged for ongoing and forthcoming projects. In August 2008, Afghan President Hamid Karzai visited New Delhi. This visit further strengthened bilateral relations, and Prime Minister Singh pledged further aid for Afghanistan.

On 18 October 2009, the Indian Embassy in Kabul was attacked again by a car bomb, little more than a year after the previous attack. The attack killed at least 17 people. Another attack conducted by the same Pakistan-based terrorist organisation took place at the Arya guest house where Indian doctors were staying, resulting in the death of 18 people. India's pledge to rebuild Afghanistan has reached a total of US$2 billion in May 2011 after Manmohan Singh arrived to Kabul for a two-day visit.

The September 2011 assassination of former Afghan president Burhanuddin Rabbani was condemned by India, which stated that, "Tragically, the forces of terror and hatred have silenced yet another powerful voice of reason and peace in Afghanistan. We unreservedly condemn this act of great brutality," and reiterated the steadfast support of the people and government of India in Afghanistan's "quest for peace and efforts to strengthen the roots of democracy".

India promised to stand by the people of Afghanistan as they prepare to assume the responsibility for their governance and security after the withdrawal of international forces in 2014. In October 2011, Afghanistan signed its first strategic pact with India. The military assistance will include training of Afghan security personnel. During his visit to India, Karzai told the media that "This strategic partnership is not directed against any country. This strategic partnership is to support Afghanistan." He also stated that "Pakistan is our twin brother, India is a great friend. The agreement we signed with our friend will not affect our brother." He also added that "However, our engagement with Islamabad has unfortunately not yet yielded the result that we want." Both sides will launch Partnership Council, topmost body to implement the Strategic Partnership Pact in May,2012.

On 22 May 2014 the Indian consulate in Herat was attacked by 3 militants equipped with AK-47s, RPGs, hand grenades and suicide vests. "Our premises have been repeatedly attacked by those who do not support India's development work in Afghanistan. The attack will not dilute India's development assistance and its contribution to rehabilitation and reconstruction of Afghanistan," India's ambassador to Kabul Amar Sinha said at the time.

Economy

India seeks to expand its economic presence in Afghanistan as the international coalition fighting the Taliban withdraws combat forces through 2014. Especially, it wants to improve transport connectivity and economic collaboration with countries in Central and South Asia. India has already invested US$10.8 billion in Afghanistan as of 2012. More such projects are likely to come up after Nato's withdrawal. This includes setting up Iron ore mines, a 6 MTPA steel plant (by SAIL—Steel Authority of India Limited), an 800 MW power plant, Hydro-electric power projects, transmission lines, roads etc., India and Iran are set to ink a transit agreement on transporting goods to landlocked Afghanistan. The Indian government is investing more than US$100 million in the expansion of the Chabahar port in south-eastern Iran which will serve as a hub for the transportation of transit goods. Besides as a goodwill gesture, India is also constructing a new Parliament complex for the Afghan government at a cost of INR 710 crores (USD 115 million). This building will be inaugurated in October 2015.

Bibliography

Ahmad, Imtiaz: *State and Foreign Policy: India's Role in South Asia*, New Delhi, Vikas, 1993.

Anthony, J. Parel : *Hind Swaraj or Indian Home Rule*, Cambridge University Press, 1925.

Anurag Gangal : *Contemporary Global Problems : A Gandhian Perspective*, Jammu, Vinod, 1995.

Ashton, S.R.: *British Policy Towards the Indian States, 1905-1939*, London: Curzon, 1982.

Atri, Ajit : *Gandhi's View of Legal Justice*, New Delhi, Deep and Deep Pub., 2007.

Barber B.R.: *Strong Democracy. Participatory Politics for a New Age*. Berkeley, University of California Press, 1984.

Behari, Madhuri: *Indian Trade since Independence: Chronology of Events*, Delhi, D.K. Publications, 1983.

Bhambhri, C.P. : *Indian Politics Since Independence*, 1999.

Budge I: *The New Challenge of Direct Democracy*, Oxford, Polity Press, 1996.

Carl J. Friedrich: *Constitutional Government and Democracy*, Boston, Ginn, 1950.

Gaur, Mahendra : *Indian Political Parties Annual*, Delhi, Kalpaz Pub., 2006.

Gehlot, N. S.: *Indian Government and Politics*. New Delhi: Rawat Publications, 1996.

Ghosh, Arun : *Indian Industrialization: Structure and Policy Issues*. New York: Oxford University Press, 1992.

Henken, Louis, *Foreign Affairs and the Constitution*, NY, 1972.

Imtiaz, A.: *State and Foreign Policy: India's Role in South Asia*, New Delhi, Vikas, 1993.

Jeevan Nair : *Encyclopaedia of Indian Government and Politics*, 2000.

Jha, Prem Shankar: *India: A Political Economy of Stagnation*, Bombay, Oxford University Press, 1980.

Jones, W.H.: *The Government and Politics of India*, London, Hutchinson, 1971.

Maheshwari, Shriram: *Rural Development in India: A Public Policy Approach*, New Delhi, Sage, 1995.

Mathur, Krishan D.: *Conduct of India's Foreign Policy*. New Delhi: South Asian Publishers, 1996.

Max Beloff: *Foreign Policy and the Democratic Process*, Baltimore, Johns Hopkins University Press, 1955.

Mclean, I.: *Democracy and New Technology*, Cambridge, Polity Press, 1989.

Metcalf, Thomas R.: *Land, Landlords and The British Raj: Northern India in the Nineteenth Century*, Berkeley, UCP, 1976.

Morris-Jones, W.H.: *The Government and Politics of India*, London, Hutchinson, 1971.

Narula, Sanjay : *Indian Politics*, New Delhi, Murari Lal and Sons, 2007.

Nehru, Jawaharlal , *Towards A Socialistic Order,* New Delhi, 1956.

Noorani, A.G. : *Indian Political Trials : 1775-1947*, New Delhi, Oxford University Press, 2005.

Patnaik, Naveen: *A Second Paradise: Indian Courtly Life, 1590-1947*, Garden City, New Jersey, Doubleday, 1985.

Prasad, Lal Bahadur : *Indian Political System and Law,* New Delhi, Shree, 2005.

Prem Shankar: *India: A Political Economy of Stagnation,* Bombay, Oxford University Press, 1980.

Probyn, Mr. : *Indian Coinage and Currency,* Effingham Wilson, London, 1897.

Pruthi, R.K. : *Indian Political Thought,* New Delhi, Mohit Pub., 2007.

Ram, S. and R. Kumar : *Encyclopaedia of Indian Freedom Struggle,* Commonwealth Pub., New Delhi, 2008.

Saksena, N.S.: *India: Towards Anarchy, 1967-1992*, New Delhi, Abhinav, 1993.

Seligman, E. R. A. : *Currency Inflation and Public Debts,* New York, 1922.

Tomlinson, B. R.: *The Economy of Modern India, 1860–1970.* New York: Cambridge University Press, 1993.

Vohra, Ranbir. *The Making of India: A Historical Survey.* Armonk, N.Y.: M. E. Sharp, 1997.

Yasin, Mohammad : *Indian Politics : Processes, Issues and Trends,* New Delhi, Kanishka, 2004.

Zaidi,A.M. and S.G. Zaidi: *The Foundations of Indian Economic Planning,* New Delhi, 1979.

Index

❑❑❑